Safe Area GORAŽDE

by Joe Sacco

FANTAGRAPHICS BOOKS

DEDICATION
This book is dedicated to the town of Gorazde,
where I spent some of my happiest moments.

FANTAGRAPHICS BOOKS
7563 Lake City Way NE
Seattle, WA 98115

Edited by Kim Thompson
Design and Art Direction by Carrie Whitney
Gary Groth and Kim Thompson, publishers

"Born in the U.S.A." written by Bruce Springsteen
"Dead Flowers" written by Mick Jagger and Keith Richards
"Helter Skelter" written by John Lennon and Paul McCartney
"Hotel California" written by Don Henley, Glenn Frey, and Don Felder
"More Than I Can Say" written by J.I. Allison and Sonny Curtis
"One" written by Bono
"Proud Mary" written by John Fogerty
"Sounds of Silence" written by Paul Simon
"Twist and Shout" written by Burt Russell and Phil Medley

To receive a free catalog of Joe Sacco books and comics, call 1-800-657-1100 or write us at Fantagraphics Books, 7563 Lake City Way
NE, Seattle, WA 98115; you can also visit the Fantagraphics website at www.fantagraphics.com.

First hardcover printing: June, 2000
Second hardcover printing: September, 2000
Third hardcover printing: February, 2001
First softcover printing: November, 2001

ISBN: 1-56097-470-2

Printed in China

INTRODUCTION BY CHRISTOPHER HITCHENS

In Sarajevo in the summer of 1992, when the journalistic community (who had already annexed the British phrase "the hacks" as their collective noun) met in the bar of the disfigured Holiday Inn — and that phrase itself suggests the surreal nature of things, with a Holiday Inn being disfigured rather than disfiguring — there were all sorts of competitive anecdotes about near-misses, random encounters, and different styles of flak-jacket. Every now and then, I noticed, they also spoke of a place that might be even more frightening than Sarajevo itself. There was apparently this town, once not far off but now, with the blockade, as unimaginably difficult of access as Dubrovnik on the coast, or distant Zagreb. (Thus was the Balkanization of the mind slowly accomplished by common speech about "areas," "districts," and the still more alien "zones.") It took me a while to connect the name of this place to the spelling on my map, because when they discussed it — infrequent faint radio transmissions, rumors of mayhem and rape, of famine and even of cannibalism — foreign hacks distributed the emphasis differently each time. Gore-aj-day, Gorr-as-dee. Anyway, the somewhat homely title denoted a location more comprehensively fucked-up and fucked-over than Sarajevo, and thus to be looked up to, or looked down upon, according to choice, or mood.

Having persisted so long as an affront to civilization, and having ended so abruptly with the most compromising compromise that Holbrookian statecraft could confect, the siege of Sarajevo and the obliteration of the civilian "safe havens" at Srebrenica and Zepa have passed into an area of the semi-conscious. In a dim fashion, people apprehended that the mass graves of the latter were the price — and the pressure — for Bosnian signature at Dayton. Yet did this not after all constitute peace? Even a peace "process"? How excellent it is, then, that just as we are all forgiving ourselves, Joe Sacco steps forward to clear his throat, and our vision. How excellent it is, too, that he should have hit upon unfashionable, inaccessible old Gorazde and not one of the war's more chic or celebrated spots.

The first thing that one must praise is the combination of eye and ear. I personally always fail at physical description on the page, though I can sometimes catch the nuance of a voice. And I'm referring only to verbal capacity.

Sacco's combined word-illustration makes me remember that distinctive Bosnian domestic architecture — the gable ends and windows — with a few deft strokes. You know where you are, in other words, and it's not in some generic hotspot. Then the additional details, such as the unforgettable "bear's paw" scar that a mortar-shell makes on a pavement. And — more easily replicated but still impressive — the forlorn look of a wood-built house that's been reduced by fire to a silhouette and a brick chimney stack. These, in Bosnia, became as suggestive as church-steeples or minarets (more distinctive than the latter, actually, since most mosques were deliberately dynamited by Serbian chauvinists during periods of "cease-fire").

As to the ear, I haven't seen it more candidly admitted that the Bosnian war was in so many ways a carnival of embarrassment. On one side was a host of international volunteers, aid-workers, charity-artists, and of course hacks, who all desperately wanted to avoid the charge of being voyeuristic or starry-eyed. This sometimes led to a sort of protective cynicism; sometimes to an idealism that did not quite dare to speak its name. Then there were the actual inhabitants, heirs to a long tradition of hospitality and gusto, who knew that foreign sympathy was their main hope but didn't want to become absolute whores for it. Language was a sort of barrier, but it often seemed to be put there only as a test of the local plum brandy. This could lead to unintentional awkwardness and forced bonhomie. ("You are American?" "No." "French?" "No." "Ah — you are German — we like Deutschemarks very much ha ha ha." "No." "Where you from?" "England." "English people very good.")

Joe Sacco was evidently no blissed-out internationalist, still less a furry member of any mujahidin, but nor — though he draws himself into his panels as if he wanted us to forgive him a little — was he some affectless, disengaged Zelig. Bosnians are made of human materials and thus make bad subjects for romanticization, yet he found out by dint of punctilious observation, and succeeds in making plain, that they had no aggressive intentions towards their neighbors. Towards their "neighbors," that is to say, whether as contiguous former Yugoslav republics or as people living next door. Bosnia threatened nobody: Bosnians were defined by their long and easy-going habit of coexistence. Those who butchered and dispersed them had to lie and shriek, as a thug or rapist will psych himself up to do something foul. If this is not the entire story, it is still the indispensible element without which no truthful story can be told. Sacco tells it through the microcosm of Gorazde, and we're in his debt.

A microcosm needs its context, and again I found myself impressed by his encapsulations. The historical and geographic inserts are objective, and do not omit the moments when Bosnians, and Bosnian Islam, were historically compromised (most notably in the Second World War). The Bosnians we meet in these pages are not heroic — though some of them are exemplary — and their greeds and needs are recognizable to any American or European; recognizable to the point of banality. Well then, Sacco seems to be saying, will you turn away from the extermination and dispossession of those who are so much like your own unlovely self? He at any rate could not do so; good for him.

Where there is bile in these pages — and I could quite frankly have done with several more pints and quarts of it — it is not directed at "the Serbs." Even in their extremity, Bosnian victims referred to Serbo-fascists as "Chetniks" and thus honorably agreed to loathe them under a political and historical and not an ethnic rubric. No, the contempt is reserved for the temporizing, buck-passing, butt-covering "peacekeepers" who strove to find that swamp of low moral and "middle" ground into which the innocent end up being shoveled by the aggressive. Why was that road from Sarajevo to Gorazde so impassable? It had been wide open through several decades of inefficient state socialism, after all. Why did NATO armies, readied through the same decades to launch a thermonuclear war on a moment's notice, find it inconvenient to face down a flimsy roadblock manned by a rabble of drunken racists? Nobody who witnessed this miserable spectacle will ever forget it; nor will he wonder how some of the worst deeds in human history came to be committed in plain sight, and without shame. It became essential for the post-Cold War gatekeepers to define Chetniks and Bosnian civilians as equivalent — echoing the propaganda of Milosevic, their "partner in peace" until 1999 — because otherwise the shame might become unsupportable.

I now, having disburdened myself, feel rather shy about saying that Mr. Sacco is also funny, and ironic, and self-mocking. We have been told that "it takes a village" and — never mind the implication for now — it probably does. A village or small town like Gorazde can mature for years in history's cask, ripening away for all its provincialism. The large majority of its citizens may be content or at any rate reconciled. But the awful and frightening fact about fascism is that it "takes" only a few gestures (a pig's head in a mosque; a rumor of the kidnap of a child; an armed provocation at a wedding) to unsettle or even undo the communal and human work of generations. Normally the fascists don't have the guts to try it; they need the reassurance of support from superiors or aid from an outside power and the need to know that "law," defined nationally or internationally, will be a joke at the expense of their victims. In Bosnia they were granted all three indulgences. But even at the edge of those medieval paintings of breakdown and panic and mania, when people still thought the heavens might aid them, there was often the oblique figure at the edge of the scene, who might have hoped to record and outlive the carnage and perhaps to rebuild the community. Call him the moral draughtsman, at least for now, and be grateful for small mercies.

AUTHOR'S NOTE ABOUT PRONUNCIATION

I have opted to leave out the Bosnian-language accents on the names of people and towns; however, my modest lay-person's pronunciation guide for the most prominent places follows:

Gorazde sounds more or less like "go-RAJH-duh" (the "Z" is a soft "J" like the second "g" in "garage")

Visegrad rhymes with "FISH-a-grad"

Foca rhymes with "GOTcha"

Srebrenica is pronounced "sre-bre-KNEE-(t)sa"

Zepa is pronounced "JHEPP-ah," with a soft "J" sound (see above)

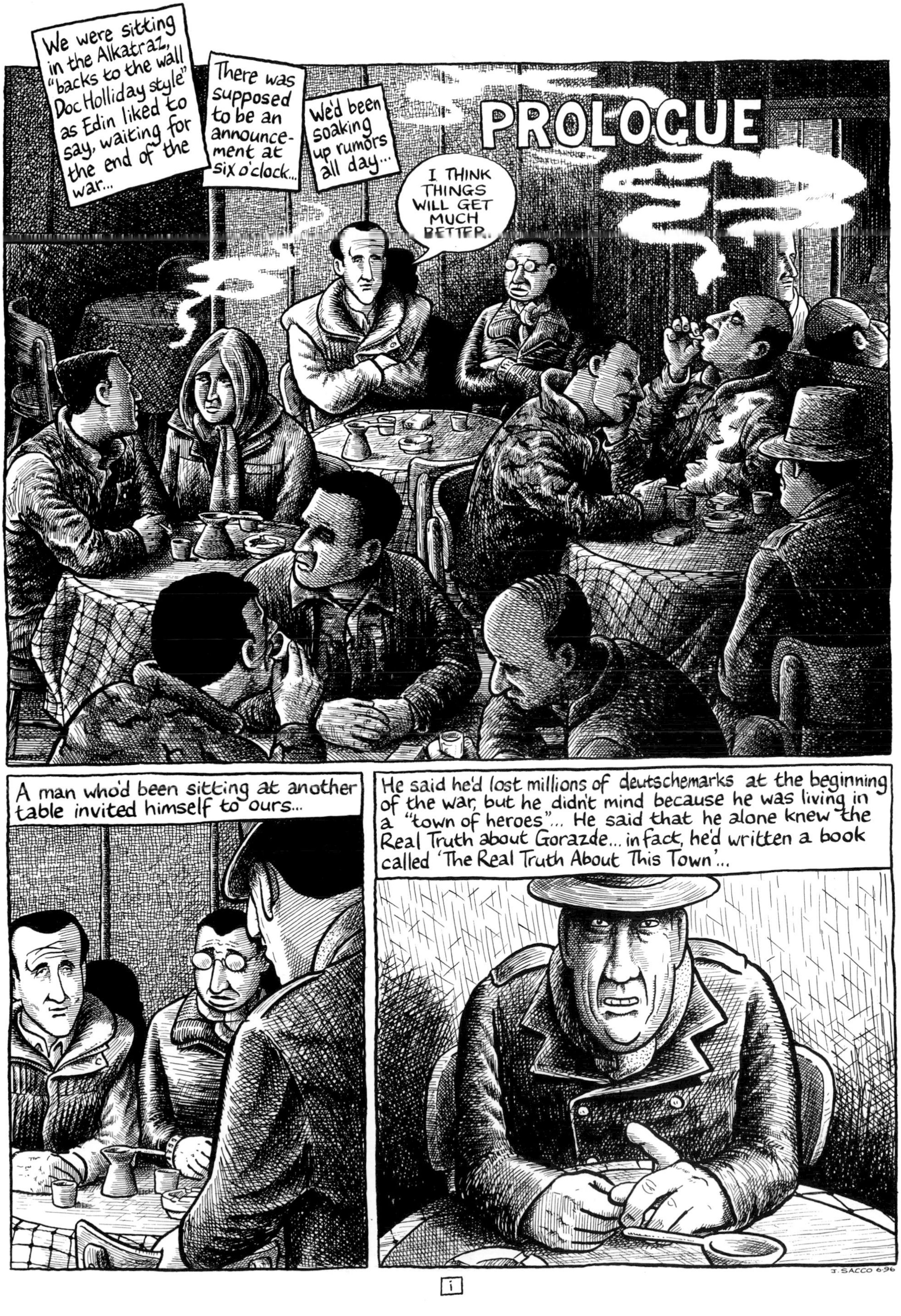
We were sitting in the Alkatraz, "backs to the wall Doc Holliday style" as Edin liked to say, waiting for the end of the war...
There was supposed to be an announcement at six o'clock...
We'd been soaking up rumors all day...
PROLOGUE
I THINK THINGS WILL GET MUCH BETTER.
A man who'd been sitting at another table invited himself to ours...
He said he'd lost millions of deutschemarks at the beginning of the war, but he didn't mind because he was living in a "town of heroes"... He said that he alone knew the Real Truth about Gorazde... in fact, he'd written a book called 'The Real Truth About This Town'...
J. SACCO 6·96

He was putting himself at my disposal, I could ask him anything I liked, go ahead, he said...

I asked him what made him think he knew the Real Truth...

He said he'd seen everything... During the worst of the shelling, he said, while everyone was in their cellars, he was out in the streets. He couldn't be touched. He <u>couldn't</u>. His dreams told him so...

He said he'd been believing in his dreams since 1957... For example, yesterday he had dreamed he'd receive a letter, and today he received the letter!

And if I were a real journalist, he said, who sought the Real Truth, I would visit him and look over his manuscript about Gorazde, and he would explain everything...

I never visited that man. In fact, after that evening I avoided him completely...

Meanwhile, six o'clock came and went and there was no announcement... None at midnight, nor in the morning, nor by early afternoon when an announcement had been rescheduled... Milosevic, Tudjman, and Izetbegovic were still behind closed doors in Dayton, Ohio, and maybe the war was going to go on forever...

J. SACCO 6-96

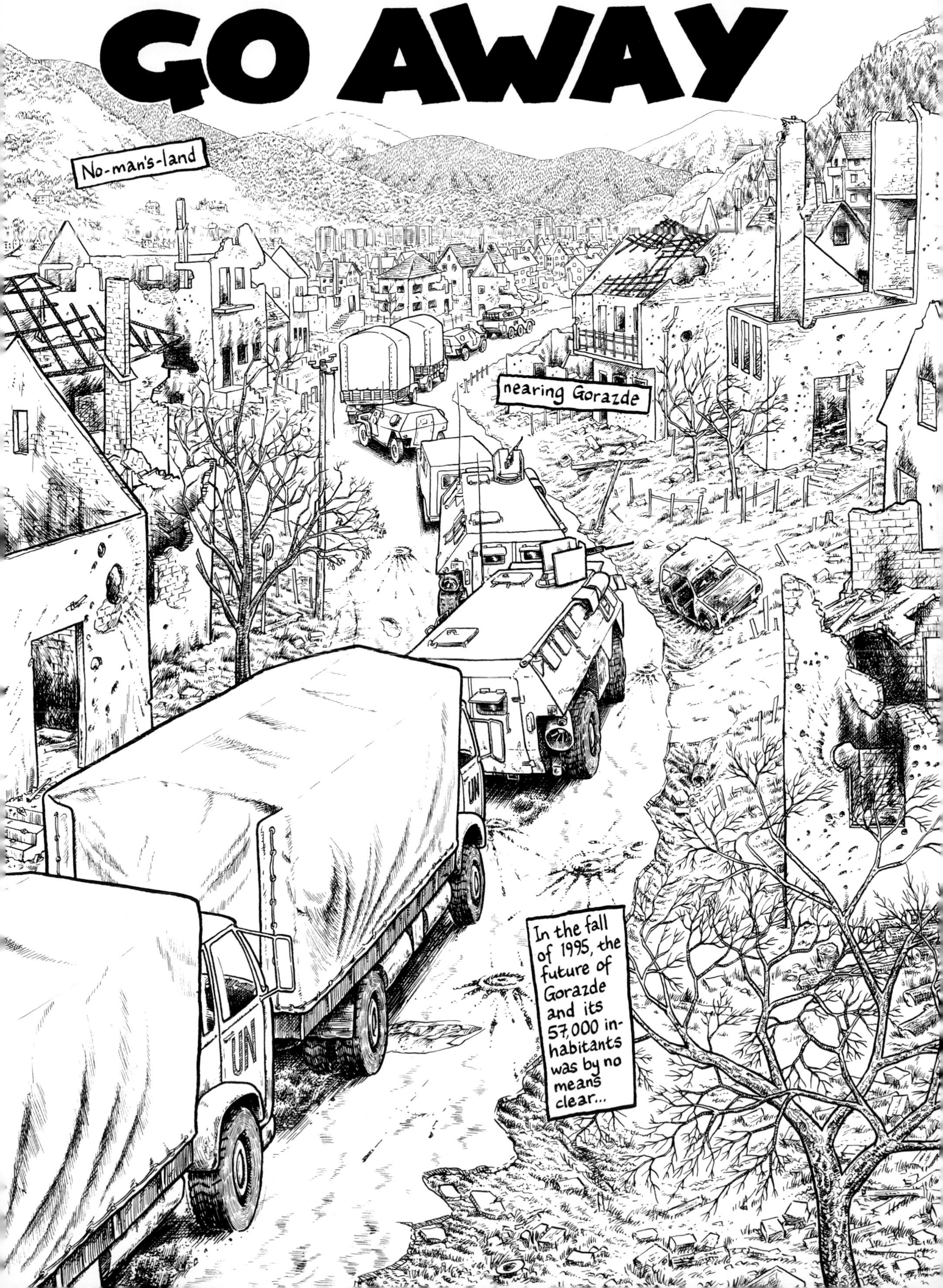
GO AWAY
No-man's-land
nearing Gorazde
In the fall of 1995, the future of Gorazde and its 57,000 inhabitants was by no means clear...

It was an enclave. It was surrounded by separatist Serb forces, it had been since the beginning of the Bosnian War more than three and a half years ago. And it was a U.N.-designated safe area...

The two other eastern enclaves, Srebrenica and Zepa, also designated safe areas, had been abandoned by the U.N. in the summer. The victorious Serbs entered Srebrenica and Zepa, and, in the aftermath, horrible stories had emerged...

When British and Ukranian U.N. peacekeepers pulled out of Gorazde shortly thereafter, Gorazdans thought they, too, had been abandoned...

J. SACCO 10 96

But now, following a massive NATO bombing campaign against them, the Serbs were compelled under the terms of a cease-fire to allow regular U.N. relief convoys through their territory and into Gorazde...

meanwhile, comprehensive peace talks were set to take place in Dayton, Ohio...

Foreign journalists, endlessly discussing possible Dayton scenarios, pondered the sticky problem of Gorazde's presence deep in Serb-held land. Some felt that a peace settlement would be facilitated if the Bosnian government traded the enclave to the Serbs for more territory around the capital, Sarajevo...

J. SACCO 11-96

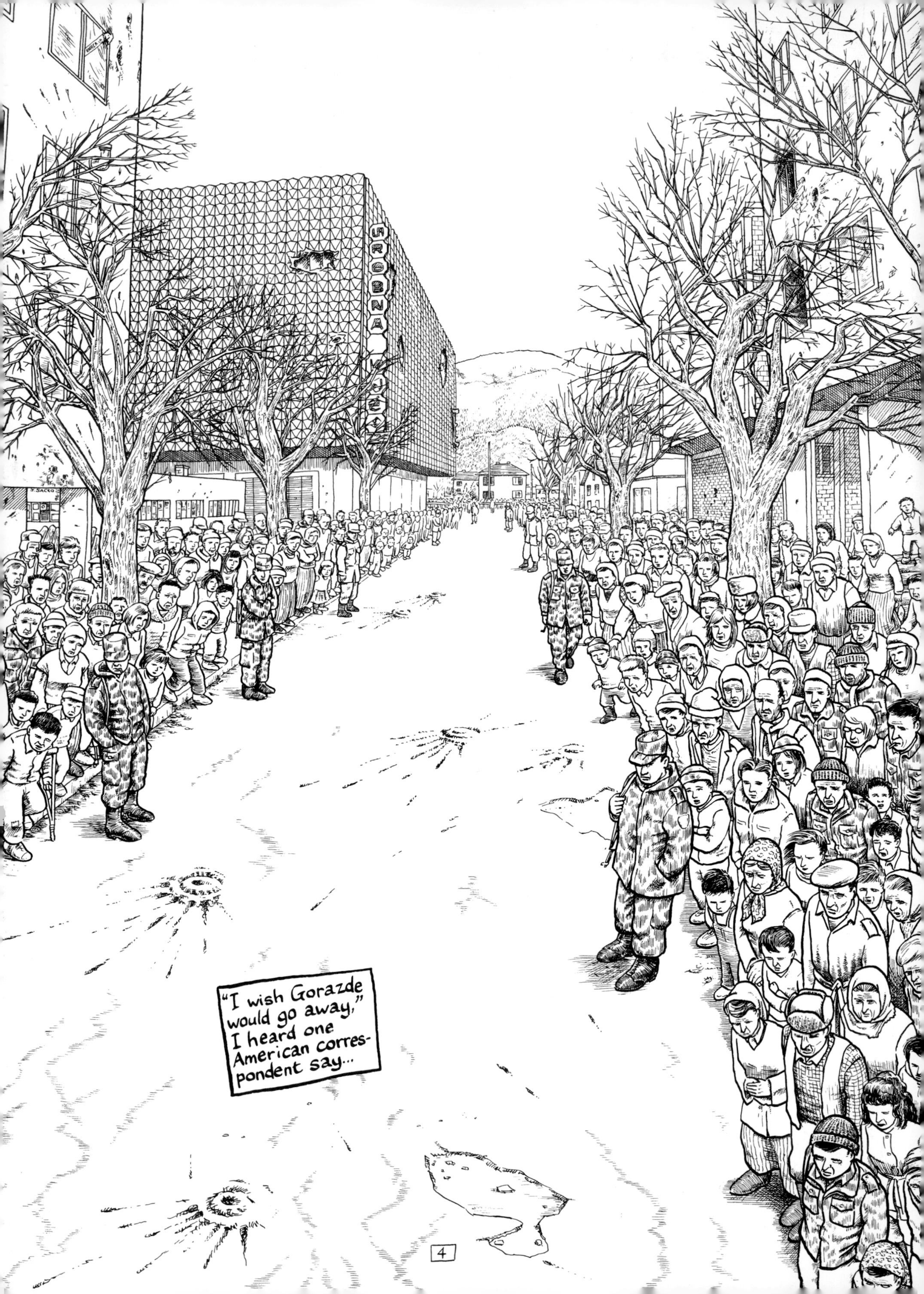
"I wish Gorazde would go away," I heard one American corres-pondent say...

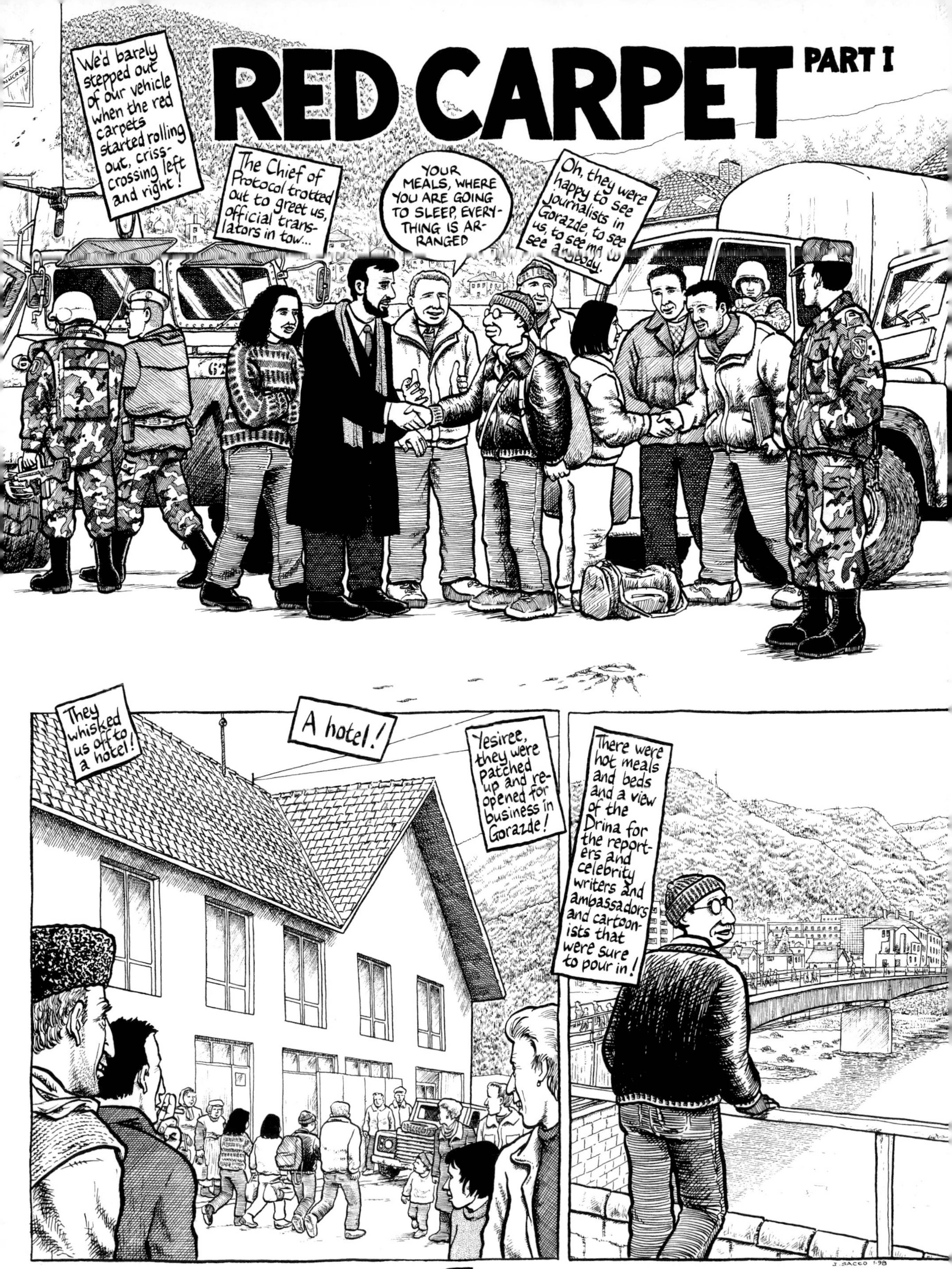
RED CARPET PART I
We'd barely stepped out of our vehicle when the red carpets started rolling out, criss-crossing left and right!
The Chief of Protocol trotted out to greet us, official translators in tow...
YOUR MEALS, WHERE YOU ARE GOING TO SLEEP, EVERYTHING IS ARRANGED
Oh, they were happy to see journalists in Gorazde, to see us, to see ma
see anybody.
They whisked us off to a hotel!
A hotel!
Yesiree, they were patched up and re-opened for business in Gorazde!
There were hot meals and beds and a view of the Drina for the reporters and celebrity writers and ambassadors and cartoonists that were sure to pour in!
J. SACCO 1-98

My colleagues and I, we were prancin' and dancin', giggly in Gorazde, glorious by association!

Gorazde!

which had just wrested the spotlight from that media darling Sarajevo!

Gorazde!

which was getting CNNed! NPRed! BBCed!

But its proverbial 15 minutes were ticking away!

Pretty soon no one was gonna remember Gorazde!

Gora-wuh?

Hunh?

We didn't have a moment to lose!

PART II

Pretty soon we were in someone's living room, awash in coffee, getting an overview of the last three and a half years...

The hunger?

Awful!

The prices and fortunes wiped out?

Hoo boy!

The shells coming in?

You wouldn't believe it!

(Maybe you won't when I get to it.)

But I was trying to break the ol' ice-aroo with Emira, the 19-year-old translator who'd been assigned to us for the afternoon.

SO WHAT DO YOU DO AROUND HERE FOR FUN?

I DON'T HAVE FUN.

J. SACCO 1-98

6

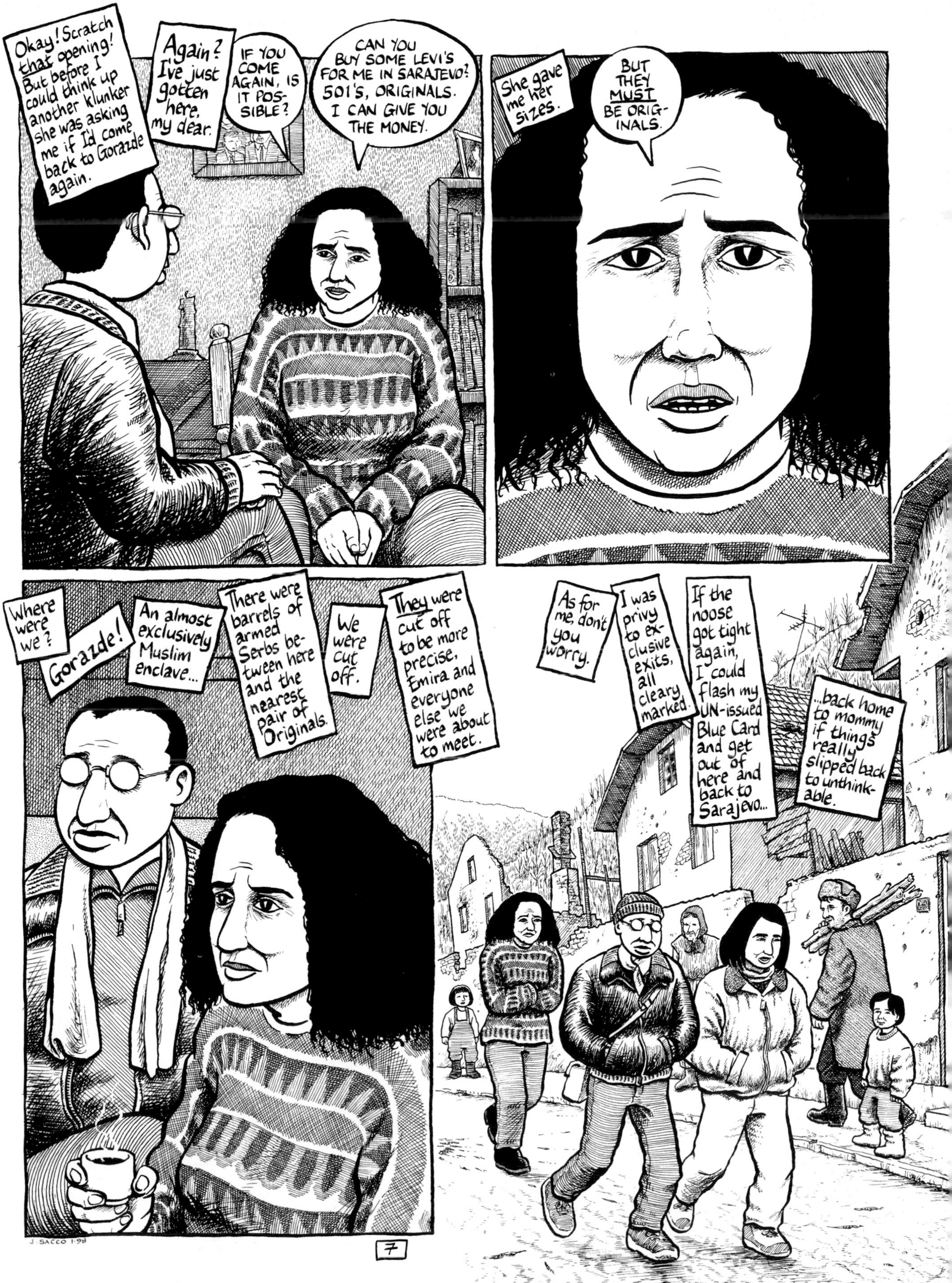

Okay! Scratch that opening! But before I could think up another klunker she was asking me if I'd come back to Gorazde again.
Again? I've just gotten here, my dear.
IF YOU COME AGAIN, IS IT POSSIBLE?
CAN YOU BUY SOME LEVI'S FOR ME IN SARAJEVO? 501'S, ORIGINALS. I CAN GIVE YOU THE MONEY.
She gave me her sizes.
BUT THEY MUST BE ORIGINALS.
Where were we?
Gorazde!
An almost exclusively Muslim enclave...
There were barrels of armed Serbs between here and the nearest pair of Originals.
We were cut off.
They were cut off to be more precise, Emira and everyone else we were about to meet.
As for me, don't you worry.
I was privy to exclusive exits, all cleary marked.
If the noose got tight again, I could flash my UN-issued Blue Card and get out of here and back to Sarajevo...
...back home to mommy if things really slipped back to unthinkable.
J. SACCO 1·98

A couple hours later, you couldn't have dragged me out of Gorazde.

I was having a ball, man, drunk on moonshine brandy and letting loose with some nutto locals ready to turn the presence of a few foreign journalists into a major swingfest.

This fellah, Edin—he said he was a school teacher—he'd organized the party.

Later he turned out to be our main man, my main man, worth his weight in satellite phones to journalists who wanted the scoop on Gorazde, and not just the scoop. We wanted some laughs, too, a chandelier to swing from if available.

Edin's friend Nina was hosting us, promising homemade pizza.

J. SACCO 7-98

Her son, Mela, was all decked out to receive the foreigners...

He was some kid, a subscriber to the maximum-body-contact school of hospitality...

...and a real charmer with the English he'd picked up from British peacekeepers a few months before—

CHETNIK IS ASSHOLE.

Nina's husband was hamming it up with a toy microphone, singing his heart out over a turbo-folk video while we laughed and hooted.

Okay okay, maybe this shindig doesn't sound like much, just a bunch of drinks and decibels in Bumfuck, The Balkans.

But our new pals...

they partied like the resurrected...

not like there was no tomorrow, but because there was a tomorrow...

they'd been so desperate for so long, and, apparently, just weeks ago, so doomed, that now—

J. SACCO 1-98

9

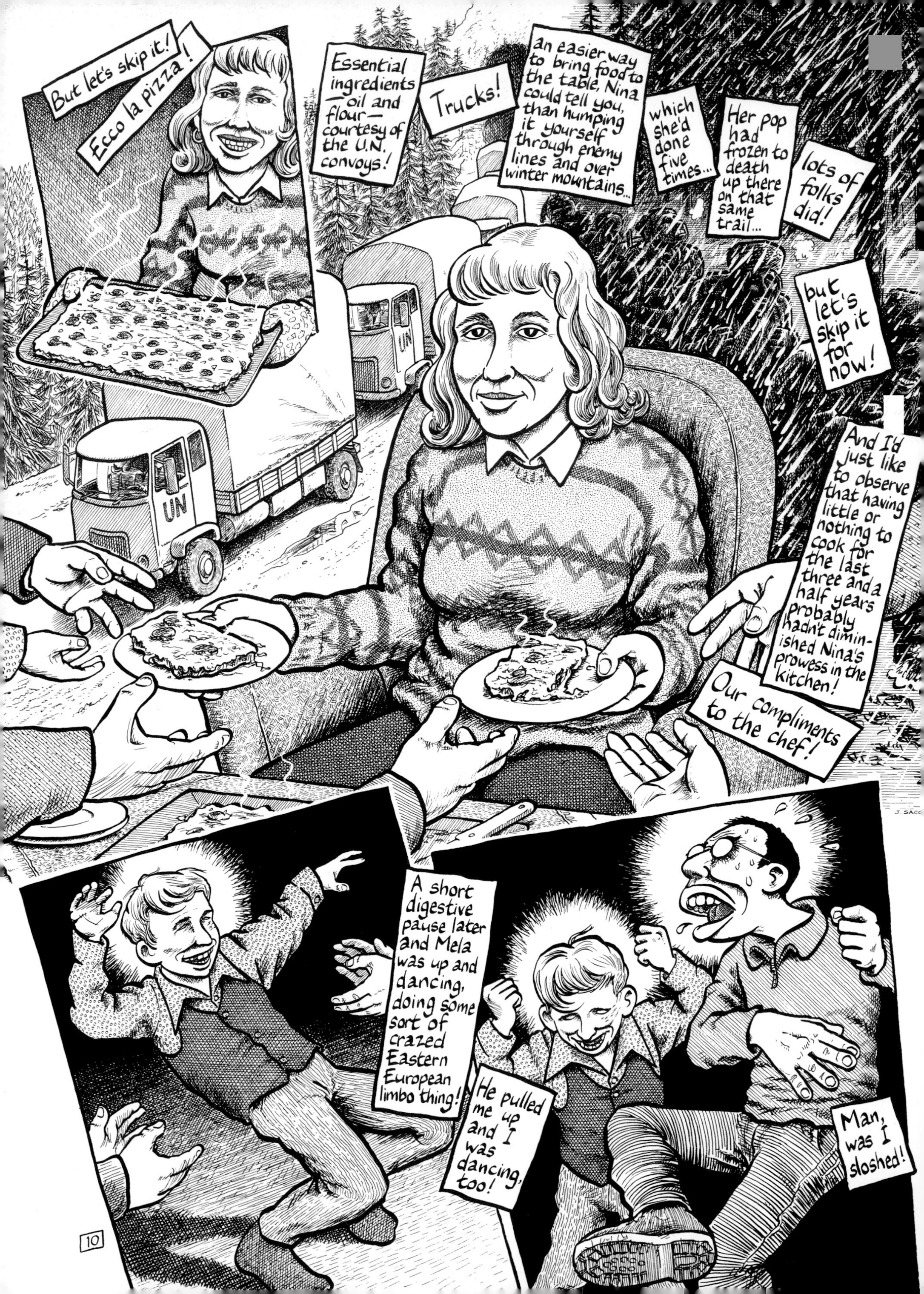
Ecco la pizza!
But let's skip it!
Essential ingredients—oil and flour—courtesy of the U.N. convoys!
Trucks!
an easier way to bring food to the table, Nina could tell you, than humping it yourself through enemy lines and over winter mountains...
which she'd done five times...
Her pop had frozen to death up there on that same trail...
lots of folks did!
but let's skip it for now!
And I'd just like to observe that having little or nothing to cook for the last three and a half years probably hadn't diminished Nina's prowess in the kitchen!
Our compliments to the chef!
J. SACCO
A short digestive pause later and Mela was up and dancing, doing some sort of crazed Eastern European limbo thing!
He pulled me up and I was dancing, too!
Man, was I sloshed!

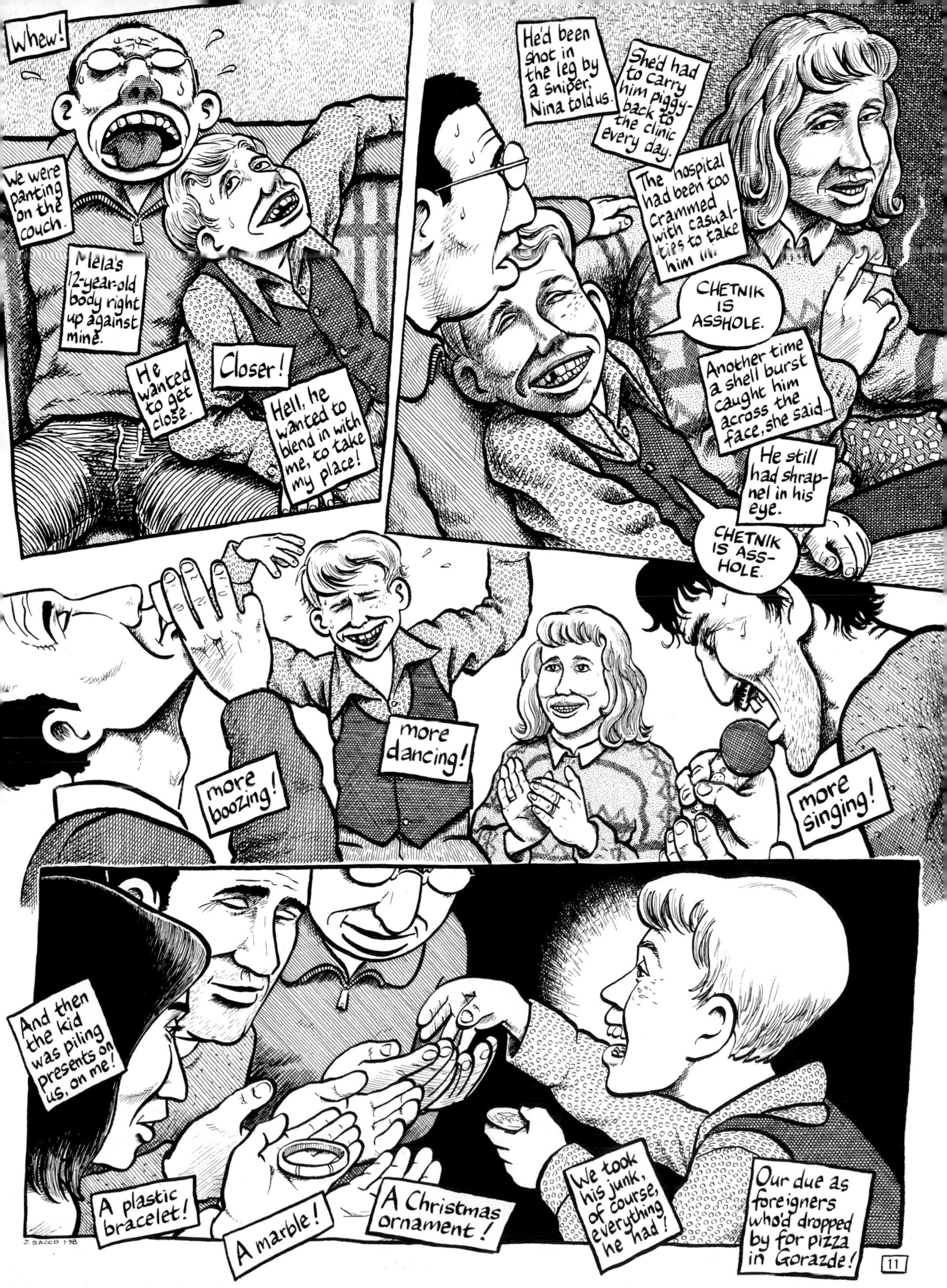
Whew!
We were panting on the couch.
Mela's 12-year-old body right up against mine.
He wanted to get close.
Closer!
Hell, he wanted to blend in with me, to take my place!
He'd been shot in the leg by a sniper, Nina told us.
She'd had to carry him piggy-back to the clinic every day.
The hospital had been too crammed with casualties to take him in.
CHETNIK IS ASSHOLE.
Another time a shell burst caught him across the face, she said...
He still had shrapnel in his eye.
CHETNIK IS ASS-HOLE.
more boozing!
more dancing!
more singing!
And then the kid was piling presents on us, on me!
A plastic bracelet!
A marble!
A Christmas ornament!
We took his junk, of course, everything he had!
Our due as foreigners who'd dropped by for pizza in Gorazde!
J. SACCO 1.98

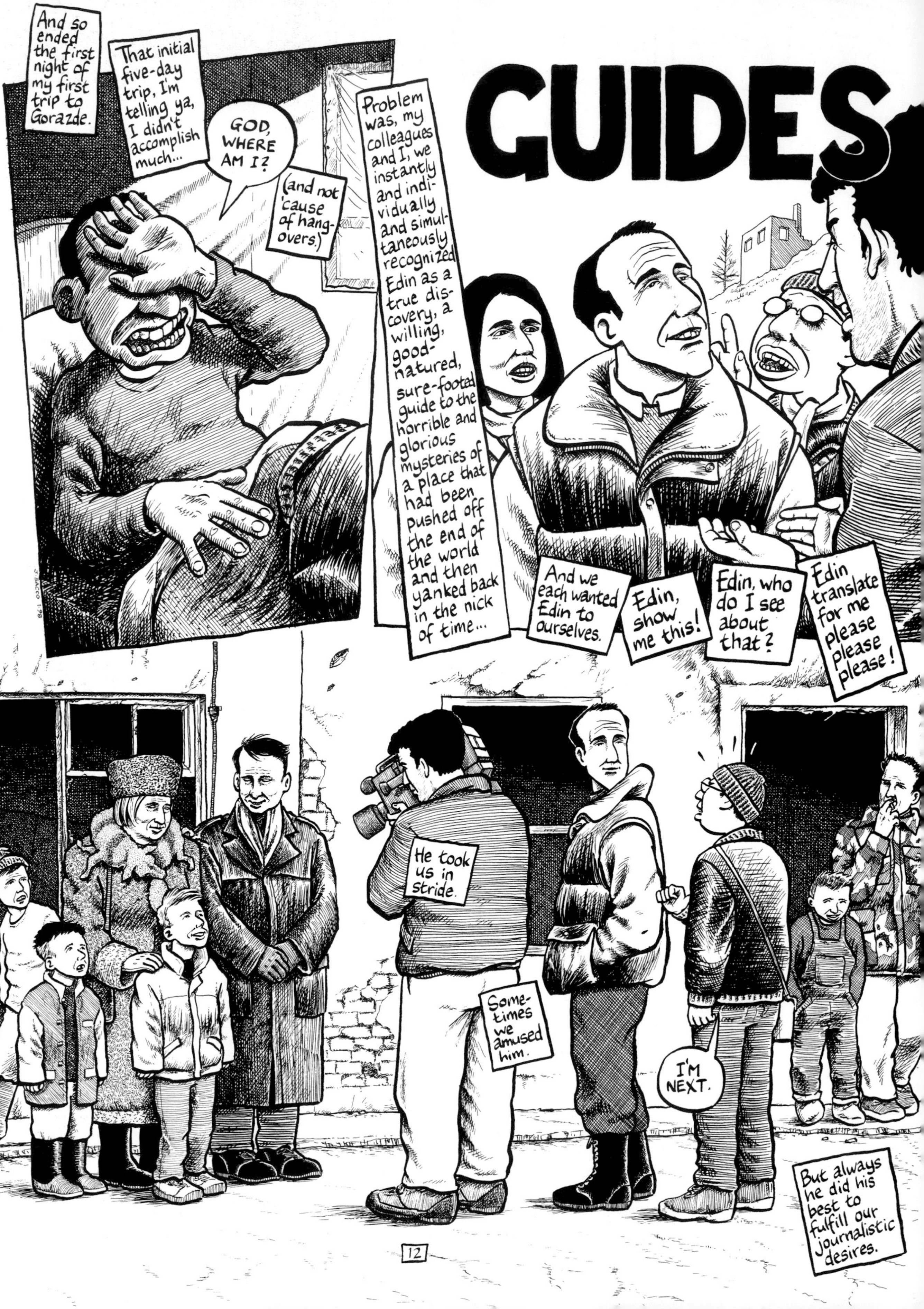
And so ended the first night of my first trip to Gorazde.
That initial five-day trip, I'm telling ya, I didn't accomplish much...
GOD, WHERE AM I?
(and not 'cause of hang-overs.)
Problem was, my colleagues and I, we instantly and indi-vidually and simul-taneously recognized Edin as a true dis-covery, a willing, good-natured, sure-footed guide to the horrible and glorious mysteries of a place that had been pushed off the end of the world and then yanked back in the nick of time...
GUIDES
And we each wanted Edin to ourselves.
Edin, show me this!
Edin, who do I see about that?
Edin translate for me please please please!
He took us in stride.
Some-times we amused him.
I'M NEXT.
But always he did his best to fulfill our journalistic desires.

Edin seemed to know everyone, to have his foot in every door...

he could smooth our way with the police and at the municipality...

he could make the necessary introductions...

and at the end of the day he knew the nearest good time...

All that and he taught at the technical school, too.

Once he invited us into his trigonometry class and—

YOU CAN ASK THEM ANY QUESTION.

But we asked instead if they had any questions for us...

WHY DID YOU COME TO GORAZDE?

J. SACCO 1-98

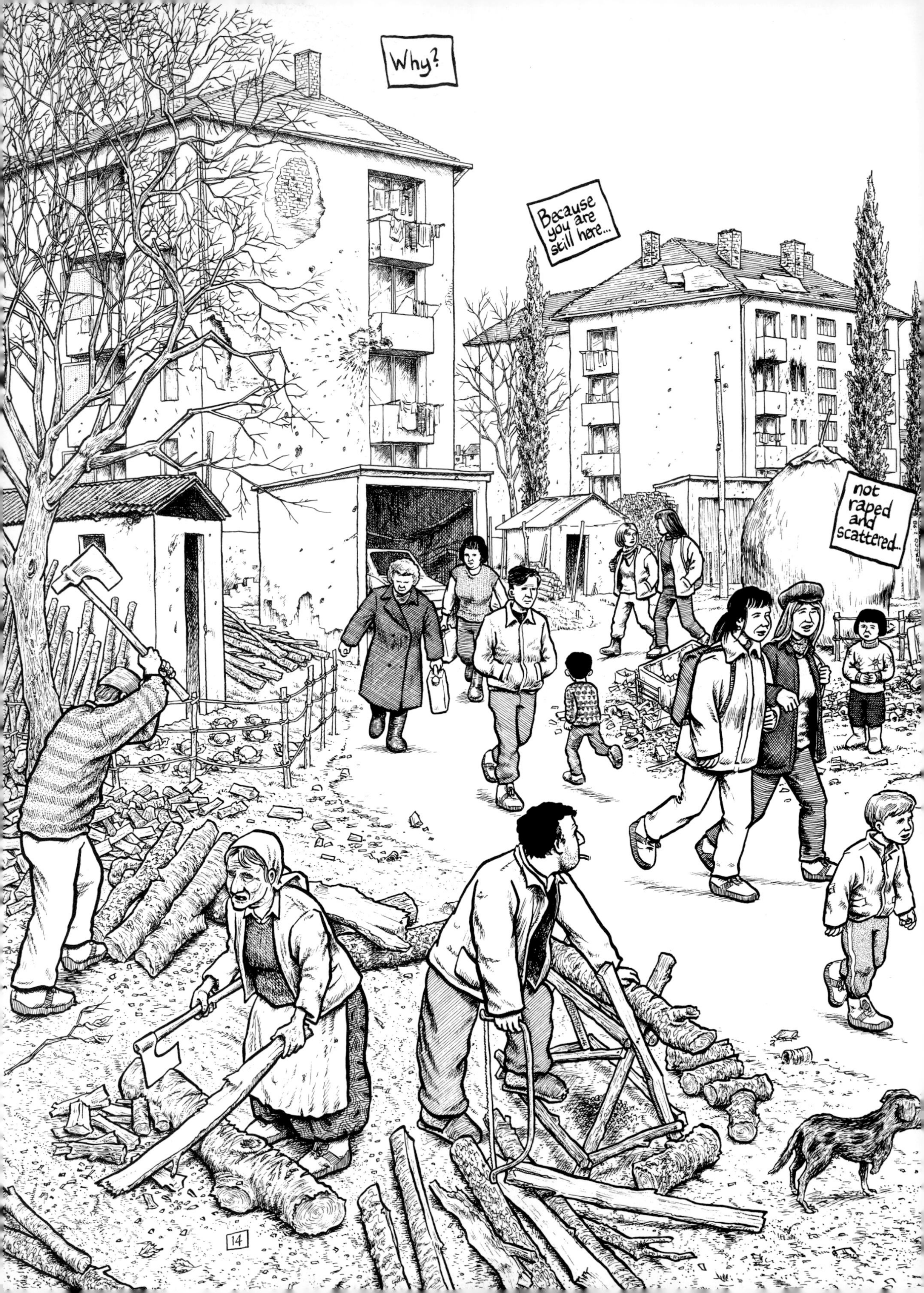
Why?
Because you are still here...
not raped and scattered...

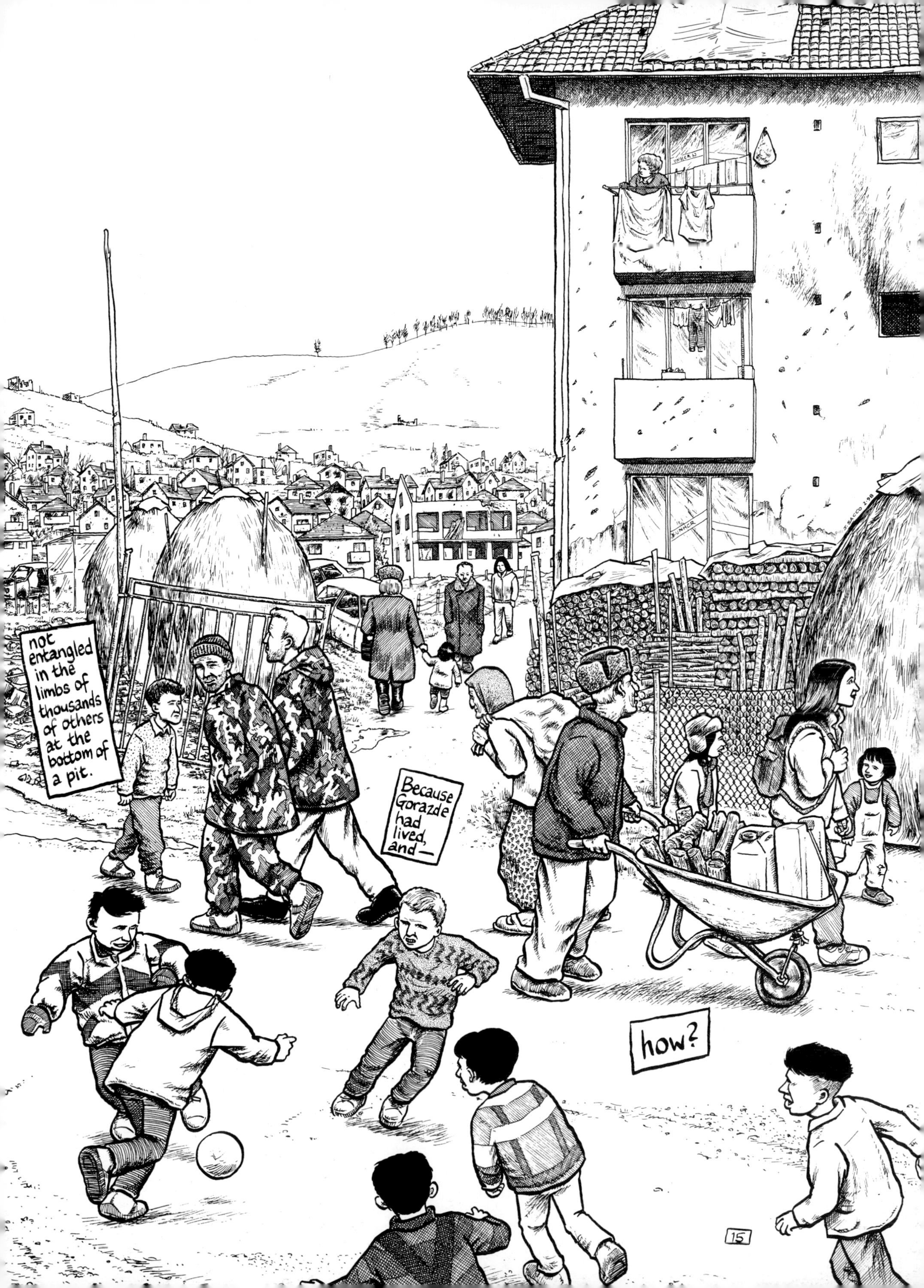
not entangled in the limbs of thousands of others at the bottom of a pit.
Because Gorazde had lived, and—
how?

And I came back three times, and each time I sought out Edin to help me put the pieces of the story together...

And sometimes he showed me the pieces that were visible...

MARKS IN THE ROAD WHERE A SERB TANK HAD STOPPED AND TURNED.

and sometimes he showed me the pieces hidden away...

FOOTBRIDGE UNDER THE SECOND BRIDGE, BUILT TO SHIELD PEDESTRIANS FROM SNIPERS.

and sometimes the pieces he showed me were his own...

THE CAR OF ONE OF HIS BEST FRIENDS, KILLED ON THE FIRST DAY OF THE FIRST ATTACK ON GORAZDE.

16

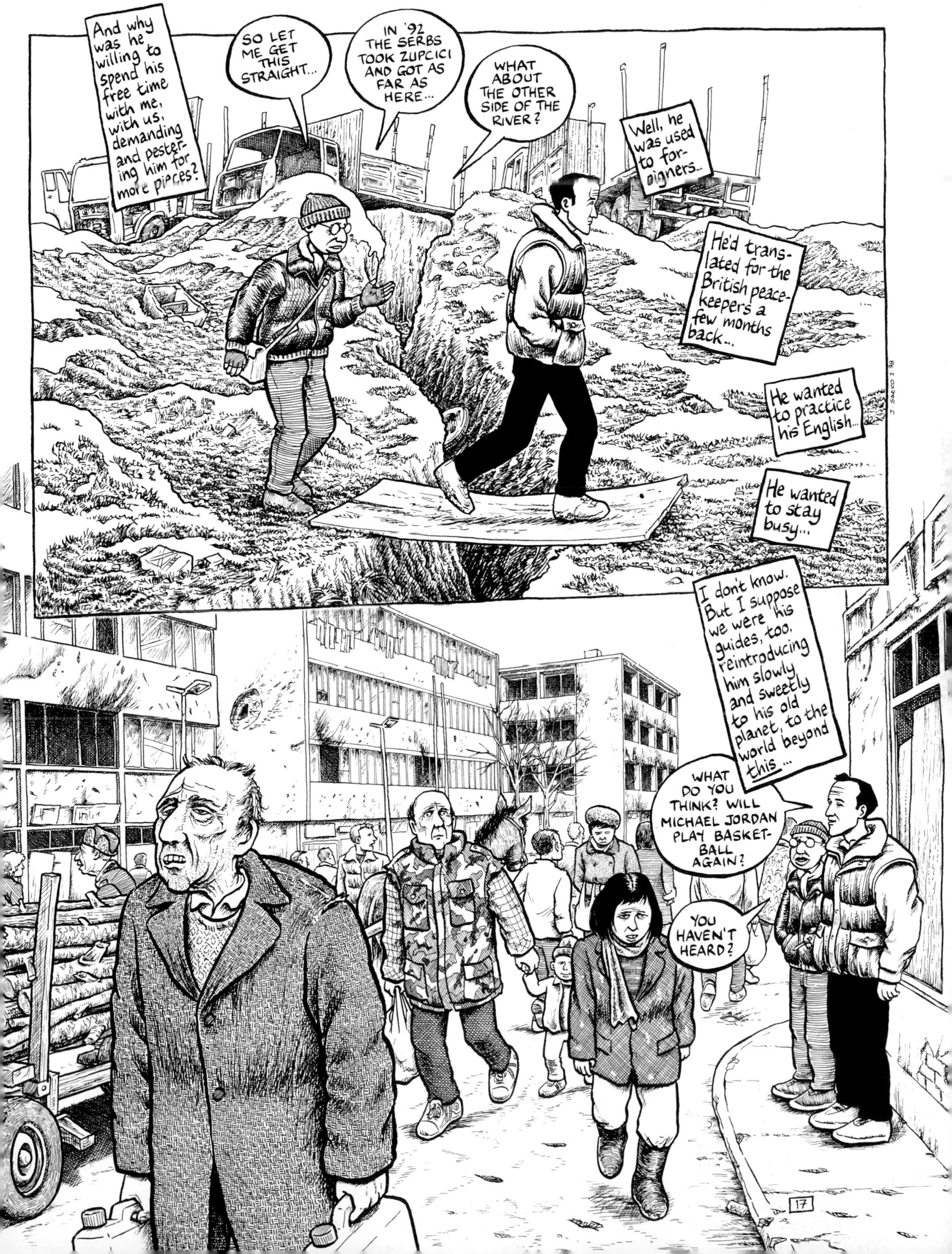
And why was he willing to spend his free time with me, with us, demanding and pestering him for more pieces?
SO LET ME GET THIS STRAIGHT...
IN '92 THE SERBS TOOK ZUPCICI AND GOT AS FAR AS HERE...
WHAT ABOUT THE OTHER SIDE OF THE RIVER?
Well, he was used to foreigners...
He'd translated for the British peacekeepers a few months back...
He wanted to practice his English...
He wanted to stay busy...
J. Sacco 2 '98
I don't know. But I suppose we were his guides, too, reintroducing him slowly and sweetly to his old planet, to the world beyond this...
WHAT DO YOU THINK? WILL MICHAEL JORDAN PLAY BASKETBALL AGAIN?
YOU HAVEN'T HEARD?

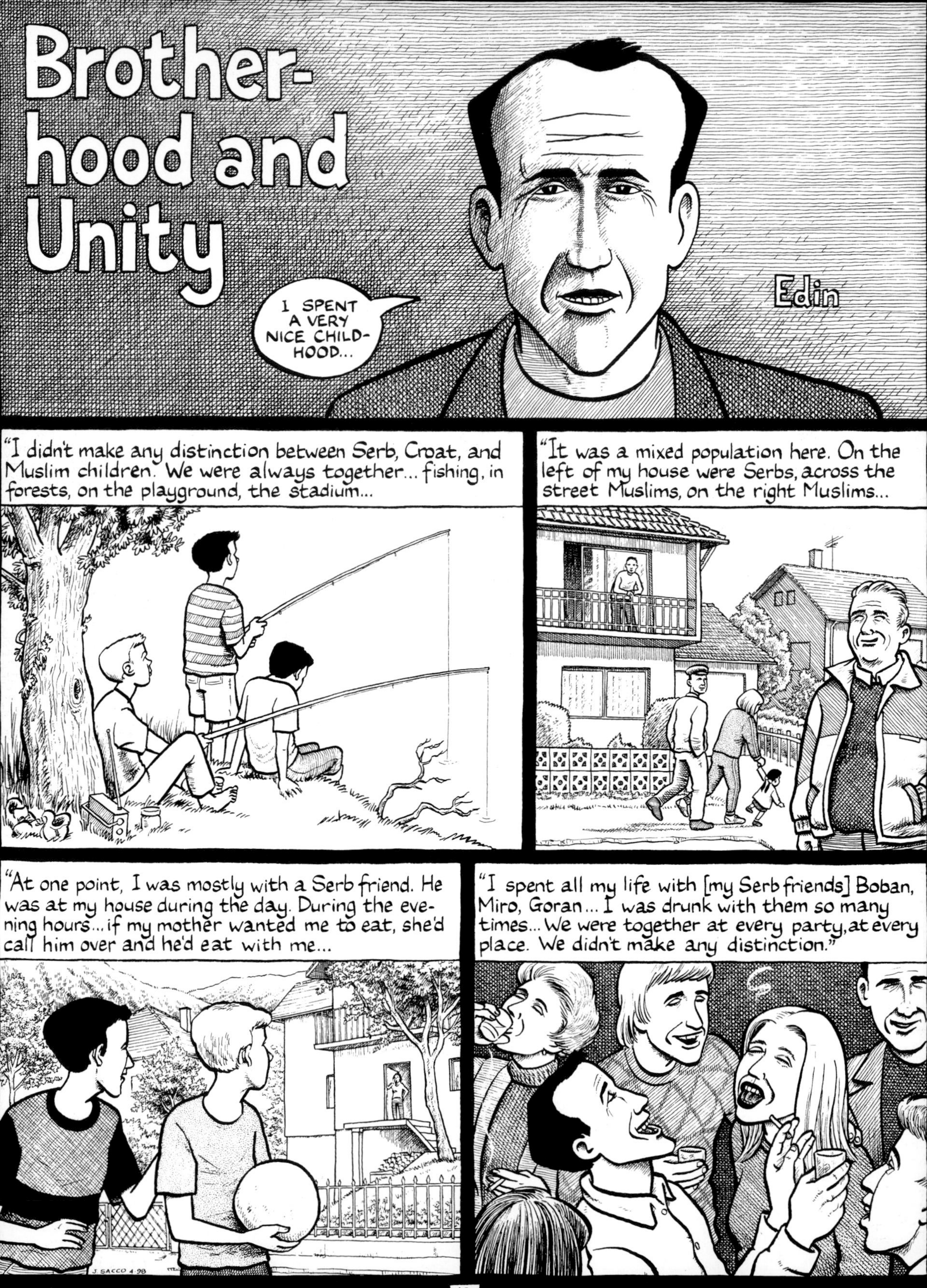
Brotherhood and Unity
Edin
I SPENT A VERY NICE CHILDHOOD...
"I didn't make any distinction between Serb, Croat, and Muslim children. We were always together... fishing, in forests, on the playground, the stadium...
"It was a mixed population here. On the left of my house were Serbs, across the street Muslims, on the right Muslims...
"At one point, I was mostly with a Serb friend. He was at my house during the day. During the evening hours... if my mother wanted me to eat, she'd call him over and he'd eat with me...
"I spent all my life with [my Serb friends] Boban, Miro, Goran... I was drunk with them so many times... We were together at every party, at every place. We didn't make any distinction."
J. SACCO 4-98

Modern Yugoslavia was fashioned out of the wreckage of the Kingdom of Yugoslavia after World War II by the Communist resistance leader Josip Broz, better known as Tito.

AUSTRIA
HUNGARY
Slovenia
ROMANIA
Croatia
Vojvodina
Bosnia
Serbia
Monte-
negro
Kosovo
BULGARIA
Macedonia
ITALY
ALBANIA
GREECE
ADRIATIC SEA

YUGOSLAVIA BEFORE THE BREAK-UP, SHOWING THE REPUBLICS AND AUTONOMOUS AREAS

Of the six Yugoslav republics constituted by Tito, Bosnia was the most ethnically diverse. It contained large populations of Croats, Serbs, and Muslims. Each of these ethnic groups has a particular history and cultural background, but they are all South Slavs and speak essentially the same language. Their chief distinguishing characteristic is religious. Croats are Roman Catholics; Serbs are Orthodox Christians; and Muslims are generally descended from those Slavs who converted to Islam during a 500-year Ottoman occupation.

CROATIA
Kupa
Sava
Una
BIHAC
BANJA LUKA
Vrbas
Sava
Bosna
BRCKO
BIJELJINA
DOBOJ
Drina
Sava
BOSNIA
TUZLA
ZVORNIK
JAJCE
SERBIA
TRAVNIK
VITEZ
ZENICA
SREBRENICA
VISOKO
ZEPA
SARAJEVO
VISEGRAD
ROGATICA
GORAZDE
FOCA
Drina
MOSTAR
Neretva
MONTE-NEGRO

Some of Bosnia's larger cities, like the capital Sarajevo, were particularly well mixed, and enjoyed a rich and often touted spirit of tolerance.

Gorazde is in the Drina Valley in Eastern Bosnia, where villages and towns were populated predominantly by Muslims and Serbs.

J. GACCO 3-98

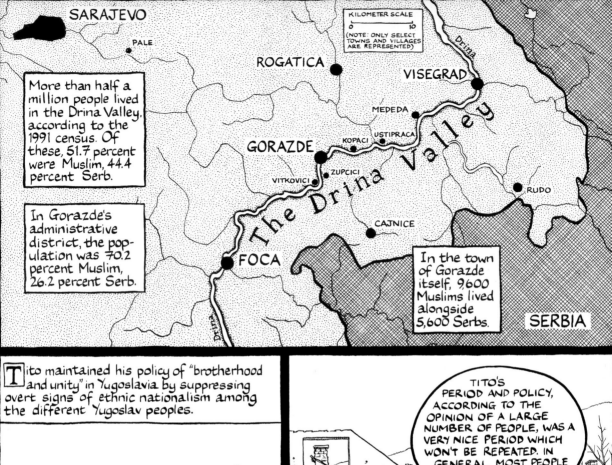

SARAJEVO

PALE

ROGATICA

VISEGRAD

MEDEDA

KOPACI USTIPRACA

GORAZDE

VITKOVICI · ZUPCICI

RUDO

CAJNICE

FOCA

The Drina Valley

Drina

Drina

KILOMETER SCALE
0   10
(NOTE: ONLY SELECT
TOWNS AND VILLAGES
ARE REPRESENTED)

SERBIA

More than half a
million people lived
in the Drina Valley,
according to the
1991 census. Of
these, 51.7 percent
were Muslim, 44.4
percent Serb.

In Gorazde's
administrative
district, the pop-
ulation was 70.2
percent Muslim,
26.2 percent Serb.

In the town
of Gorazde
itself, 9,600
Muslims lived
alongside
5,600 Serbs.

Tito maintained his policy of "brotherhood
and unity" in Yugoslavia by suppressing
overt signs of ethnic nationalism among
the different Yugoslav peoples.

If Tito managed to create something of a
Yugoslav identity, he did so without defusing
or allowing for an airing of the nationalities'
grievances. Those grievances would be
exploited by politicians jockeying for power
once President-for-life Tito was gone.

TITO'S
PERIOD AND POLICY,
ACCORDING TO THE
OPINION OF A LARGE
NUMBER OF PEOPLE, WAS A
VERY NICE PERIOD WHICH
WON'T BE REPEATED. IN
GENERAL, MOST PEOPLE
REGRET THE END
OF THIS PER-
IOD.

IT IS
MY OPINION
AS WELL.

For although
Tito's rule was
authoritarian, in
his Yugoslavia Croats,
Serbs, and Muslims
had lived together
peacefully for half
a century, and this
after the extra-
ordinary blood-
letting between
them in World War II.

J. SACCO 4-98

More than a million Yugoslavs died in the war, mostly at the hands of other Yugoslavs.

When the Axis powers occupied and dismembered the Kingdom of Yugoslavia in 1941, they installed Croatian fascists, the Ustasha, in their own state, which was expanded to include Bosnia. The fury with which the Ustasha carried out their genocidal program of wholesale slaughter, forced religious conversion, and expulsion of the Serb population left even the Nazis aghast. Ustasha victims fed the ranks of two competing resistance groups, the Chetniks and the Partisans.

The Chetniks were a somewhat loose alliance of groups of Serb nationalists and royalists who typically sought the establishment of a Greater Serbia cleansed of non-Serbs. The Chetniks waged a ruthless war against Bosnia's Croat and Muslim citizenry, whom they viewed as Ustasha collaborators, and against the Partisans, whom they saw as likely post-war rivals.

The Partisans, the Communist resistance force led by Tito, also were a predominantly Serb group (Tito himself was half-Croatian, half-Slovenian), but they welcomed a growing number of Muslim and Croatian recruits as disillusionment with the Ustasha regime increased and Chetnik outrages continued. The Partisans fought a generally defensive war against Axis forces and waged an aggressive campaign against the Chetniks, whom they eventually crushed.

Bosnia's Muslims could be found on all sides of the conflict. A few even allied themselves with the Chetniks. Others joined in the Ustasha persecution of the Serbs. Several thousand volunteered with the Germans for a Muslim S.S. division which carried out anti-Serb atrocities.

As chaos spread, some Muslims formed autonomous defense units for protection against any and all threats, and in greater and greater numbers Muslims joined the multi-ethnic Partisans, which led to more Chetnik reprisals.

Hundreds of thousands of Serbs were killed in the war, mostly by the Ustasha, but the Muslims lost a greater percentage of their population, mostly in Chetnik attacks and massacres, many of which took place in Eastern Bosnia.

THERE WAS PLENTY OF KILLING IN THE WAR, MUSLIMS BY CHETNIKS.

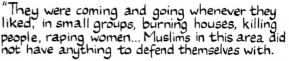

"They were coming and going whenever they liked, in small groups, burning houses, killing people, raping women... Muslims in this area did not have anything to defend themselves with.

"The Chetniks raped and slaughtered... so many of my cousins and Muslims in this area. The worst things happened in Foca. The village of my family, Bucije ...over the River Drina, the Chetniks completely blew up, and whomever they found they killed. We're talking about the men...

"When people heard that these groups were coming, as fast as possible they were hiding themselves or escaping somewhere. My grandfather hid himself with the help of his wife for nearly one year under the cows' shed in the ground...

"In that time, Muslims...escaped from Gorazde... They organized themselves in groups and ran from one place to the other because of the traitors, the Chetniks and the Ustasha. My grandparents were able to go to Brcko and Visoko.

"My grandfather and grandmother sometimes tried to explain to me what happened during World War II, but I did not listen, or listened with one ear."

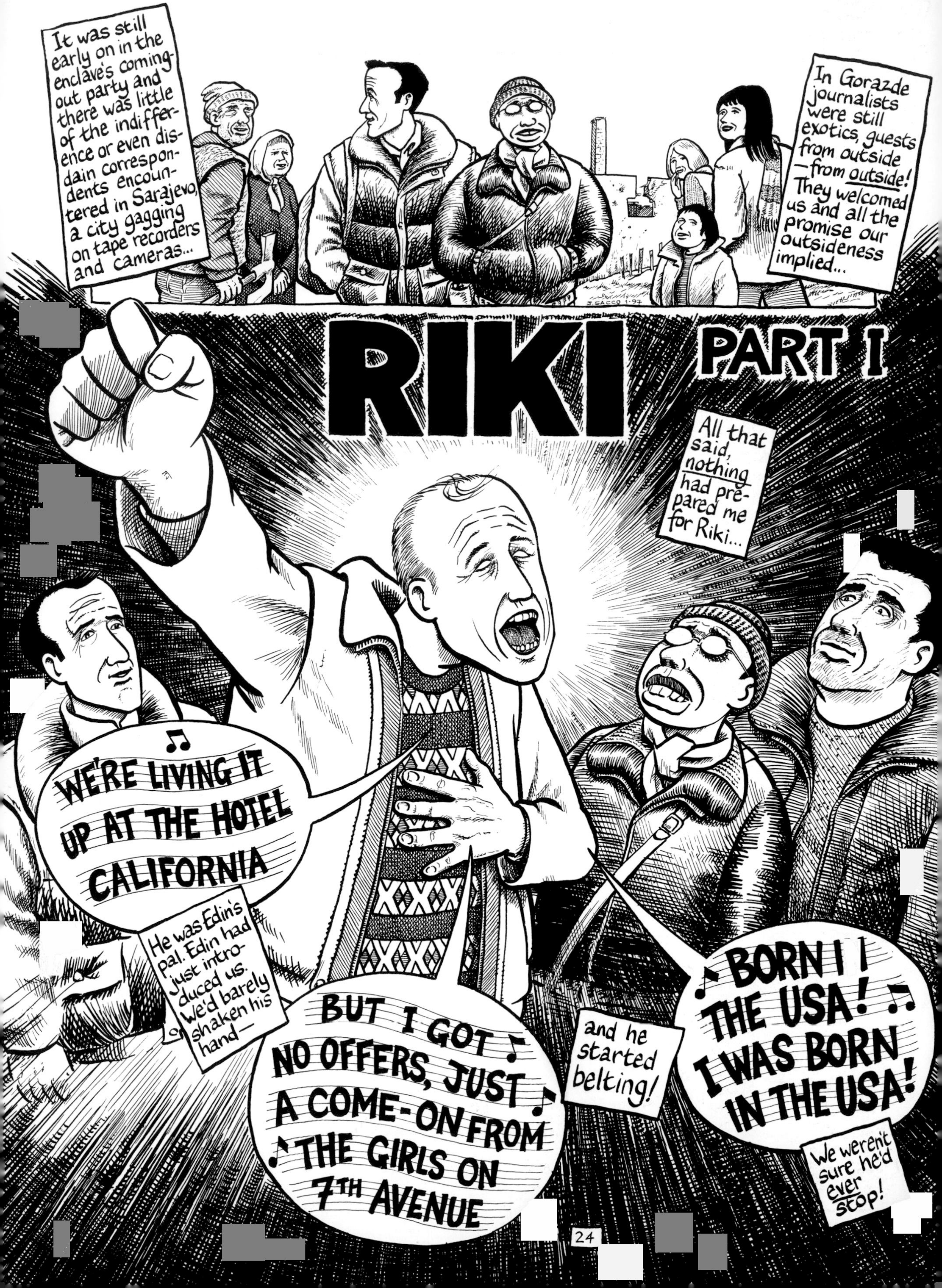
It was still early on in the enclave's coming-out party and there was little of the indifference or even disdain correspondents encountered in Sarajevo, a city gagging on tape recorders and cameras...
In Gorazde journalists were still exotics, guests from outside —from outside! They welcomed us and all the promise our outsideness implied...
J. SACCO 1·97
RIKI
PART I
All that said, nothing had prepared me for Riki...
WE'RE LIVING IT UP AT THE HOTEL CALIFORNIA
He was Edin's pal. Edin had just introduced us. We'd barely shaken his hand—
BUT I GOT NO OFFERS, JUST A COME-ON FROM THE GIRLS ON 7TH AVENUE
and he started belting!
BORN I
THE USA! I WAS BORN IN THE USA!
We weren't sure he'd ever stop!

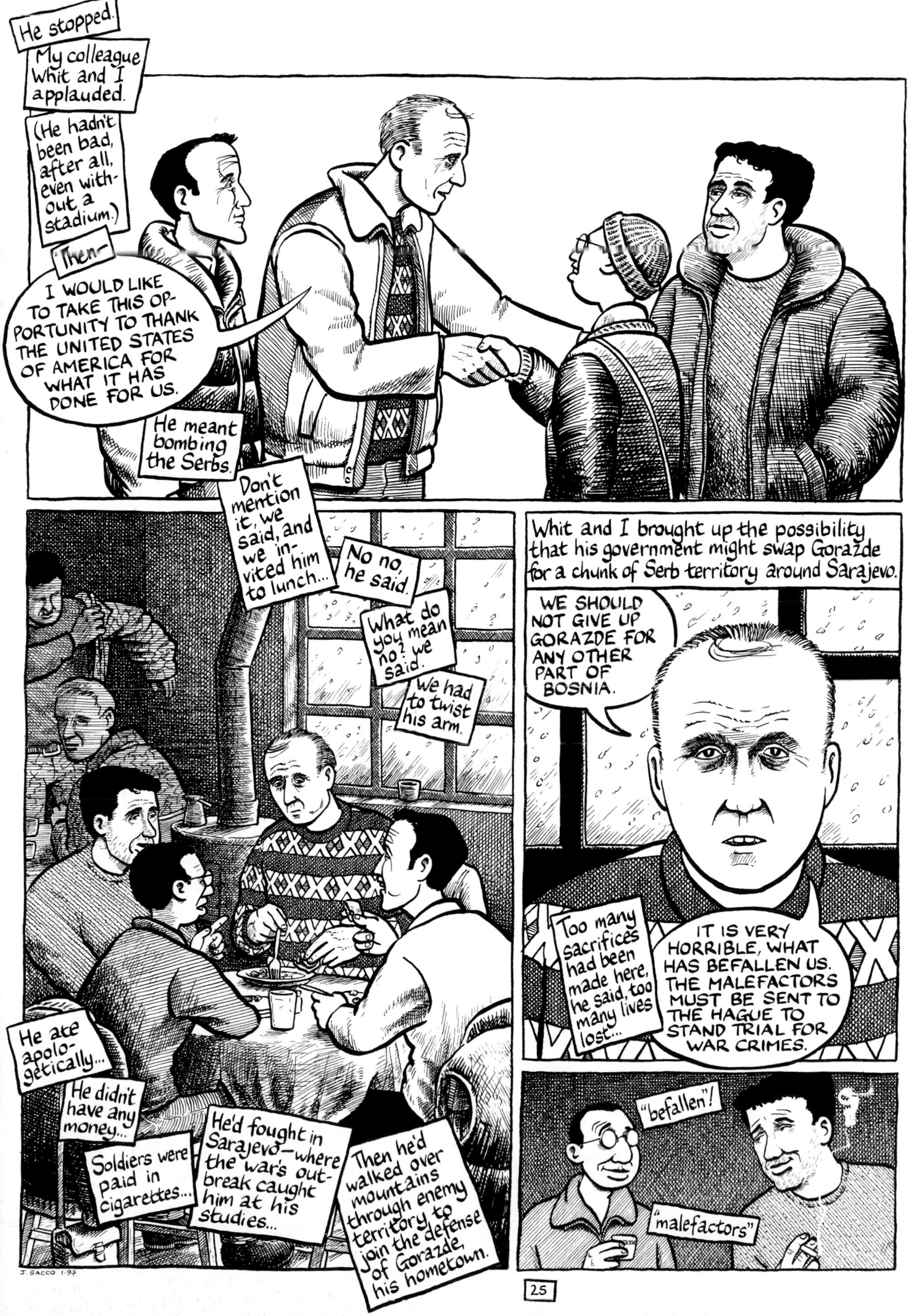
He stopped.
My colleague Whit and I applauded.
(He hadn't been bad, after all, even without a stadium.)
Then—
I WOULD LIKE TO TAKE THIS OPPORTUNITY TO THANK THE UNITED STATES OF AMERICA FOR WHAT IT HAS DONE FOR US.
He meant bombing the Serbs.
Don't mention it, we said, and we invited him to lunch...
No no, he said.
What do you mean no? we said.
We had to twist his arm.
He ate apologetically...
He didn't have any money...
Soldiers were paid in cigarettes...
He'd fought in Sarajevo—where the war's outbreak caught him at his studies...
Then he'd walked over mountains through enemy territory to join the defense of Gorazde, his hometown.
Whit and I brought up the possibility that his government might swap Gorazde for a chunk of Serb territory around Sarajevo.
WE SHOULD NOT GIVE UP GORAZDE FOR ANY OTHER PART OF BOSNIA.
Too many sacrifices had been made here, he said, too many lives lost...
IT IS VERY HORRIBLE, WHAT HAS BEFALLEN US. THE MALEFACTORS MUST BE SENT TO THE HAGUE TO STAND TRIAL FOR WAR CRIMES.
"befallen"!
"malefactors"
J. SACCO 1·97

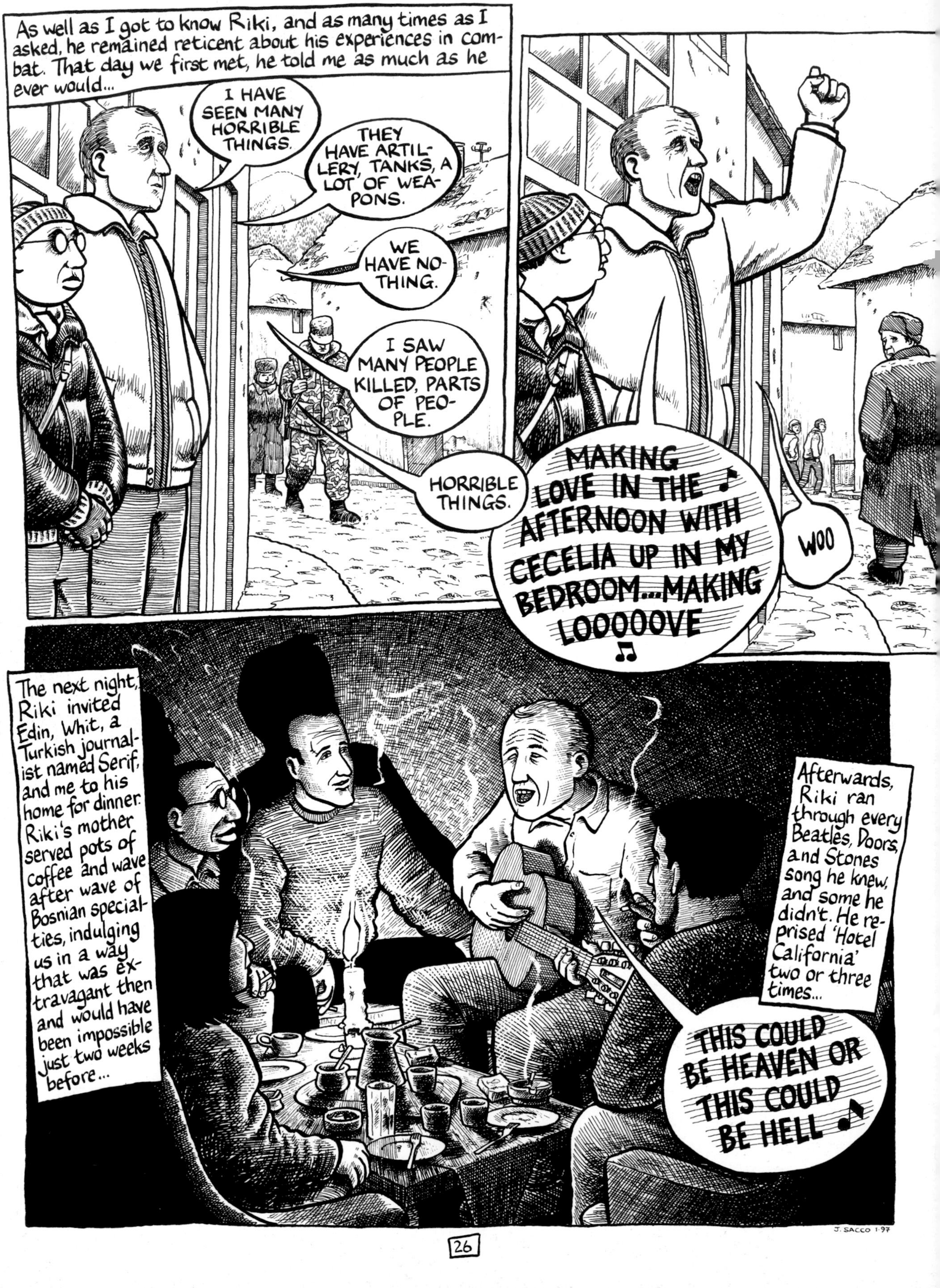

As well as I got to know Riki, and as many times as I asked, he remained reticent about his experiences in combat. That day we first met, he told me as much as he ever would...
I HAVE SEEN MANY HORRIBLE THINGS.
THEY HAVE ARTILLERY, TANKS, A LOT OF WEAPONS.
WE HAVE NOTHING.
I SAW MANY PEOPLE KILLED, PARTS OF PEOPLE.
HORRIBLE THINGS.
MAKING LOVE IN THE AFTERNOON WITH CECELIA UP IN MY BEDROOM...MAKING LOOOOOVE
WOO
The next night, Riki invited Edin, Whit, a Turkish journalist named Serif, and me to his home for dinner. Riki's mother served pots of coffee and wave after wave of Bosnian specialties, indulging us in a way that was extravagant then and would have been impossible just two weeks before...
Afterwards, Riki ran through every Beatles, Doors, and Stones song he knew, and some he didn't. He reprised 'Hotel California' two or three times...
THIS COULD BE HEAVEN OR THIS COULD BE HELL
J. SACCO 1·97

Then he and Edin regaled us with Bosnian folk and patriotic songs...

They'd been room-mates before the war at the University of Sarajevo where both had studied mechanical engineering...

It got late and we were quieting down...

the three of us who were outsiders began speculating about Gorazde's future...

their future...

land swap?

evacuation?

Like most foreigners in Bosnia, we enjoyed weaving our theories...

Then Serif, perhaps the most charming journalist in all of Bosnia, who, as a Turkish national, had passed through Serb territory to reach Gorazde at some peril, began a gentle, sleepy summation of how she'd come to cover the war for ten days and stayed two years...

27

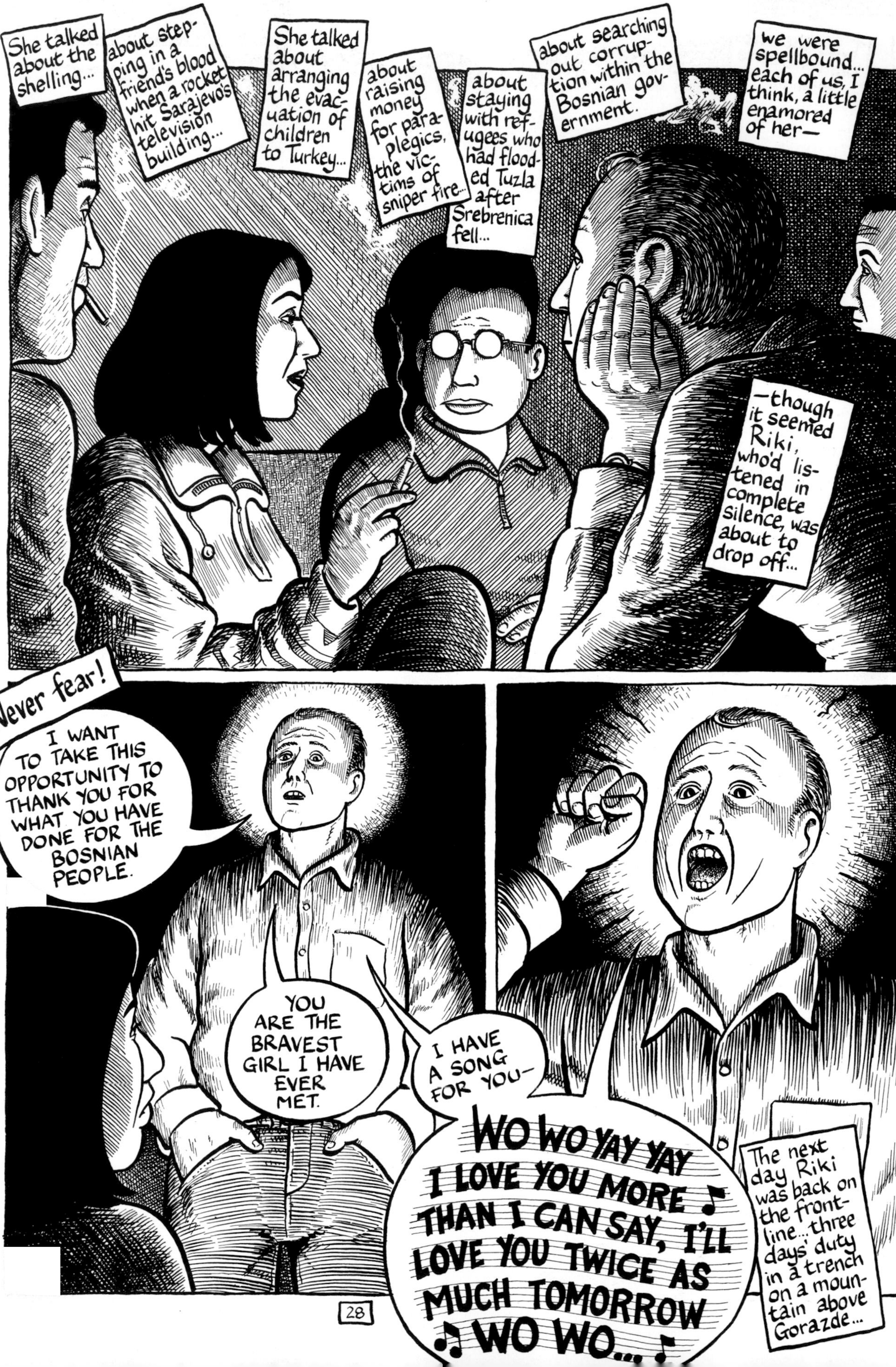
She talked about the shelling...
about stepping in a friend's blood when a rocket hit Sarajevo's television building...
She talked about arranging the evacuation of children to Turkey...
about raising money for paraplegics, the victims of sniper fire...
about staying with refugees who had flooded Tuzla after Srebrenica fell...
about searching out corruption within the Bosnian government.
we were spellbound... each of us, I think, a little enamored of her—
—though it seemed Riki, who'd listened in complete silence, was about to drop off...
Never fear!
I WANT TO TAKE THIS OPPORTUNITY TO THANK YOU FOR WHAT YOU HAVE DONE FOR THE BOSNIAN PEOPLE.
YOU ARE THE BRAVEST GIRL I HAVE EVER MET.
I HAVE A SONG FOR YOU—
WO WO YAY YAY I LOVE YOU MORE THAN I CAN SAY, I'LL LOVE YOU TWICE AS MUCH TOMORROW WO WO...
The next day Riki was back on the front-line... three days' duty in a trench on a mountain above Gorazde...
J. SACCO 2/97

CLOSE

Twice the Serbs had come close to eliminating Gorazde. In '92 and '94 their troops pushed into the town it-self...

Edin took me to the hospital where I asked if there'd been panic during the '94 offensive...

Yes, one nurse admitted, among patients and staff...

What did I expect?!

See that house?!

The white one?!

THE CHETNIKS WERE THERE!

And they were here in '92, at the bus station, a five-minute walk from the second bridge, which spans the Drina in the middle of town...

And across the first bridge, they'd once been on this ridge for months, "almost close enough to stone us," someone told me...

J. SACCO 12-96

It seemed to me, from up there, that the Serbs had been close enough to stone the town...

The Serbs still had a bead on Gorazde...

Edin and I would walk around, me asking which hills they had controlled and when, which hills they still controlled...

Several weeks before a sniper had shot this five year old from that hill, which had been recaptured only recently...

The man who had rescued the boy told us his own three-year-old son had been fired on from up there, too, while crossing the road...

J SACCO 12-96

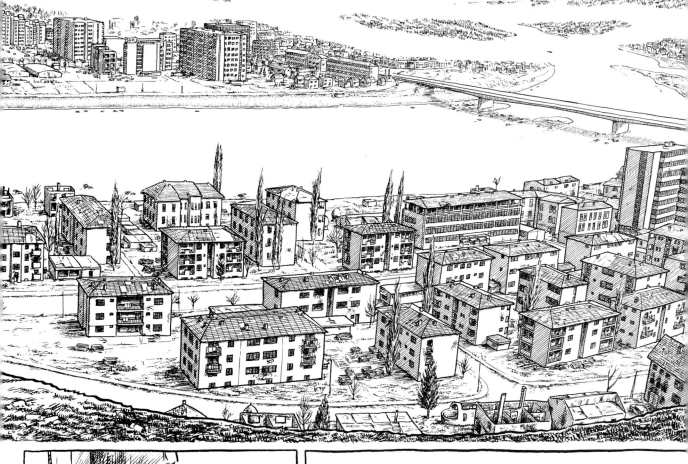

This woman, a refugee from Rudo, told us, "All last summer till these last days, it wasn't possible to go from here..."

THEY WERE SHOOTING, SNIPERS, FROM HERE, FROM THERE.

She lived with her husband in one room made habitable in an abandoned, burned-out house...

The house was so close to the checkpoint immediately behind the front line that the soldiers there had complained they could hear her nagging and had told her to cut it out. But she hadn't been nagging, she said...she'd raised her voice because her husband was nearly deaf...

J. SACCO 12-96

Their place, I'm telling you, it wasn't up to code. To get to it, you had to climb upstairs and cross a room whose floor seemed ready to give way.

After the Serbs had come through in '94, they set the place on fire.

WE ESCAPED JUST AHEAD OF THEM. WE HAD TO STOP EVERY 15 MINUTES BECAUSE MY HUSBAND CAN HARDLY WALK.

I asked why she lived in such a vulnerable area which twice had been overrun by the Serbs...

There was the garden, she said—

AND THERE WASN'T ANY ROOM DOWNTOWN. THERE WAS NO SPACE IN THE REFUGEE CENTERS. I LOOKED A LOT OF TIMES THERE.

Her neighborhood, Kokino Selo ("Chicken Village"), was home to refugees from all over eastern Bosnia who had escaped to Gorazde and found space to live only at its devastated fringes...

Edin was one of Kokino Selo's original inhabitants. He and his family lived three houses from the checkpoint, on the fringe of Gorazde's fringes...

By the way, I'd moved in with Edin and made his place home base on my visits. That hotel I told you about? A war-zone racket! Freezing in there to boot! Edin's house, at least, had one heated room and plenty of couch space.

Actually, Edin's place was mostly a shambles. It had been torched by his Serb neighbors.

But Edin and his father and brother had repaired a few rooms, making it one of the most habitable ruins in the area... Five stars by the standards of Kokino Selo!

In the back, the family field stretched downwards from the house to the Drina river...

J. SACCO 3·98

In '92, through this apple tree orchard planted by his grandfather, Edin's Muslim neighbors had crawled to the river under the fire of attackers who included some of Edin's Serb neighbors.

The Serbs now controlled the river bank directly opposite and could plainly see whoever was walking around in the field.

SERB-CONTROLLED EAST BANK

Before the cease-fire, Edin said, when snipers were still shooting, the family tended to the animals and the garden at night or during the morning mists.

Aren't you scared way out here, I asked Edin, so close to the enemy, in a part of the pocket that had been overrun by the Serbs twice already?

WE'VE GOT EVERYTHING HERE. A BIG GARDEN. PLENTY OF FRUIT. VEGETABLES. EGGS. THE COW GIVES US MILK, CHEESE.

J. SACCO 3-98

One evening, while Edin and I were sitting around digesting, she rushed in from the balcony. She could hear the Serbs singing across the river.

Edin and I stepped out there but couldn't hear a thing.

Two or three times, Edin told me, his old Serb neighbors had called to him from the other bank...

THEY WERE ASKING, "HOW IS YOUR FAMILY? WHAT IS THE CONDITION OF OUR HOUSES, WHO IS LIVING IN THEM NOW?"

Did you answer?

NO.

I HAD NO INTEREST TO SPEAK WITH THEM.

Disintegration

Dr. Alija Begovic

A NEIGHBOR FROM CHILDHOOD, A SERB FRIEND... JUST A FEW DAYS BEFORE EVERYTHING STARTED, HE SAID, 'WHAT DO YOU THINK? HOW CAN THIS PROBLEM BE SOLVED?'

"I told him the only solution was to stay together... that we have to build a Chinese Wall around Gorazde and live together."

"He said we can't live together, that the only solution is to separate the peoples."

"I understood then their aim was to clear this area."

Little more than a decade after Tito's death in 1980, Yugoslavia began to come apart, and the driving figure in the break-up and the tragedies that followed was the man who would become Serbia's president, Slobodan Milosevic. He had exploited and encouraged Serb nationalism and sense of victimhood to consolidate his power in Serbia and extend his influence over Serbs living in the other republics.

...AGAIN WE ARE IN BATTLES AND QUARRELS. THEY ARE NOT ARMED BATTLES, THOUGH SUCH THINGS SHOULD NOT BE EXCLUDED YET.

J. SACCO 4-98

Through a series of political intrigues Milosevic stripped Serbia's Kosovo and Vojvodina provinces of their autonomy and took control of their votes in the rotating Yugoslav presidency that had replaced Tito's rule.

Slovenia and Croatia, their own nationalism roused and wary of Milosevic's growing power, declared their independence from Yugoslavia in 1991. Slovenia, which did not have a significant Serb population, was permitted to leave the federation after a ten-day conflict. In Croatia, however, a brutal war broke out as a large Serb minority —whose interests and sensitivities had been run roughshod by the Croatian leadership— carved out its own statelet.

In this they were supported by Milosevic and the heavy guns of the JNA (Yugoslav People's Army), which had evolved from a federal institution into an instrument for achieving a Greater Serbia, a state that would encompass Serbs living beyond Serbia's borders.

In the territory they consolidated, the Serbs brutally cleansed themselves of Croatian civilians.

The Serbs were convinced they were preempting their own victimization by what they perceived to be a resurgent Ustasha state. Their nationalist leaders had used the ethnic crimes of the past to fuel a new cycle of ethnic violence in order to shatter the notion of "brotherhood and unity" forever.

Bosnia was now at a crossroads. It could remain in a rump Yugoslavia consisting of a chauvinistic, dominant Serbia and Serbia's close ally Montenegro or seek independence and risk its own war.

YUGOSLAV REPUBLICS THAT ACHIEVED INDEPENDENCE IN 1991

SLOVENIA

CROATIA

BOSNIA

SERBIA

MONTE-NEGRO

MACEDONIA

RUMP YUGOSLAVIA IN EARLY 1992

In Bosnia's first free election in 1990, voters mostly had cast their ballots along ethnic lines, bringing three nationalist parties to power. These parties formed a coalition government but worked toward different ends. The Serb party (SDS) wanted Bosnia to remain in Yugoslavia; the Croat (HDZ) and Muslim (SDA) parties wanted Bosnia to break away.

ASSEMBLY AND GOVERNMENT BUILDING OF THE BOSNIAN REPUBLIC

J. SACCO 4-98

The man named to head Bosnia's rotating presidency was Alija Izetbegovic, who was also leader of the Muslim party.

I WOULD SACRIFICE PEACE FOR A SOVEREIGN BOSNIA-HERZEGOVINA, BUT FOR THAT PEACE I WOULD NOT SACRIFICE SOVEREIGNTY.

Brushing aside arguments that an independent Bosnia could remain an inclusive, multi-ethnic society, the Serb party stoked fears among Serbs that they would be living as a minority dominated by Muslims who were bent on creating an Islamic republic. Despite the fact that the ethnic groups were largely intermingled, the SDS argued that only an ethnic division of Bosnia would avert war.

Serbs began establishing autonomous areas, and their party leader, Dr. Radovan Karadzic, had this warning for the protesting Muslim leadership.

YOU WANT TO TAKE BOSNIA-HERZEGOVINA DOWN THE SAME HIGHWAY OF HELL AND SUFFERING THAT SLOVENIA AND CROATIA ARE TRAVELING... AND DO NOT THINK THAT YOU WILL NOT PERHAPS MAKE THE MUSLIM PEOPLE DISAPPEAR BECAUSE THE MUSLIMS CANNOT DEFEND THEMSELVES IF THERE IS WAR...

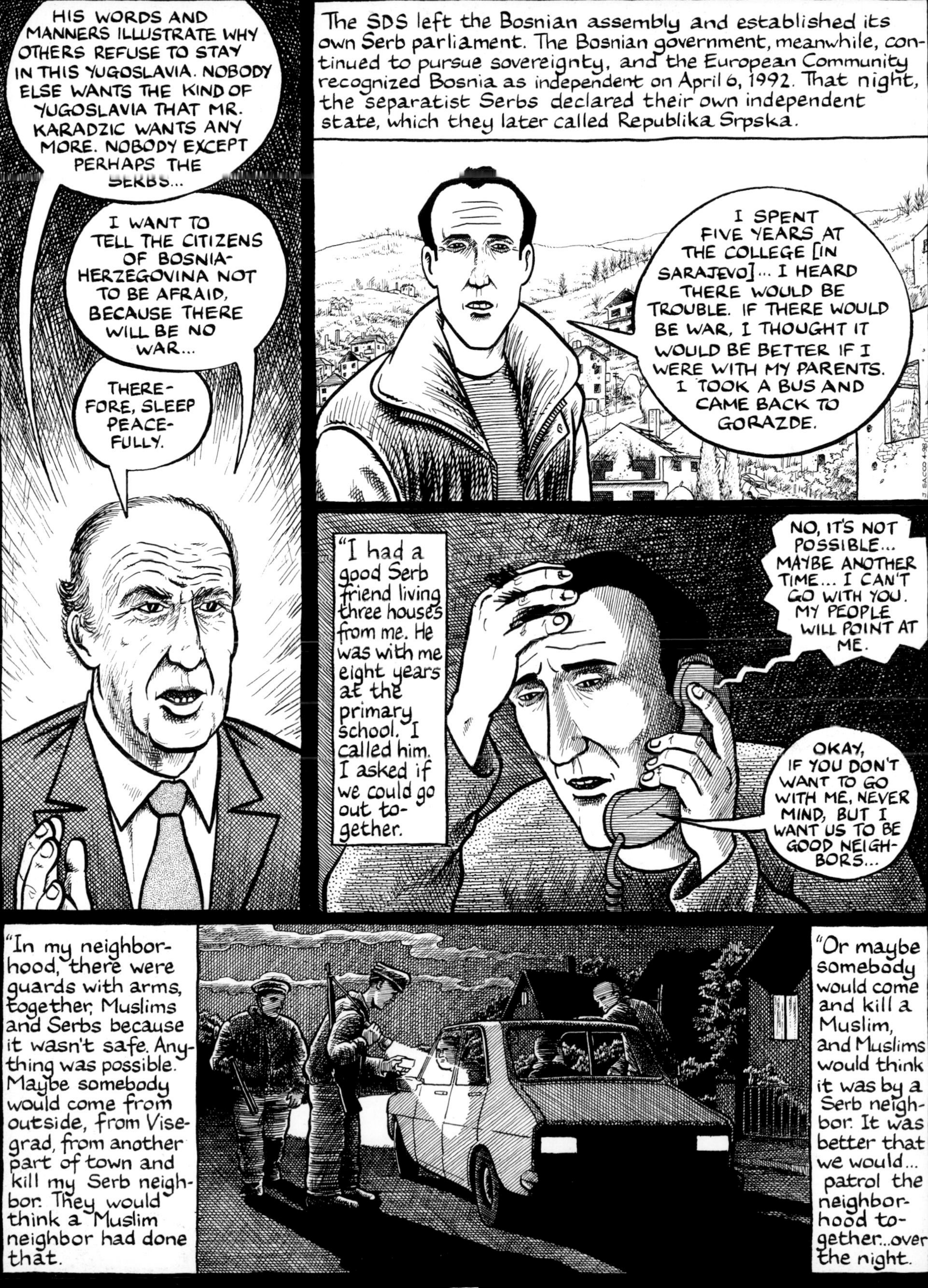
HIS WORDS AND MANNERS ILLUSTRATE WHY OTHERS REFUSE TO STAY IN THIS YUGOSLAVIA. NOBODY ELSE WANTS THE KIND OF YUGOSLAVIA THAT MR. KARADZIC WANTS ANY MORE. NOBODY EXCEPT PERHAPS THE SERBS...
I WANT TO TELL THE CITIZENS OF BOSNIA-HERZEGOVINA NOT TO BE AFRAID, BECAUSE THERE WILL BE NO WAR...
THEREFORE, SLEEP PEACEFULLY.
The SDS left the Bosnian assembly and established its own Serb parliament. The Bosnian government, meanwhile, continued to pursue sovereignty, and the European Community recognized Bosnia as independent on April 6, 1992. That night, the separatist Serbs declared their own independent state, which they later called Republika Srpska.
I SPENT FIVE YEARS AT THE COLLEGE [IN SARAJEVO]... I HEARD THERE WOULD BE TROUBLE. IF THERE WOULD BE WAR, I THOUGHT IT WOULD BE BETTER IF I WERE WITH MY PARENTS. I TOOK A BUS AND CAME BACK TO GORAZDE.
"I had a good Serb friend living three houses from me. He was with me eight years at the primary school. I called him. I asked if we could go out together.
NO, IT'S NOT POSSIBLE... MAYBE ANOTHER TIME... I CAN'T GO WITH YOU. MY PEOPLE WILL POINT AT ME.
OKAY, IF YOU DON'T WANT TO GO WITH ME, NEVER MIND, BUT I WANT US TO BE GOOD NEIGHBORS...
"In my neighborhood, there were guards with arms, together, Muslims and Serbs because it wasn't safe. Anything was possible. Maybe somebody would come from outside, from Visegrad, from another part of town and kill my Serb neighbor. They would think a Muslim neighbor had done that.
"Or maybe somebody would come and kill a Muslim, and Muslims would think it was by a Serb neighbor. It was better that we would... patrol the neighborhood together... over the night.

"Every day it was the same, ordinary life, but it was possible to feel something in the air — trouble.

"Every day tensions increased...because leaders of this town argued on the radio...trying to find a solution for both nationalities.

"In some coffee bars, all the people were Muslim, and 15 meters away another coffee bar was full of Serbs....I didn't feel comfortable going alone into a Serb coffee bar.

"I asked a lot of Serbs ... good friends, others...for the reason...and always it was answered, 'Why don't you want to live with us in the same country, with Montenegro and Serbia?'

"My friend said to me—

YOU CAN'T EXPECT GOOD RELATIONS BETWEEN US IN THE NEAR FUTURE. YOU WILL TRY TO KILL ALL THE SERBS IN BOSNIA AND MAKE A MUSLIM COUNTRY.

"I told him that wasn't true, and if it <u>was</u> true, I didn't want to live in a Muslim country.

"The last days before the war you didn't hear, 'Hello, how are you, neighbor?'"

J. SACCO 2-97

War broke out in north-eastern Bosnia in the towns of Bijeljina and Zvornik in early April 1992. In a pattern already established in Croatia, paramilitary groups from Serbia, Milosevic's JNA, and local Serb nationalists began ethnically cleansing areas of their non-Serb inhabitants. The Bosnian government was totally unprepared to fight a war and further hampered by a standing U.N. arms embargo on the former Yugoslavia.

The Serb bombardment of Sarajevo had begun, but Gorazde was still quiet.

Bahra

BEFORE THE WAR I SAW A LOT OF SERBS PUTTING THEIR FAMILIES ON BUSES TO BELGRADE, AND I SAID TO MY HUSBAND, 'SOMETHING IS GOING TO HAPPEN.'

NO, DON'T BE FOOLISH, THERE WON'T BE ANYTHING. THERE IS GOING TO BE NO WAR HERE.

"I was working in a factory and I asked my manager, who was a Serb, 'Is something going to happen? Have you sent your family somewhere?'

NO.

I WISH I HAD A PLACE TO SEND THEM—

BECAUSE THERE IS GOING TO BE NO LIFE TOGETHER BETWEEN SERBS AND MUSLIMS, NOT JUST HERE IN GORAZDE, BUT EVERYWHERE IN BOSNIA.

SO, IF YOU CAN, SEND YOUR FAMILY ANYWHERE, JUST TO BE SAFE.

"We had guards in our neighborhood...to keep out infiltrators. One of those guards saw a Serb neighbor... taking crates of guns from a truck and putting them into his cellar.

"But he said the crates had meat and cheese for the market, not to be afraid.

"After that the Muslims of the neighborhood had a meeting and decided to remove their families to Sarajevo.... We went in buses.

"(The daughter and son-in-law of that guy later turned out to be snipers in Gorazde.)

"We came to a JNA checkpoint in Ustipraca, and... they checked our documents and our luggage and let us go.

"In the center of town we were stopped again. Again they entered — the Serb police — and asked for our documents.

"When we got to Rogatica Serb police checked us again and let us go.

"They saw a young couple, a husband and wife.... They took them from the bus.... They never came back.

"Our driver was a Serb, so we decided to collect money and give it to him so that he'd manage that no one would stop us again. So there were checkpoints, but no one was stopping us....

J. SACCO 2'

42

"Only at Sokolac, one guy... from Arkan's unit*... entered and asked for documents.

"He saw my mother's ID was from Visegrad.

DO YOU HAVE A HOUSE IN VISE-GRAD?

NOT ONE. TWO HOUSES.

WHAT IF SOMEONE BURNS YOUR HOUSES?

I THINK I WAS GOOD WITH ALL MY NEIGHBORS, AND NO ONE WILL BURN MY HOUSES.

HOPEFULLY THERE ARE STILL PEOPLE LIKE THAT.

"We continued... and all the forest around the road was full of Chetniks and JNA soldiers. They were together.

"So my mother said to my son, 'Hide behind the curtains of the bus, and if they ask how old you are, say you are 11....'

WHY?

BECAUSE THEY CAN TAKE YOU FROM THE BUS.

"I couldn't believe it when we came to Sarajevo, when I put my foot on the ground... I said, 'Dear God, has it finally happened that we are saved?'

"We went to a relative of ours.... After that house was shelled...we moved to a refugee center.

" Then the first list of killed people from Gorazde came, and the first name on the list was my husband's."

*ARKAN: A NOTORIOUS PARAMILITARY LEADER FROM SERBIA.

THE DEEP DARK

Every morning, before tending to the animals, Edin's mom would tiptoe into the room where I slept to get the wood fire going in the stove.

Water was boiled and dinner heated on the stove.

Clothes were dried above it.

The stove provided the house's only heat.

I loved that stove.

When I came down with a wicked case of the dog, Edin's mom heated bricks on the stove and then wrapped them in cloth and put them under my feet.

YOU LOOK LIKE OUR AUNT.

Radiation, convection, conduction, I accepted the stove's heat graciously, any way it came.

IT'S GOING TO BE FUCKING COLD TODAY.

Like yesterday, like tomorrow.

Gorazde's wood stoves were going all out!

44

J. SACCO 5-98

People had to go far for their wood. The trees on nearby hills had already been cut down.

These men had hauled their load some four or six kilometers to town. They told me that the six of them, carrying and chopping for ten days, could supply a family with wood for four months. They were helping each other stock up.

This woman, who lived alone with her child, had fuel only for a few more days. She'd collected her batch in the forest herself, carried it to the road, and managed to bring it down in someone else's wheelbarrow...

THIS WAR, IT'S LIKE THAT.

J. SACCO 10-96

The civil authorities used to consider that older couple in Kokino Selo priority one for firewood disbursement. But they'd been dropped to priority three and now received none.

Fortunately, a young neighbor was helping out.

The first fall snows had come and with them an ever-present sound of chopping and sawing.

46

J. SACCO 12-96

The sound conspicuously <u>absent</u> in Gorazde was traffic. And, in that way at least, after the noise (and speed and belching fumes) of Sarajevo, Gorazde almost <u>did</u> seem like a safe area.

Only 10 vehicles were still in operation—not counting those coming with convoys and belonging to relief organizations—according to the district's Secretary of Industry. Before the war, he said, the town had 9,000 registered vehicles. He estimated that 80 percent had been destroyed. The rest were stored away for safer times when fuel would be readily available.

If it now seemed strangely pre-industrial, the Gorazde area once provided 10,000 factory jobs.

But those workplaces were gone. The outlying chemical, cement, and heavy machinery plants had been destroyed, for example, and a textile factory was a ruin housing refugees.

J. SACCO 12·96

47

In addition, Gorazde had been without running water or electricity since the war's beginning. The Visegrad hydroelectric plant was in Serb hands.

No street lamps, the overcast nights were jet black. Edin and I would stumble back to his place from our nightly coffee bar rounds, listening to our footsteps or maybe to voices in front of us, getting nearer, nearer, and then to the soft whishing of people unseen passing by.

Edin called the blackness "the deep dark."

Some light showed through a window here or there

—a small bulb powered by a car battery, perhaps, or a kerosene lamp—

But if the light pulsated, most probably its source was one of the contraptions floating on the Drina...

"Mini centrales" they called them. Dozens of the fragile devices were tied along the river banks and under the bridges.

They were fashioned out of wood, barrels, parts of cars, bits of washing machines, and other scraps...

The river turned their paddle-wheel generators, and electric wire brought a modest current into a small percentage of Goražde's homes...

THE RIVER IS HIGH. WE WILL HAVE GOOD POWER TONIGHT.

Edin's mini-centrale served both his and his neighbor's home...

48

J. SACCO 1-97

To prevent sudden power surges from burning out the television set, Edin regulated the current by turning on lights as necessary...

More often, power fluctuations caused lights to flicker and the VCR to shut itself off.

Typically, Edin would pop up every five or ten minutes to restart 'American Ninja II' or whatever other video his brother had dug up for our late evening's entertainment.

Edin had built four mini-centrales during the war. The first had broken down, the second was lost in territory captured by the Serbs, the third had been stripped by a thief...

The fourth had its own problems...

On this occasion, Edin's brother removed branches clogging the paddle wheels and discovered that the differential gears weren't turning well...

WE CAN'T WATCH A VIDEO. NEVER MIND, WE STILL HAVE SOME ELECTRICITY.

They'd taken advantage of the cease-fire to bring the mini-centrale downstream and closer to home...

I pointed out that if the cease-fire didn't hold, they'd hardly be able to repair it under the guns of the Serbs across this part of the river—

that they'd have a hell of a time getting it back upstream then.

YES! YOU'RE RIGHT ABOUT THAT!

We had a good laugh...

Edin and I were always having a good laugh about something...

J. SACCO 1-97

49

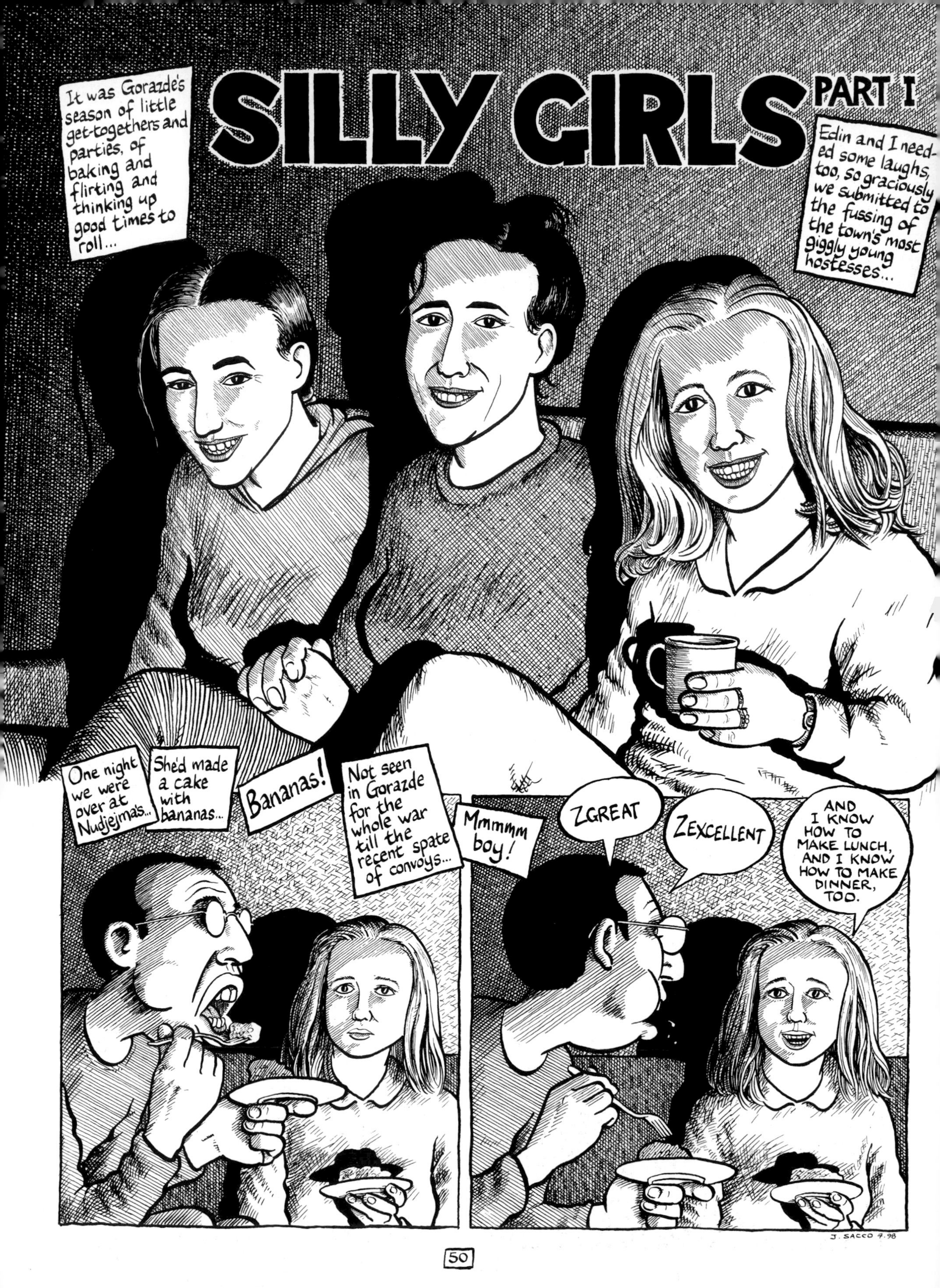
It was Gorazde's season of little get-togethers and parties, of baking and flirting and thinking up good times to roll...
SILLY GIRLS PART I
Edin and I needed some laughs, too, so graciously we submitted to the fussing of the town's most giggly young hostesses...
One night we were over at Nudjejma's...
She'd made a cake with bananas...
Bananas!
Not seen in Gorazde for the whole war till the recent spate of convoys...
Mmmmm boy!
ZGREAT
ZEXCELLENT
AND I KNOW HOW TO MAKE LUNCH, AND I KNOW HOW TO MAKE DINNER, TOO.
J. SACCO 4.98

I had to remind her...

DO YOU MAKE CAKE FOR YOUR BOYFRIEND?

NO, ONLY FOR YOU AND EDIN.

WHAT'S IN HIS MIND IS, HE'S OLD ENOUGH TO BE HER FATHER.

It is? I am?

THAT'S RIGHT.

She was sweet 16...

her boyfriend was 19...

two, three months they'd been going steady, and already things were rocky...

Sabina, Kimeta's sis, claimed to take this love stuff in stride...

She had no intention of marrying any time soon...

NOT BEFORE I'M 20.

He's THE POETIC TYPE.

She put on her jacket and periodically disappeared into the dark and mud seeking signs of her boyfriend.

Hell, they were all in the middle of boy trouble. Kimeta's sweetheart had been badly wounded ages ago, he'd been Medivac'd and was recuperating in Dublin.

WE'VE BEEN TOGETHER FOR 32 MONTHS.

Well, she'd been together for 32 months. He'd found a new squeeze along the way...

J. SACCO 9-98

And there he was! ahhhhhhhhhh Dude!

And just as advertised—

just like that—

Dude got poetic!

Dude was giggly, too...

DO YOU KNOW WHERE YOU'VE COME?

He was a refugee from Visegrad. His father had been slaughtered by the Serbs, his brother killed in action.

He was alone.

In the morning he was going back to the front.

IS OUR FIGHT JUST?

Yes, I said, your fight is just.

J. SACCO 8-98

52

DO THEY KNOW ABOUT GORAZDE IN AMERICA?

Yes, I lied.

WILL THERE BE PEACE?

I don't know, I said truthfully.

IT'S BETTER NOW, BUT I'M WORRIED ABOUT THE SPRING.

Because in the spring armies begin to march...

And in the spring of '92, Nudjejma's house was burned down in a Serb offensive...

The cups and plates we were using...

the couches and chairs we were sitting on...

the house...

all of it belonged to a family that'd fled to Australia before the war...

Her family had lost most all it owned...

But so what?

Once, she told me, she came home, found the front door blasted through by shrapnel, her parents bleeding inside...

Now that—

that...

J. SACCO 9.98

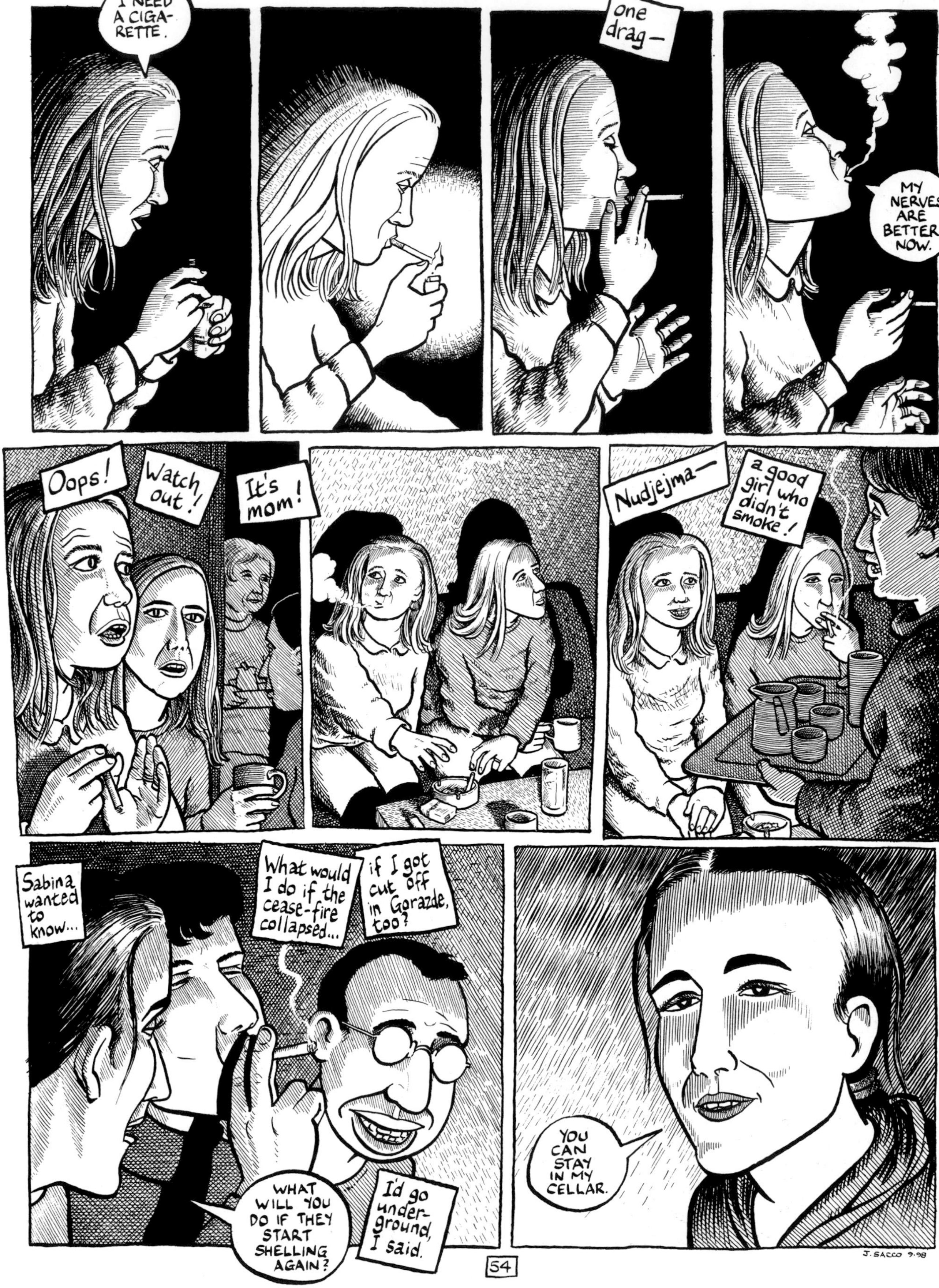
I NEED A CIGA-RETTE.
one drag—
MY NERVES ARE BETTER NOW.
Oops!
Watch out!
It's mom!
Nudjejma—
a good girl who didn't smoke!
Sabina wanted to know...
WHAT WILL YOU DO IF THEY START SHELLING AGAIN?
I'd go under-ground, I said.
What would I do if the cease-fire collapsed...
if I got cut off in Gorazde, too?
YOU CAN STAY IN MY CELLAR.
J. SACCO 9·98

DO YOU LIKE SABINA? ARE YOU INTERESTED IN SABINA?

SURE.

BUT SHE'S TAKEN ALREADY.

NO ONE LIKES MUSLIM GIRLS.

?

Meanwhile, on the other side of the table, Kimeta unfolded the handkerchief and divided the polished stones...

It was time to look into the future...

not for signs of peace or the sound of marching in the spring...

YOU ARE EMPTY.

YOUR BOYFRIEND IS EMPTY...

BUT SOON YOU WILL FIND HAPPINESS WITH SOMEONE NEW.

‹I DID IT TO MAKE HER FEEL BETTER.›

J. SACCO 7-98

55

I told them I'd be leaving Goražde soon, that I'd return in a few days, a couple of weeks...

was there anything they wanted from Sarajevo?

JEANS!

Orders and sizes poured in:

Levi's!

Original 501's!

American-made!

Make no mistake!

I warned them jeans were 110 marks! 140!

Don't worry, they'd get the dough!

Relatives were sending money in parcels!

What was there to spend it on in Goražde?

But hold on!

WEREN'T BOTH OF YOU TALKING ABOUT GOING TO AMERICA TO STUDY MEDICINE?

WOULDN'T IT BE BETTER IF YOU SPENT THAT MONEY ON SOME BOOKS TO LEARN ENGLISH?

WOULDN'T THAT SHOW MORE CHARACTER?

yes...

yes, of course it would, they agreed...

They were a couple of silly girls.

J. SACCO 9-98

THE BLUE ROAD

Gorazde was in love with me. People I didn't know hailed me by name. Whole high school classes jumped up when I entered the room. Drunks offered me the town slut. Soldiers wanted to talk girls, and girls wanted to flirt, they wanted me to carry them off to a Gap outlet in the sky.

I'd like to tell you it was me they loved, but that wouldn't be the Real Truth. What really made 'em swoon was how I'd gotten there, not by foot and over mountains through enemy minefields, but by road— the Blue Road, the U.N. route to Gorazde.

YOU, ME, AMERICA?

The Blue Road —so-named because U.N. soldiers wore blue helmets—wound from Sarajevo to Gorazde through areas "cleansed" of Muslims. And that was the rub: The Blue Road was entirely in Serb-held territory.

SARAJEVO
Blue Road
Blue Road
ROGATICA
USTIPRACA
SERB-CONTROLLED TERRITORY
KOPACI
GORAZDE ENCLAVE
GORAZDE
Drina
BOSNIAN GOVERNMENT-CONTROLLED TERRITORY
KILOMETER SCALE
0   5   10   15

SACO '97

SERB NATION-A-LIST SALUTE

UN

It was not the happiest of trails.

Although obliged by the October '95 cease-fire to allow unhindered access to Gorazde, the Serbs were throwing up roadblocks, holding up convoys, sometimes turning them back.

On my second trip to Gorazde, the escorting French peacekeepers assigned me to a civilian truck with a Bosnian driver.

The Serbs at the Ustipraca roadblock were keeping us an unusually long time.

BONJOUR.

J. SACCO 4·97

WE 'AVE A LEETLE PROBLEM.

The Serbs were demanding to examine the contents of the trucks. The Frogs had refused and were on the radio with their brass in Sarajevo. The Serbs were in contact with theirs in Pale.

YOUR DRIVER IS MUSLIM, SO IF A SERB WANTS TO LOOK IN THE TRUCK, DON'T LET HIM INTO THE CABIN.

I was not warming to the idea of holding the door closed against the Serb soldiers moving around us, but the driver, who had infinitely more to worry about, took our predicament in stride.

After two hours, the Serbs dropped their demand and the convoy proceeded.

A few kilometers further up, in Kopaci, a rock smashed through the windshield of a truck ahead of us and into a driver's face.

Accessibility to Gorazde diminished even further over the next few days.

By late November, UNPROFOR* was threatening to use its Rapid Reaction Force against the Serbs to make sure the route remained open.

J. SACCO 4.97

*UNPROFOR: UNITED NATIONS PROTECTION FORCE

You get the picture—passage via the Blue Road was a little iffy to say the least... and there were those in Gorazde who bristled at the idea of a lifeline to Sarajevo subject to constriction by the Serbs.

FUCK THE BLUE ROAD!

THE BOSNIAN ARMY MUST MAKE ITS OWN CORRIDOR!

ALL THE WAY TO FOCA!

Still, as tenuous as it was, the Blue Road had so far meant a considerable infusion of goods into Gorazde.

Convoys were bringing in flour, beans, peas, milk powder, other essentials.

Humanitarian organizations were delivering medical supplies, second-hand clothes, shoes...

THINGS HAVE IMPROVED BIT BY BIT OVER THE LAST TWO OR THREE WEEKS, AND I HAVE ENJOYED EVERY LITTLE THING.

The influx of goods meant that prices in Gorazde, perhaps the world's highest, had plummeted... Coffee was no longer 1000 dm a kilo... Salt, which had fetched 100dm a kilo on the black market in mid-October, was $\frac{1}{50}$ the price a month later.

A pack of smokes was down to 1½ dm from its 100dm high.

I'LL NEVER COMPLAIN ABOUT ANYTHING AGAIN.

J. SACCO 4 97

IN LATE OCTOBER 1995
1 dm = 70 U.S. CENTS

Perhaps the greatest of the new joys arriving with the convoys were private parcels—the first received since the beginning of the war.

Public bulletins notified the lucky recipients.

Emira saw her name on the list...

MAYBE IT'S A PACKAGE FROM MY BROTHER IN GERMANY. MAYBE HE SENT ME SOME PANTS.

HER ONLY PAIR

Lejla modelled the boots she'd just received from a relative in Sweden.

At the office of the International Committee of the Red Cross, the young women censoring letters were bored to tears reading all the outgoing requests...

"I WANT TROUSERS, I WANT SHOES, HERE ARE MY SIZES."

EVERY LETTER THE SAME.

J. SACCO 4·97

Another package arrived for Lejla and family... from Germany... this one had sat in Sarajevo almost a year.

Mean-while...

IT WASN'T ME ON THE LIST.

THE PACKAGE WAS FOR SOME-ONE WITH THE SAME NAME.

But if an expected package wasn't coming in or bringing satisfaction, the Blue Road provided a fall-back delivery system:

Me!

SHE WANTS TO KNOW WHEN YOU'RE LEAVING.

Not 'cause she'd miss me, but to add to the requests for perfumes and shoe polish and lipsticks and playing cards that'd roll in before my departures for Sarajevo.

Alma wanted a watch, a cheap one, but a wind-up, please, nothing that needed batteries...

IF WE'RE CUT OFF AGAIN, I WON'T BE ABLE TO REPLACE THEM.

Nina wanted hair color, facial cream, something for skin allergies...

I BROKE OUT AGAIN WHEN MY BROTHER WAS KILLED.

J. SACCO 9-98

62

And, of course, there were gifts and personal messages to pass back and forth between loved ones who hadn't seen each other in three and a half years...

Would I take this package to Riki's sister in Sarajevo?

In Sarajevo, Riki's sister sorted through the baby clothes sent by her parents to the granddaughter they'd never seen.

IS ANY-ONE WOUND-ED?

IS RIKI A GOOD MUSLIM?

Back in Gorazde, the first order of business was dispensing scribbled notes and packets.

YOU KNOW THIS GUY? I'VE GOT AN ENVELOPE OF DEUTSCHE-MARKS FOR HIM.

And so the cycle went...

Returning to Sarajevo tomorrow.

A message for your wife, perhaps?

TELL HER THERE'S PLENTY OF ROOM HERE. EVERYTHING'S IN GOOD CONDITION. THERE'S LOTS OF CHOPPED WOOD.

TELL HER I LOOK GOOD.

SHE SHOULD COME SOON.

Back in Sarajevo with his wife and children, I handed her a letter from the moon, told her about the chopped wood, that her husband wanted her to come soon...

J. SACCO 10-98

Come soon? But how? Assuming she or anyone could get government permission to travel the Blue Road — which seemed highly unlikely — few Muslims were ready in late '95 to entrust themselves to the good will of the Serbs along the route.

Still, in Gorazde, the Blue Road dangled the glorious possibility of people getting out some day.

Getting out!

Lejla and Ema were flirting with the notion.

After years being trapped, sealed off, they now had a glimmer of Somewhere Else...

and maybe — perhaps — that Emerald City was no longer an infinity away.

WAIT FOR US, SARAJEVO!

WE ARE COMING!

Many took heart that outsiders like me, and not just peacekeepers and humanitarian workers, could now come and go.

I'd show up and find my pals, their families, and everyone else still surrounded in the enclave just where I'd left 'em.

Oh, the happy reunions!

♪ YOU CAN CHECK OUT ANY TIME YOU LIKE, BUT YOU CAN NEVER LEAVE... ♪

J. SACCO 10-98

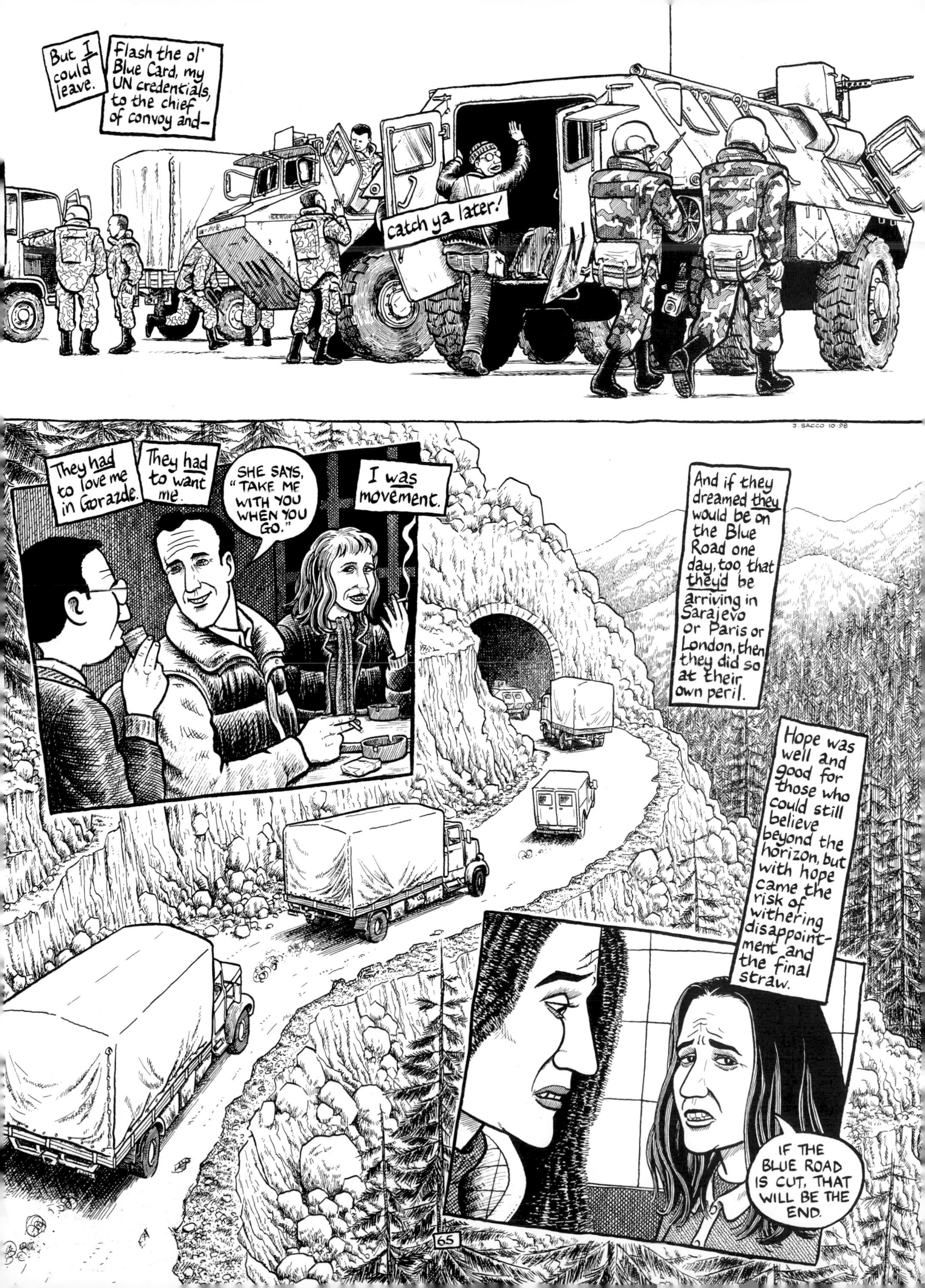
But I could leave.
Flash the ol' Blue Card, my UN credentials, to the chief of convoy and–
catch ya later!
J. SACCO 10.98
They had to love me in Gorazde.
They had to want me.
SHE SAYS, "TAKE ME WITH YOU WHEN YOU GO."
I was movement.
And if they dreamed they would be on the Blue Road one day, too, that they'd be arriving in Sarajevo or Paris or London, then they did so at their own peril.
Hope was well and good for those who could still believe beyond the horizon, but with hope came the risk of withering disappointment and the final straw.
IF THE BLUE ROAD IS CUT, THAT WILL BE THE END.

THE BLUE ROAD: AN ASIDE

I told you before, the Blue Road could get dicey. At a certain point the Serbs started demanding to check the ID's of convoy passengers.

In one incident, they blocked the return of a convoy to Sarajevo for hours because a certain journalist non grata had ridden it into Gorazde.

The French suspended journalists from their convoys and that left me stranded in Sarajevo. And you shoulda heard me, alternately bad-mouthing the Frogs and snivelling for updates from their captains and colonels.

OUI OUI... JE SUIS ME AGAIN, MON CAPITAINE.

ANY CHANGE?

ON TAKING JOURNALISTS TO GORAZDE?

MAYBE NEXT WEEK?

BUT YOU SAID THAT LAST WEEK.

The public information officer at the UNPROFOR headquarters wanted to be helpful, but—

IF THE FRENCH DON'T WANT TO TAKE YOU, YOU'RE DEAD IN THE WATER.

A lift with Russian peacekeepers wouldn't be a problem, but they had to check with—

— THE FRENCH.

J. SACCO 10-98

Days passed.

Weeks.

UNPR

One word used at a press conference was ringing in my head.

Access to Gorazde had "deteriorated."

I was wondering about Edin, Riki, the silly girls.

If I was no longer movement, where did they stand?

Eventually the Serbs eased up on their pressure.

And for the moment the French okayed journalists again.

I got back to Gorazde.

I gave out lipsticks and letters.

I did some interviews.

I had some laughs with my pals.

We were back to square one.

But I'd had a jolt, let me tell you.

It'd been my turn to understand how much more than a few kilometers of road separated me from them.

J. SACCO 10-98

67

Disappearance

"ON THE MORNING OF MAY 4, 1992, MY MOTHER SAID, 'WAKE UP! THE WAR HAS STARTED! GO INTO THE CELLAR!' I HEARD AT THAT MOMENT THE FIRING OF AN AUTOMATIC GUN.

"I TOLD HER I MUST GO WITH MY FRIENDS TO SEE WHAT WE CAN DO.

"I called my Serb friends but nobody answered, no one was in their houses...I didn't find my Serb neighbors either ...

"The phone stopped working about 9:30, 10 o'clock...

"I went to see my Muslim friends, but they didn't know anything...

"Some people went downtown to ask what's up. People who had gone to work returned quickly...They'd heard that the Serbs had left...

"It had been very organized on the Serb side..."

The night before, in a coordinated move, most of the Serbs who remained in Gorazde slipped out of town. In Edin's neighborhood, all the Serbs disappeared. They retired to predominantly Serb areas or took up positions in the surrounding hills, apparently expecting to return to their vacant homes soon.

"I heard from some women what was up downtown... a lot of bullets, snipers, destroyed shops, people taking food, clothes...looting...I heard different stories...rumors about people killed...but no one saw any victims...

"From the closest hill in my region a machine-gun was shooting all the time to the other side of the river. But they didn't shoot here for 15 days...

"We listened to the radio... Serb radio stations... always propaganda: 'We mustn't live together, we must kill all Muslim people'...something like that...

"I kept watch on empty Serb houses. I thought, if someone steals something from Serb houses, I will be accused, I can have trouble... Nobody took anything, believe me, nobody from this area...

"One morning I saw somebody moving—my Serb neighbors from three houses over, two brothers...

"I whistled to them...and one of them signalled to me to be quiet and come over...

"I thought it was possible if I go over there, they'll capture me and kill me. I told my father I was going over to see them...

"They brought out brandy and we sat outside their house...nobody could see us. They said they'd come to feed their pigs...

"I told them about two people who'd been killed downtown.

IS IT POSSIBLE TO STOP THIS FIGHTING? IF THERE ARE MORE VICTIMS, BLOODSHED, IT WON'T BE POSSIBLE TO STOP THIS WAR.

WE'RE YOUR NEIGHBORS UP THERE, BUT ALL COMMANDS ARE COMING FROM ABOVE.

"I said I would like to speak to my friend, a chief among my Serb neighbors...

YOU CAN'T SPEAK TO HIM. YOU CAN'T DO ANYTHING.

ALL COMMANDS ARE COMING FROM UP.

"My father came by because I'd been gone so long... He joined us...

WE ARE THERE SO YOU ARE SAFE.

BUT IF YOU DON'T FEEL SAFE ENOUGH, BRING YOUR FAMILY INTO MY HOUSE.

HERE. YOU CAN TAKE THE KEY.

NO. I DON'T NEED IT.

IT'S A GOOD IDEA TO STAY IN MY HOUSE.

IF YOU NEED SOMETHING, FOOD, WE HAVE EVERYTHING. THE CELLAR IS FULL.

WE NEED NOTHING.

BUT IT'S BEST IF YOU AND YOUR FAMILY GO FROM HERE.

WHY?

IT'S DANGEROUS. IT'S BETTER THAN STAYING.

J. SACCO 5-97

"We agreed to leave important messages for each other in a bag in his house.

"But after one day, two days I stopped checking. My father told me it wasn't safe...

"On May 13, there was a lot of shooting overnight... We couldn't sleep.

"My father said we must go to the center of town... In this area they could come when they wanted and kill us...

"We were a short time in town and then my father thought it would be safer in Kopaci..."

70

ARTS and LEISURE

The Piramida!

The discotheque at the end of the war!

In Sarajevo, where most everyone considered Goražde a cow town, they didn't want to believe me when I told them about the Piramida...

about its jabbing colored lights...

its rotating mirrored ball...

its video monitors.

But there it was, and I was there, shouting over the Eurobeat to Emira and Azra about all the cities and countries I'd blazed through on my way to Bosnia.

Emira, who probably hadn't ventured a few kilometers in the whole war, shouted back that she was bored out of her mind.

Bored?! From my perspective, there was nothing like shouting over thumping music to a couple of lovely ladies to make an enclave seem exciting.

WE'RE GOING HOME.

Home?

Where it was dark?

Jesus, curfew wasn't for another hour and a half; but the kids were already clearing out.

Just then my pal K shuffled in.

71

J. SACCO 11-98

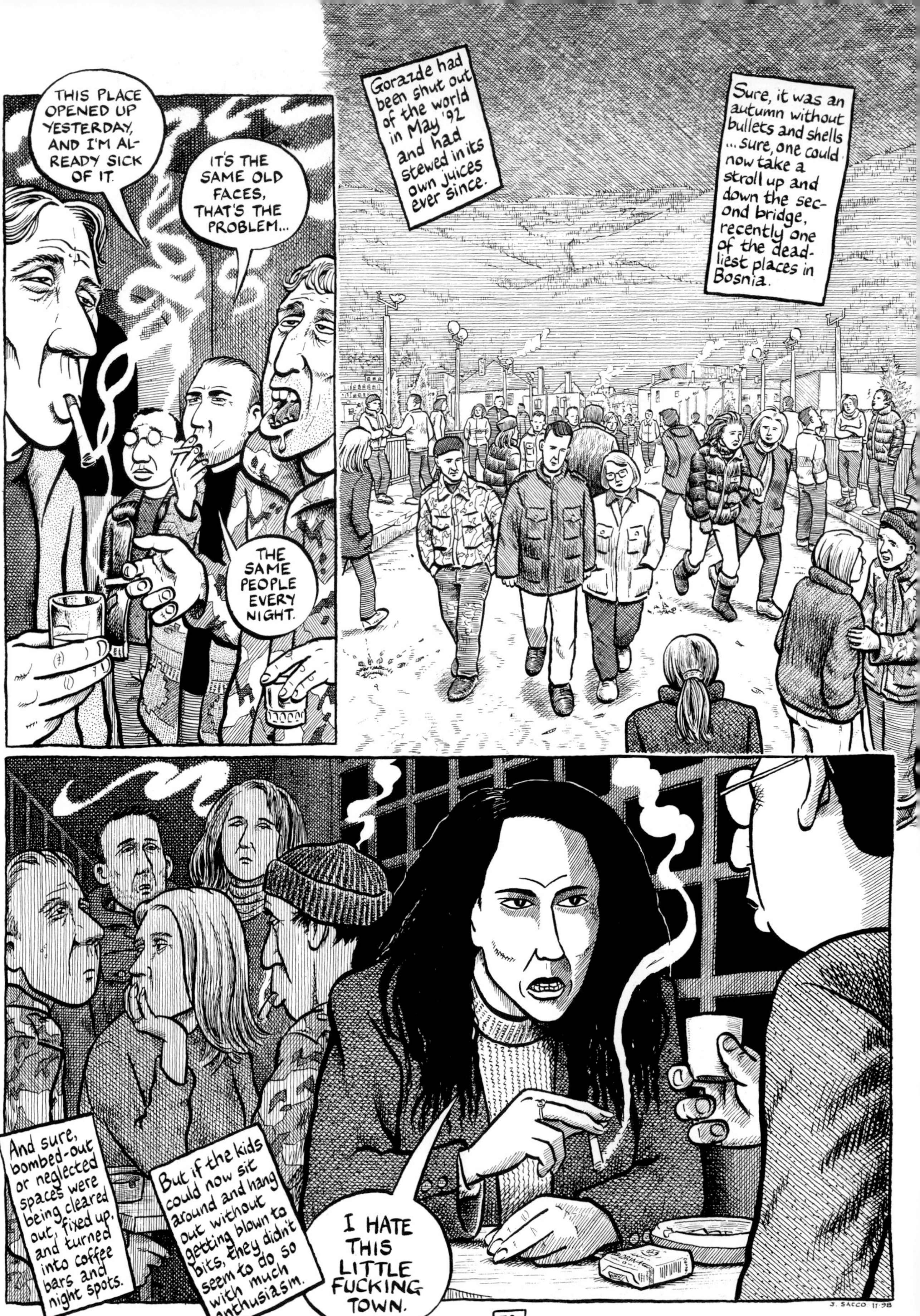
THIS PLACE OPENED UP YESTERDAY, AND I'M ALREADY SICK OF IT.
IT'S THE SAME OLD FACES, THAT'S THE PROBLEM...
THE SAME PEOPLE EVERY NIGHT.
Gorazde had been shut out of the world in May '92 and had stewed in its own juices ever since.
Sure, it was an autumn without bullets and shells ...sure, one could now take a stroll up and down the second bridge, recently one of the deadliest places in Bosnia.
And sure, bombed-out or neglected spaces were being cleared out, fixed up, and turned into coffee bars and night spots.
But if the kids could now sit around and hang out without getting blown to bits, they didn't seem to do so with much enthusiasm.
I HATE THIS LITTLE FUCKING TOWN.
J. SACCO 11.98

IT'S REALLY BORING AT HOME, SO I GO OUT AND IT'S BORING HERE, TOO.

AZRA AND I HAVE NOTHING TO TALK ABOUT.

I GOT SOME MAGAZINES FROM THE BRITISH PEACEKEEPERS WHEN THEY WERE HERE.

I READ ABOUT A FILM CALLED 'PULP FICTION.'

I REALLY WANT TO SEE THAT MOVIE.

WE WANT TO TALK ABOUT SOMETHING OTHER THAN THE WAR...

NEW FASHION...

ANYTHING NEW.

But there'd been nothing new for years, no new films, no new fashion. When I brought a few Bosnian-language magazines from Sarajevo, they were passed around and devoured. The library was so grateful to get the periodicals that it tagged them as specially donated by yours truly.

DANI DANI

The library was part of the Cultural Center, which had tried to provide Gorazde with some internal stimulus.

K. gave me the grand tour.

This room had been hit by a rocket.

Most of Gorazde's musical equipment and instruments had disappeared in a flash.

I WAS CRYING, FED UP, I WAS SEARCHING THROUGH THE RUBBLE.

I FOUND MY FRIEND ALMER'S FENDER STRATOCASTER.

UN-DAMAGED.

IT'S THE ONLY FENDER STRATOCASTER IN GORAZDE.

The library staff told me they'd lost 15,000 books in the shelling. Besides that—

SOLDIERS TAKE THEM UP TO THE FRONT AND LOSE THEM WHEN THERE'S AN ATTACK.

AND WE LOSE BOOKS, FOR EXAMPLE, WHEN PEOPLE ARE KILLED OR WOUNDED AND CAN'T RETURN THEM.

J. SACCO 11-98

73

This was the auditorium where the Center had put on youth and music festivals during the occasional cease-fire.

It was out of operation now.

Its roof had been hit earlier in the year, and the facility had sustained serious water damage.

Despite these and other setbacks, in the course of the war the Center had managed to record musicians, publish an anthology of local poetry, and show the work of the town's fine artists.

Hitko, one of the Center's directors, was still grieving over an artist friend, killed at the front, whose body fell into Serb hands and was finally exchanged on the day his exhibition opened.

THE CHETNIKS HAVE TRIED TO TURN OUR PEOPLE INTO COWS.

IF THEY'VE SUCCEEDED TO SURROUND OUR BODIES, THEY CAN'T SURROUND OUR SPIRITS.

In a backroom, Ema and Lejla were running through a script for an upcoming hand-puppet theater.

SUCH AN ACTIVITY IS A MATTER OF SURVIVAL FOR ME.

EVERY DAY I EAT BEANS UNTIL I CAN'T STAND THEM ANYMORE.

THIS MORNING I ATE THEM AGAIN.

THEN I WENT TO THE LIBRARY AND I TOOK OUT CHARLES BAUDELAIRE'S 'FLOWERS OF EVIL', AND I READ A FEW POEMS.

I'LL FEEL BETTER UNTIL THE END OF THE DAY.

TOMORROW I'LL EAT BEANS AGAIN— UNTIL I CAN'T STAND THEM ANY MORE.

THEN I'LL READ SOME MORE POEMS.

But if a few had managed to nurture their own minds and souls, all were craving an exchange with the outside.

J. SACCO 11·98

It was no wonder, then, that a foreigner was a popular thing.

I told Kuna about America's big sky, about the road stretching on and on, about running out of gas in Kansas.

I told these guys that Clyde Drexler had gone to Houston.

SMITH
F-5

ROCKETS
22

I told Haris what I remembered of 'Pulp Fiction.'

After an hour's chat about this and that, Alma told me she'd recall aspects of our conversation for a long time, that it'd keep her going for another month.

AND WHAT SHALL WE TALK ABOUT NOW? SHALL WE TALK ABOUT ART?

And I'd throw out every scrap I knew...

Stuff off the top of my head.

They gathered in my crumbs.

J. SACCO 17·98

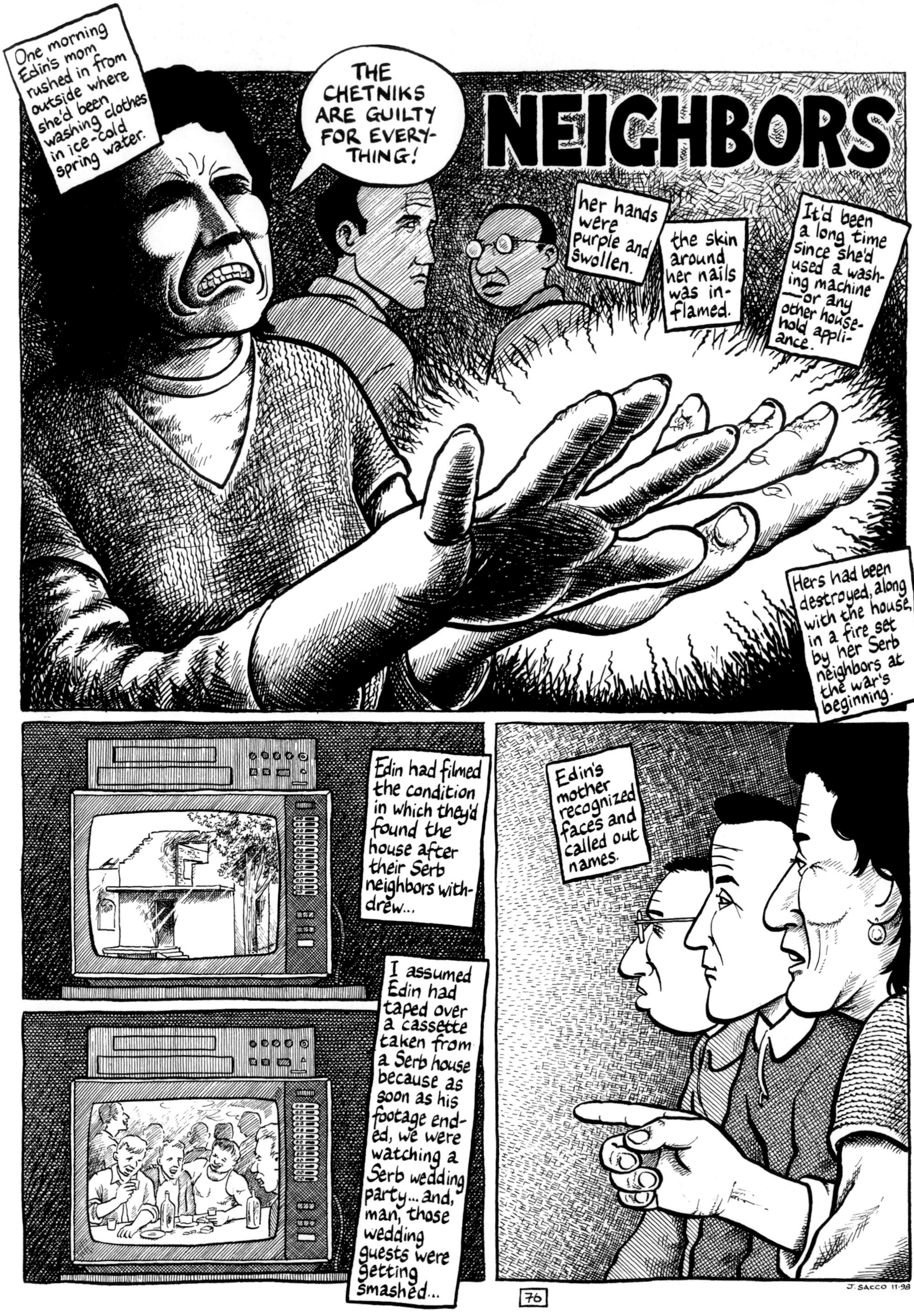

One morning Edin's mom rushed in from outside where she'd been washing clothes in ice-cold spring water.
THE CHETNIKS ARE GUILTY FOR EVERY-THING!
NEIGHBORS
her hands were purple and swollen.
the skin around her nails was in-flamed.
It'd been a long time since she'd used a wash-ing machine —or any other house-hold appli-ance.
Hers had been destroyed, along with the house, in a fire set by her Serb neighbors at the war's beginning.
Edin had filmed the condition in which they'd found the house after their Serb neighbors with-drew...
I assumed Edin had taped over a cassette taken from a Serb house because as soon as his footage end-ed, we were watching a Serb wedding party... and, man, those wedding guests were getting smashed...
Edin's mother recognized faces and called out names.
J. SACCO 11·98

By Gorazde standards, Edin's immediate family had been lucky.

No one had been killed.

But his mother almost burst into tears when reminded of the close calls:

Edin: wounded two times

her younger son, Elvir, wounded four times

her husband wounded once

She didn't understand English, but she knew when Edin and I were talking about the war.

Only once did she break in...

She said that before the war they'd done everything with their Serb neighbors.

They'd had them over for coffee, they'd celebrated Orthodox Christmas with them, they'd gone to their weddings.

She said she could live with them again, that they could come back if they wanted, that everyone must go back to his or her place...

but that it could never be the same.

never

NEIGHBORS.

NEIGHBORS.

77

J. SACCO 11-98

The First Attack

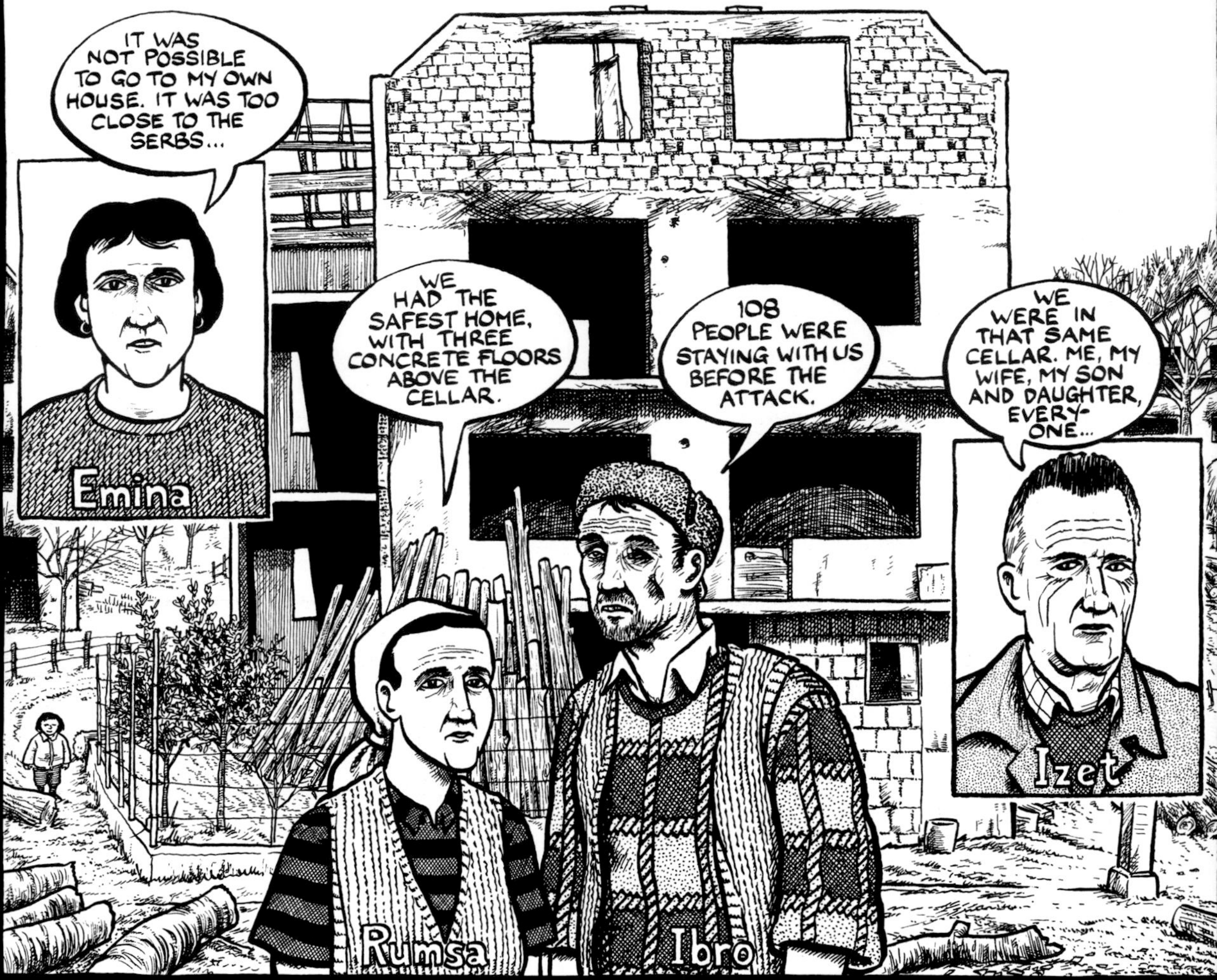
IT WAS NOT POSSIBLE TO GO TO MY OWN HOUSE. IT WAS TOO CLOSE TO THE SERBS...
Emina
WE HAD THE SAFEST HOME, WITH THREE CONCRETE FLOORS ABOVE THE CELLAR.
108 PEOPLE WERE STAYING WITH US BEFORE THE ATTACK.
WE WERE IN THAT SAME CELLAR. ME, MY WIFE, MY SON AND DAUGHTER, EVERY-ONE...
Izet
Rumsa
Ibro

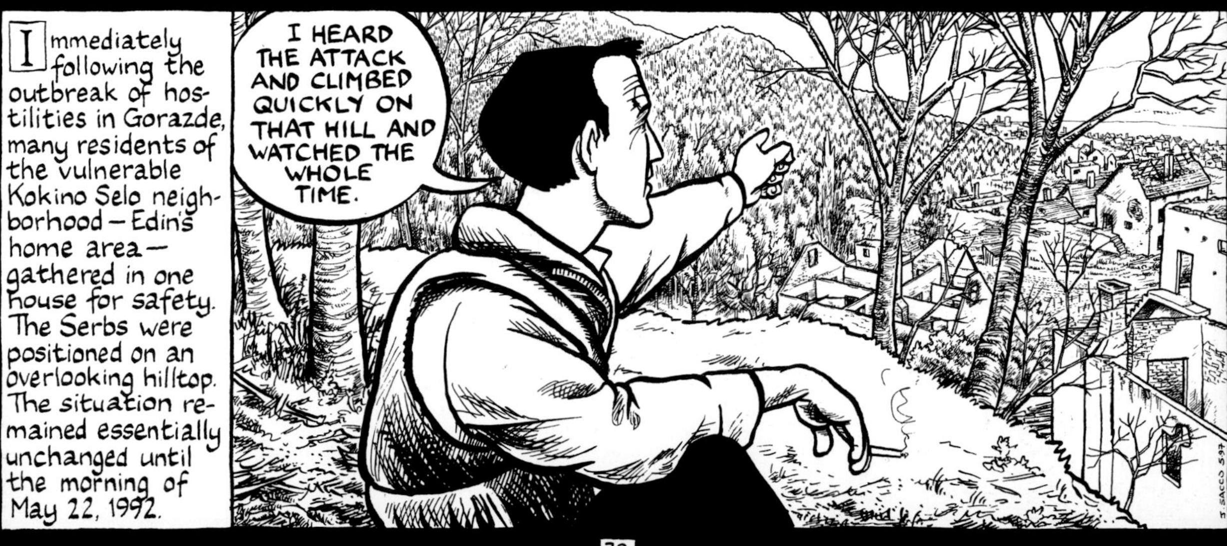
Immediately following the outbreak of hostilities in Gorazde, many residents of the vulnerable Kokino Selo neighborhood—Edin's home area—gathered in one house for safety. The Serbs were positioned on an overlooking hilltop. The situation remained essentially unchanged until the morning of May 22, 1992.
I HEARD THE ATTACK AND CLIMBED QUICKLY ON THAT HILL AND WATCHED THE WHOLE TIME.

"I only watched, I couldn't do anything... I was on guard in Kopaci, on the line, 2000 meters away, maybe more...

"There was fog and rain and I couldn't see everything. They attacked about 7 o'clock, 6:30. Everything was finished about 2 p.m...."

IZET: "I'd gone to my own house to start a fire in the oven. I was outside to get some water when an automatic gun started firing...

IT'S PROBABLY AN ATTACK!

"My son had been watching over our home with another guy, a refugee, spending the nights in the cellar...

GET OUT OF HERE!

"When the Serbs got as close as 50 meters, I recognized my neighbors...

"One of them had spent a lot of time with my youngest son, a lot of time at my house... doing homework with my son...

"I was armed with a pistol, but I didn't shoot back. It was a small gun..."

"Only 13 or 14 people were defending..."

"I got back to Ibro and Rumsa's cellar..."

WHAT DO WE DO NOW?

THEY ARE ALL AROUND US!

"We made the decision that all the women and children should escape quickly to the river..."

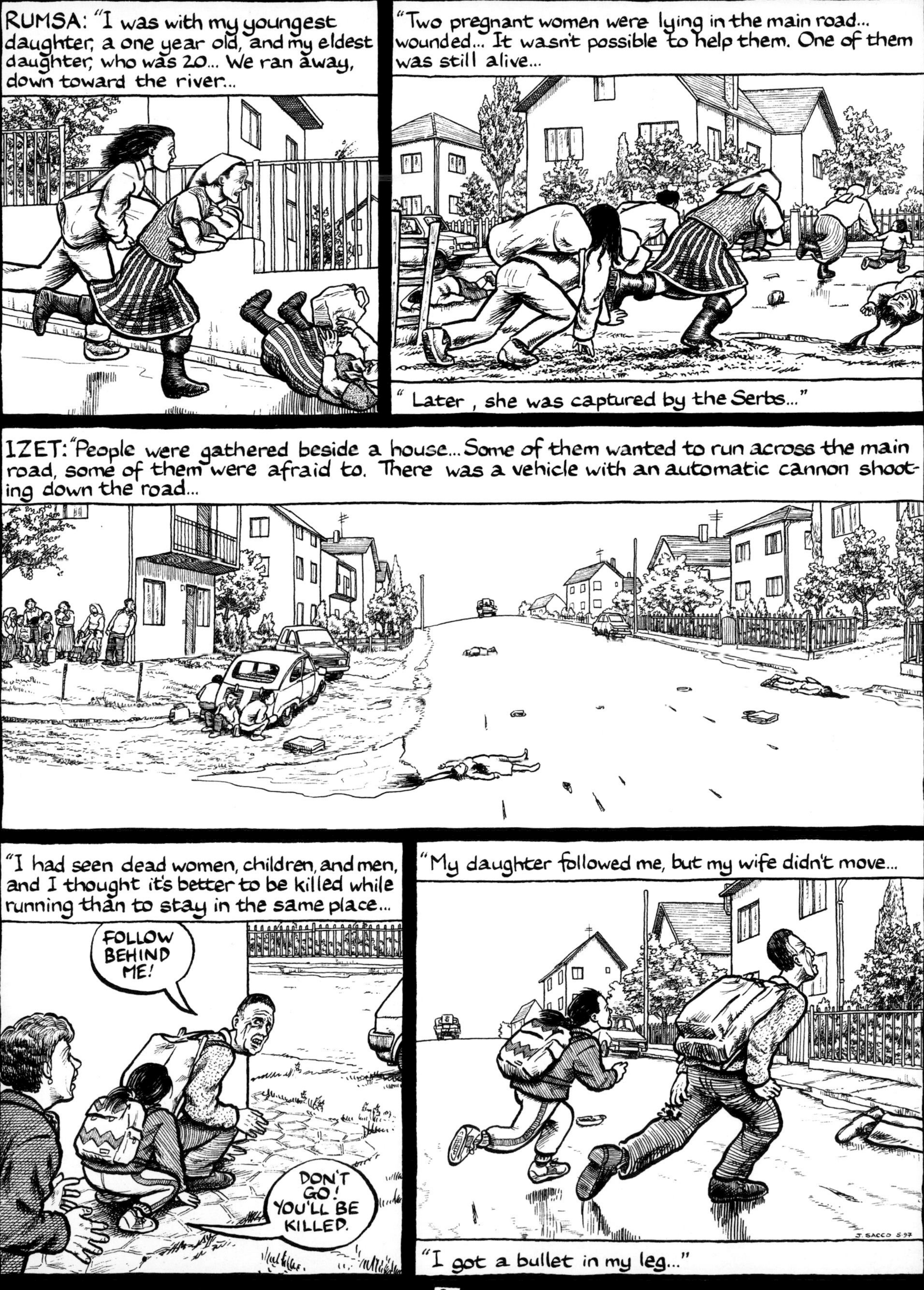
RUMSA: "I was with my youngest daughter, a one year old, and my eldest daughter, who was 20... We ran away, down toward the river...
"Two pregnant women were lying in the main road... wounded... It wasn't possible to help them. One of them was still alive...
" Later , she was captured by the Serbs..."
IZET: "People were gathered beside a house... Some of them wanted to run across the main road, some of them were afraid to. There was a vehicle with an automatic cannon shooting down the road...
"I had seen dead women, children, and men, and I thought it's better to be killed while running than to stay in the same place...
FOLLOW BEHIND ME!
DON'T GO! YOU'LL BE KILLED.
"My daughter followed me, but my wife didn't move...
J. SACCO 5·97
"I got a bullet in my leg..."

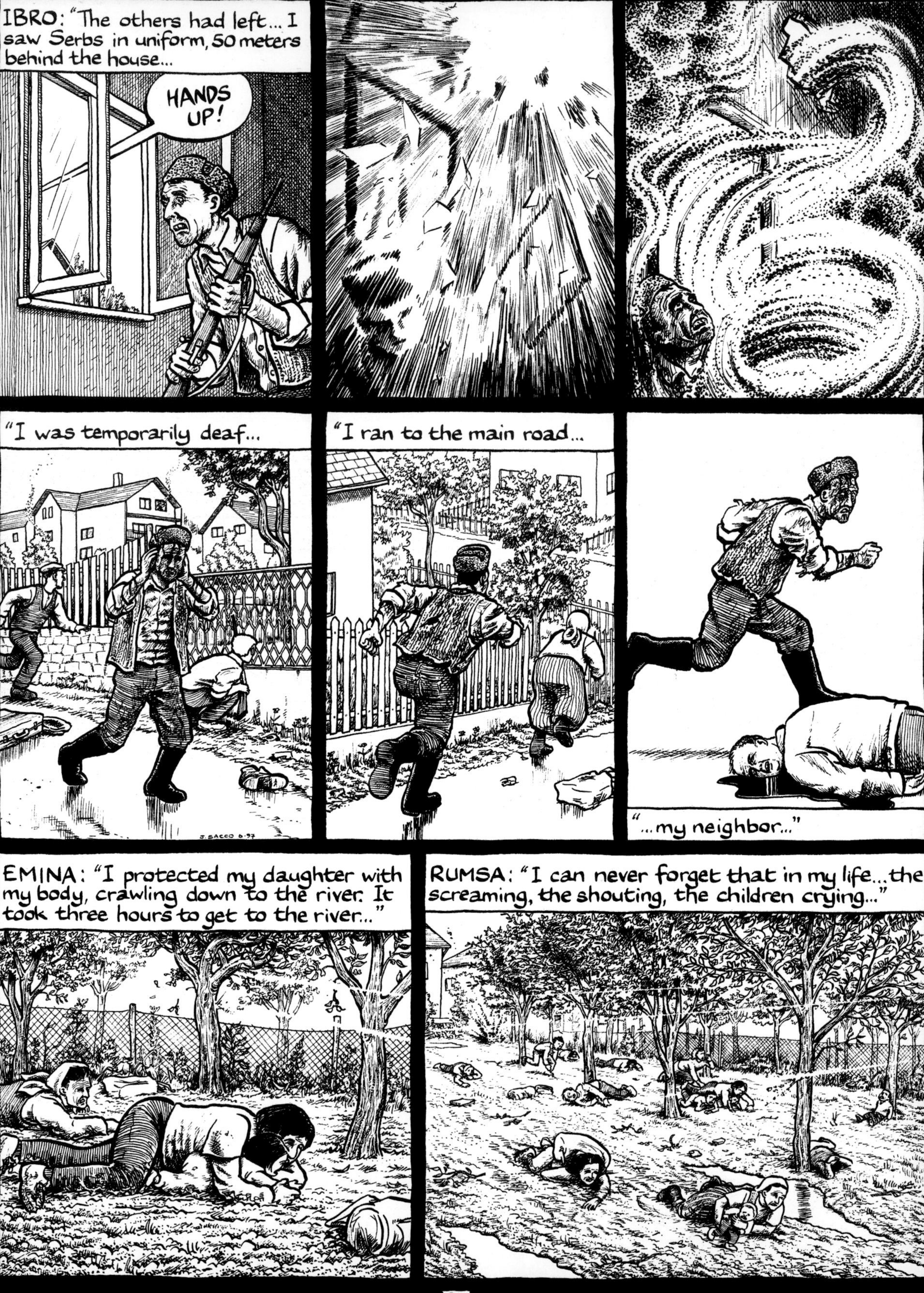
IBRO: "The others had left... I saw Serbs in uniform, 50 meters behind the house...
HANDS UP!
"I was temporarily deaf...
J. SACCO 6.97
"I ran to the main road...
"...my neighbor..."
EMINA: "I protected my daughter with my body, crawling down to the river. It took three hours to get to the river..."
RUMSA: "I can never forget that in my life... the screaming, the shouting, the children crying..."

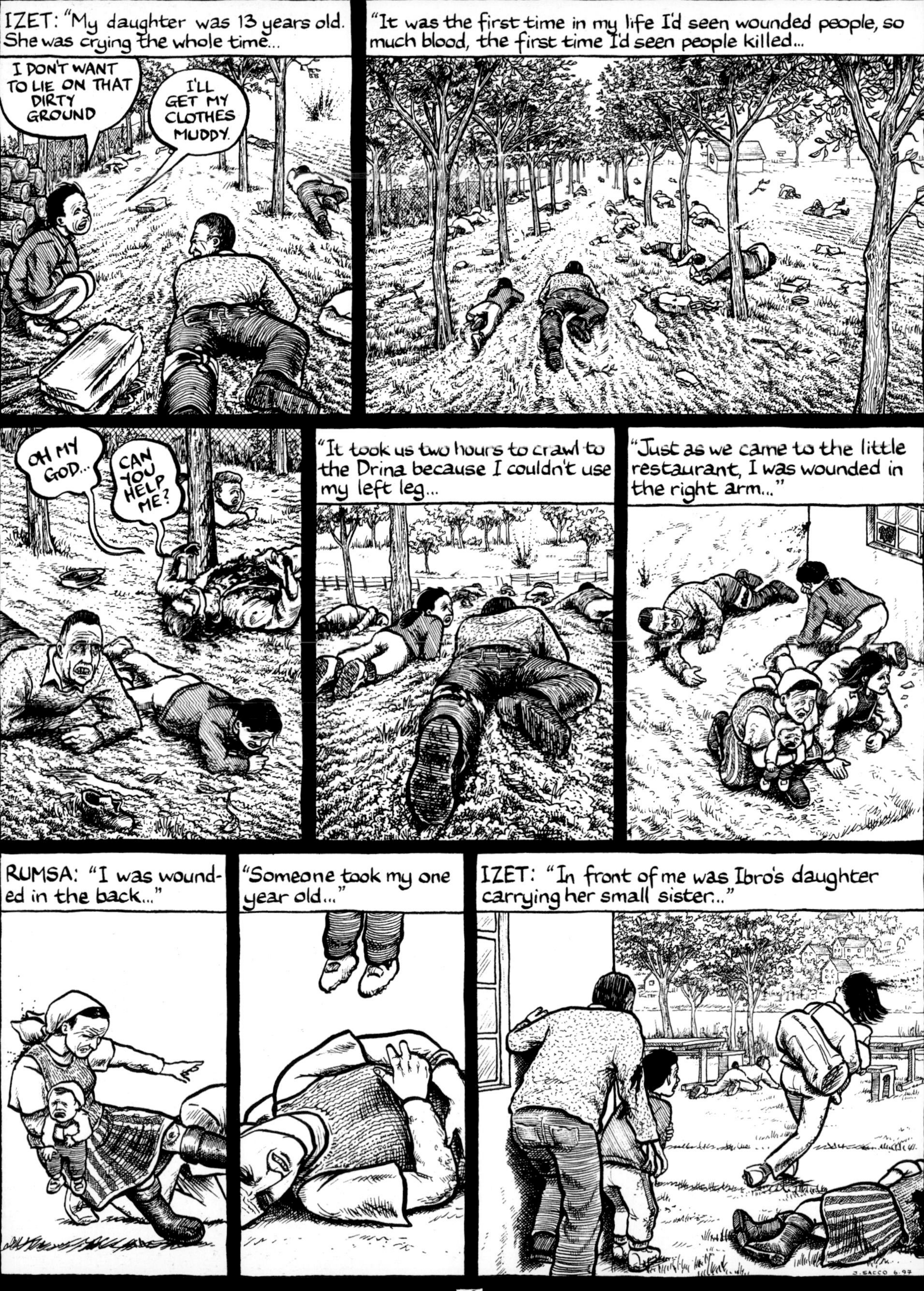
IZET: "My daughter was 13 years old. She was crying the whole time...
I DON'T WANT TO LIE ON THAT DIRTY GROUND
I'LL GET MY CLOTHES MUDDY.
"It was the first time in my life I'd seen wounded people, so much blood, the first time I'd seen people killed...
OH MY GOD...
CAN YOU HELP ME?
"It took us two hours to crawl to the Drina because I couldn't use my left leg...
"Just as we came to the little restaurant, I was wounded in the right arm..."
RUMSA: "I was wounded in the back..."
"Someone took my one year old..."
IZET: "In front of me was Ibro's daughter carrying her small sister..."
J. SACCO 6.97

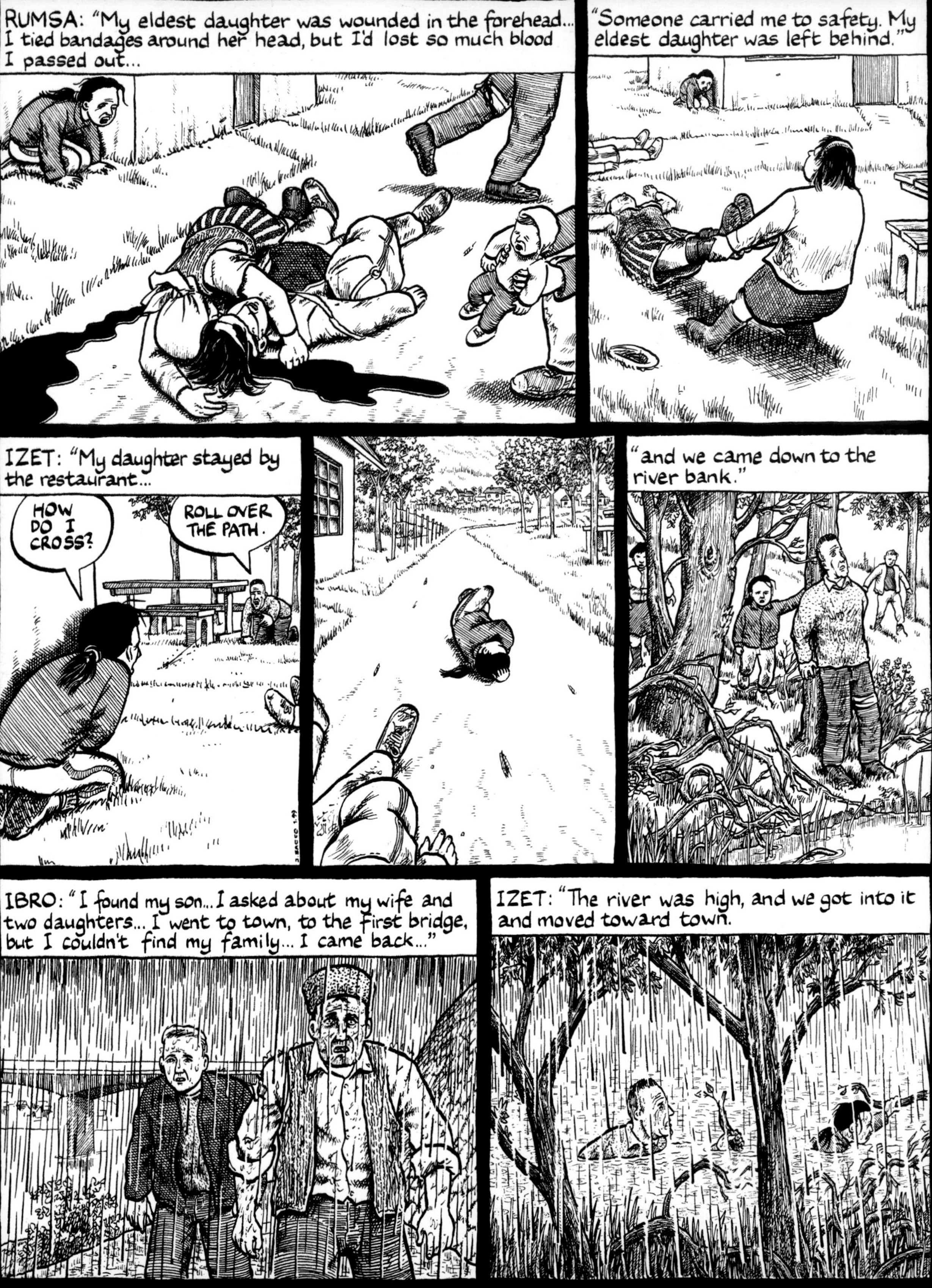

RUMSA: "My eldest daughter was wounded in the forehead... I tied bandages around her head, but I'd lost so much blood I passed out...
"Someone carried me to safety. My eldest daughter was left behind."
IZET: "My daughter stayed by the restaurant...
HOW DO I CROSS?
ROLL OVER THE PATH.
"and we came down to the river bank."
IBRO: "I found my son... I asked about my wife and two daughters... I went to town, to the first bridge, but I couldn't find my family... I came back..."
IZET: "The river was high, and we got into it and moved toward town.

"I don't like to speak about this. After 200 meters I got out because I'd lost my courage.

"I found Ibro and another man, but I didn't want to go on. So my daughter and the two men left me there."

"I changed my mind... It was raining and I couldn't use my leg, but I continued to town. I crawled all night like that."

"At 3:30 a.m. I was near the second bridge."

EMINA: "We spent nine hours in the river. We waited till after midnight... My daughter was without food or water for 24 hours, but she never cried."

MY BROTHER AND GRANDMOTHER WERE THERE WHEN THE SERBS ATTACKED... WE DIDN'T KNOW WHAT HAPPENED TO THEM FOR SEVEN OR EIGHT DAYS. WE WERE IN KOPACI.

"My brother was wounded by a shell... and he was bloody, all his body, from shrapnel... He grabbed my grandmother and ran with her on his shoulders and escaped in the direction of the river."

FIVE OF MY RELATIVES WERE MISSING AND SIX KILLED.

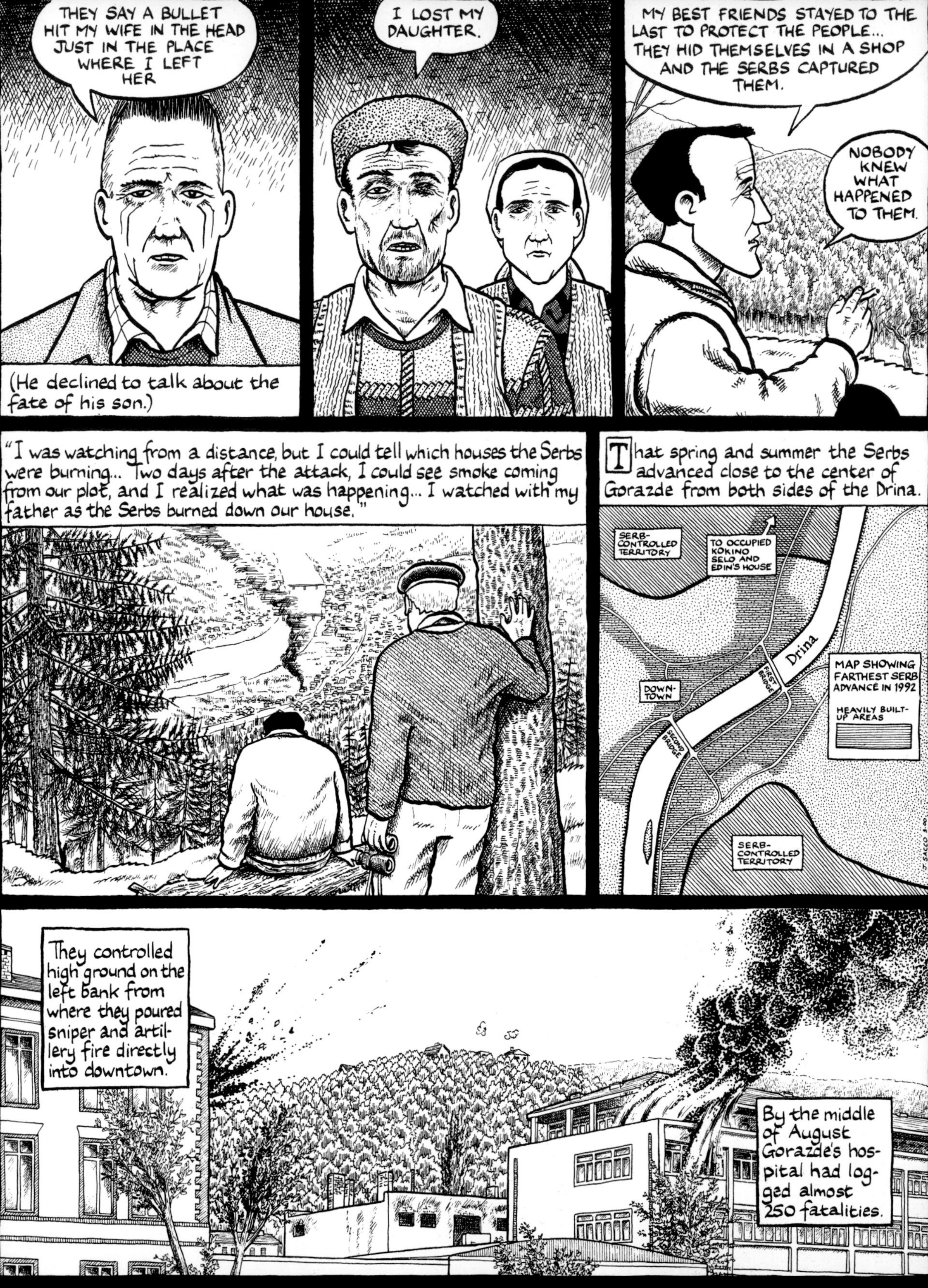
THEY SAY A BULLET HIT MY WIFE IN THE HEAD JUST IN THE PLACE WHERE I LEFT HER
(He declined to talk about the fate of his son.)
I LOST MY DAUGHTER.
MY BEST FRIENDS STAYED TO THE LAST TO PROTECT THE PEOPLE... THEY HID THEMSELVES IN A SHOP AND THE SERBS CAPTURED THEM.
NOBODY KNEW WHAT HAPPENED TO THEM.
"I was watching from a distance, but I could tell which houses the Serbs were burning... Two days after the attack, I could see smoke coming from our plot, and I realized what was happening... I watched with my father as the Serbs burned down our house."
That spring and summer the Serbs advanced close to the center of Gorazde from both sides of the Drina.
SERB-CONTROLLED TERRITORY
TO OCCUPIED KOKINO SELO AND EDIN'S HOUSE
Drina
DOWN-TOWN
FIRST BRIDGE
SECOND BRIDGE
MAP SHOWING FARTHEST SERB ADVANCE IN 1992
HEAVILY BUILT-UP AREAS
SERB-CONTROLLED TERRITORY
They controlled high ground on the left bank from where they poured sniper and artillery fire directly into downtown.
By the middle of August Gorazde's hospital had logged almost 250 fatalities.

EDIN: "I was in Kopaci during that time... I was in a unit keeping positions in a huge old building, a warehouse for corn.

"Our forces captured seven Serbs at the TV transmission tower in August. I was guarding them. I knew some of them. They weren't close friends, but sometimes we'd been together drinking. I spoke to them, trying to get information about what happened in Kokino Selo. At first they didn't want to talk. They said they didn't know what happened to my friends who'd been captured.

"Then one of those guys told me exactly who had burned down my house. It was our neighbors. Dado, three years younger than me... And one called Acko and his brother, Miro. We used to play football together. We used to go out at night, and if we didn't go out, we used to spend the evenings together on our street."

WHY DO YOU THINK THEY BURNED DOWN YOUR HOME?

I DON'T KNOW. I WOULD LIKE TO ASK THEM.

AND WHAT HAPPENED TO THOSE SERB PRISONERS?

SOME TIME LATER THEY WERE MOVED TO GORAZDE.

THEY WERE EXECUTED.

FOR SURE.

In late August and September, Bosnian forces counterattacked, and the Serbs retreated from Gorazde to avoid being cut off. Though woefully underarmed, Bosnian troops pursued the Serbs toward Visegrad in the northeast and Foca in the southwest. Meanwhile, Edin's unit advanced from Kopaci to take back territory vacated by the Serbs.

"Over the night the Serbs left in panic from Kokino Selo because they were scared we would encircle them. We realized it in the morning... About 20, 30 of us advanced down the main road toward Gorazde.

"I wanted to see if there was anything left from my house, if there was still a roof. We had hidden our TV, gold, money underground, around the house. Furs, clothes, tools... I wasn't patient... I found a bicycle in a garage... and I was the first person who came from Kopaci to Kokino Selo.

"The house was completely burned. I couldn't believe it. Only the garage was left... And whatever we'd hidden, the Serbs found. I couldn't even find a nail.

"Our soldiers had already come from the direction of Gorazde. Civilians as well.

"My dog found me... Billy! He was very happy. I started to cry.

"He stayed three months with the Serbs during their occupation. After that, if someone came to our house in uniform and armed, he would start barking very hard.

"I was very thirsty, and I went into some houses looking for something to drink, Serb houses. They were already broken into. Refugees, people from town, everyone was coming looking for food. They were robbing houses. I found some vodka...

"People were carrying out TVs. The Serbs had been collecting from Muslim homes from May till September. And I was looking for ours. It was from Germany, a couple of months old, a Grundig. My father had paid 2000 dm for it. The only one, I'm sure, in town.

IS IT A GRUNDIG? MAY I SEE IT FROM THE FRONT?

"After seven or eight televisions, I realized it was useless. I was losing time looking for the television... I took a wheelbarrow. I took vodka and a wheelbarrow.

"People were burning down Serb homes. Most of the Muslim homes had already been burned down by the Serbs.

"Some people didn't want to take anything. They just wanted to burn. They were very angry. They didn't care about anything. You couldn't say anything to anyone. People were scared and out of control.

J. SACCO 1-99

"I found my brother at our house. He had juice. We were talking, drinking.

"He had found my skis and fishing rods in the houses of the people who burned down our house.

"We found our front door at the house of a Serb neighbor. This man had three children and was very poor. My mother was always bringing them things, always inviting his wife in for a drink. He must have liked our front door.

"The same day, in the afternoon, a refugee mentioned that there was a body in a house further up than mine. I went to look with my father.

"We recognized our neighbor by his clothes. He was dead for three months. Probably they'd poured gasoline or something on him to burn him up.

"I didn't believe at that moment that it was possible, but it had been. My father couldn't eat anything in those days. It was a big shock for us, for the people who saw that...

"We found five bodies in three houses. We just couldn't believe our neighbors could do something like that, burning down our homes, killing people, burning them.

ARE YOU SURE IT WAS YOUR SERB NEIGHBORS?

MOSTLY. THAT'S FOR SURE. THEY LEFT BEHIND A NOTEBOOK. THEY LEFT IT IN SOME GARBAGE IN A STREAM ABOVE MY HOUSE. A WHOLE LIST OF NAMES, SURNAMES, AND WHAT KIND OF WEAPONS THEY CARRIED.

FIFTY-NINE OF THEM FROM MY NEIGHBORHOOD.

AND I KNEW THEM ALL.

"My father, my brother, and I decided to find materials to repair the house. We looked around the whole area, in people's homes, in warehouses, and we found brand new roofing tiles and timber. We took whatever we wanted. We found cement and lime in a Serb house. Who knows? Maybe they belonged to a Muslim...

"We cleaned the walls completely down to the bricks and put on plaster. In 40 days we fixed the roof and made two rooms livable."

Not until the following March did Izet and Gorazde discover what had happened to his son and some of the others captured by the Serbs during their first attack.

91

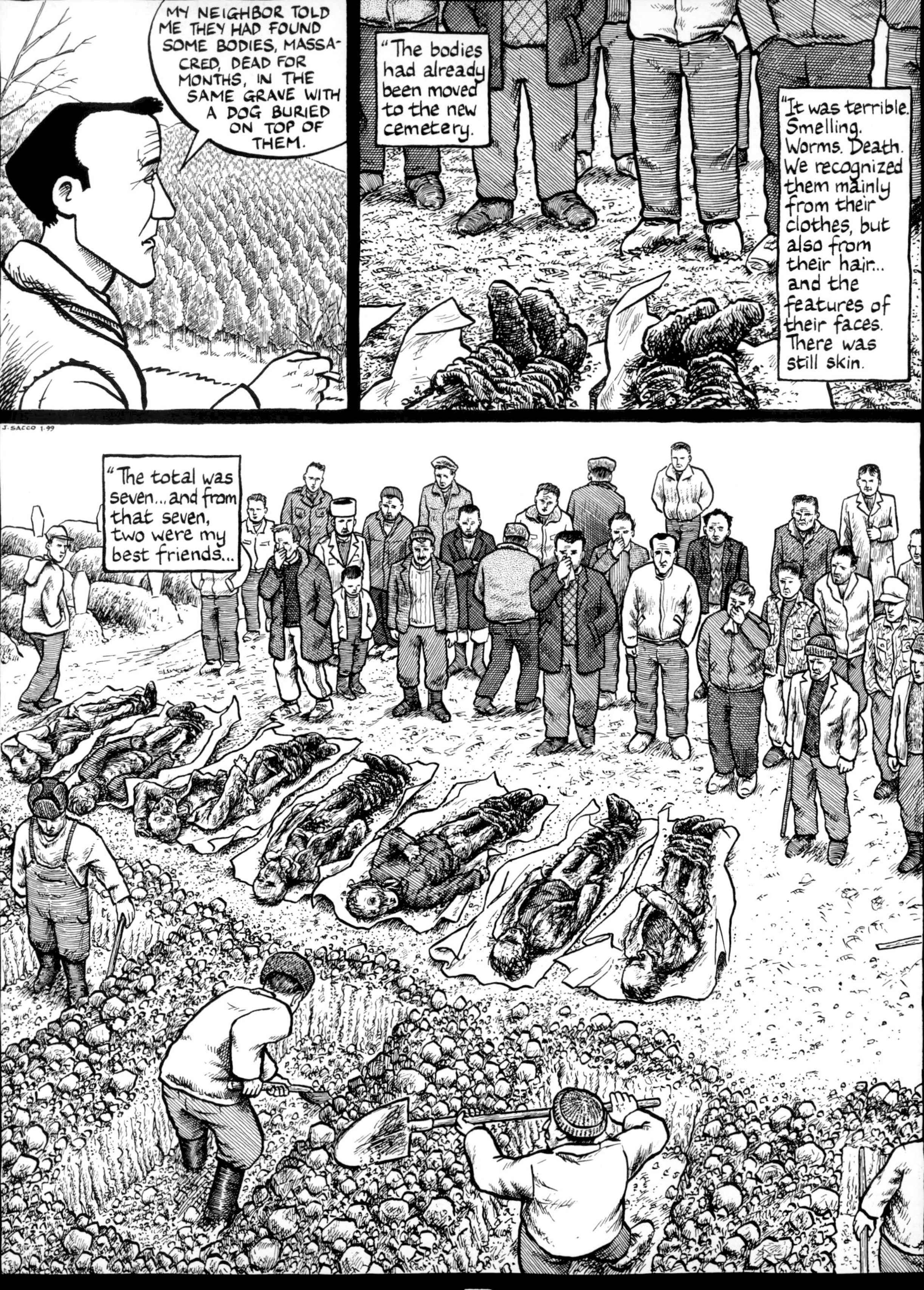
MY NEIGHBOR TOLD ME THEY HAD FOUND SOME BODIES, MASSACRED, DEAD FOR MONTHS, IN THE SAME GRAVE WITH A DOG BURIED ON TOP OF THEM.
"The bodies had already been moved to the new cemetery.
"It was terrible. Smelling. Worms. Death. We recognized them mainly from their clothes, but also from their hair... and the features of their faces. There was still skin.
J. SACCO 1-99
"The total was seven...and from that seven, two were my best friends...

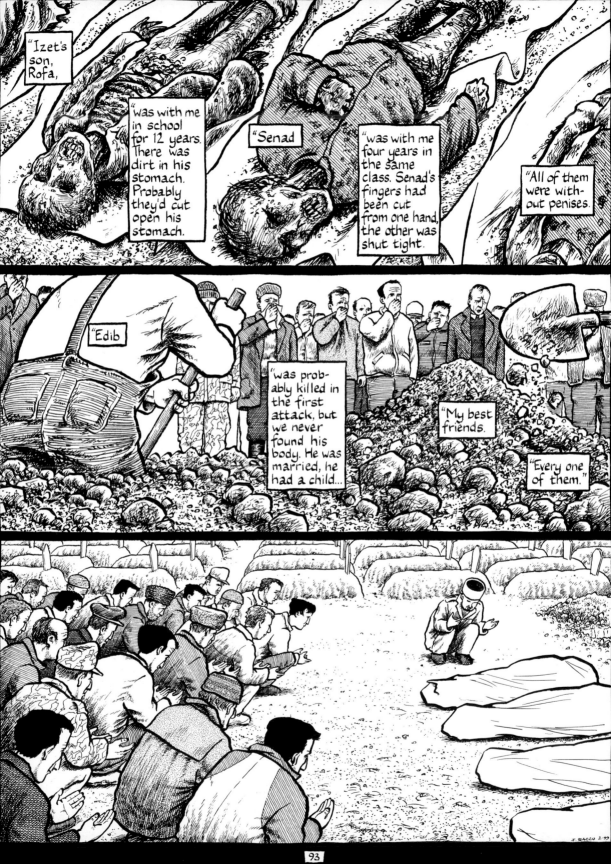

"Izet's son, Rofa,

"was with me in school for 12 years. There was dirt in his stomach. Probably they'd cut open his stomach.

"Senad

"was with me four years in the same class. Senad's fingers had been cut from one hand, the other was shut tight.

"All of them were without penises.

"Edib

"was probably killed in the first attack, but we never found his body. He was married, he had a child...

"My best friends.

"Every one of them."

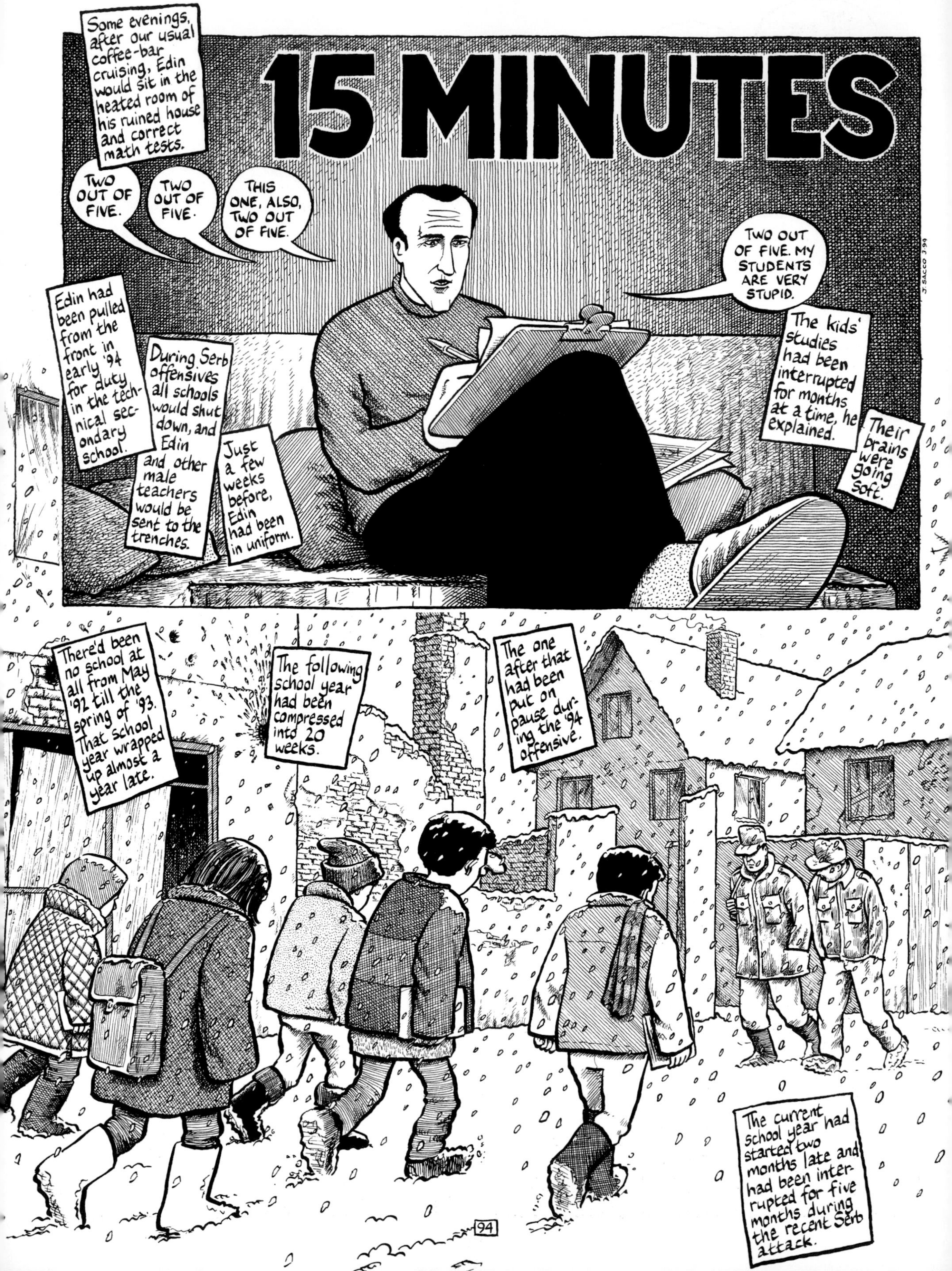

15 MINUTES
Some evenings, after our usual coffee-bar cruising, Edin would sit in the heated room of his ruined house and correct math tests.
TWO OUT OF FIVE.
TWO OUT OF FIVE.
THIS ONE, ALSO, TWO OUT OF FIVE.
TWO OUT OF FIVE. MY STUDENTS ARE VERY STUPID.
Edin had been pulled from the front in early '94 for duty in the technical secondary school.
During Serb offensives all schools would shut down, and Edin and other male teachers would be sent to the trenches.
Just a few weeks before, Edin had been in uniform.
The kids' studies had been interrupted for months at a time, he explained.
Their brains were going soft.
J. SACCO 3/99
There'd been no school at all from May '92 till the spring of '93. That school year wrapped up almost a year late.
The following school year had been compressed into 20 weeks.
The one after that had been put on pause during the '94 offensive.
The current school year had started two months late and had been interrupted for five months during the recent Serb attack.

ONE TIME, FOR EIGHT MONTHS I DIDN'T GO TO SCHOOL.

I FORGOT EVERY-THING.

I WAS WAITING FOR THE CHETNIKS TO KILL ME.

The official in charge of the enclave's sports, education, and culture department told me, "The students spent a lot of time in cellars and fighting for survival...

"and when they came back to class they would find the empty tables of their friends who were killed or wounded...

"Also, many of them lost parents, their sisters, their houses."

"After every offensive some of them had to change their living places.

"And all the time it was very danger-ous on the trip from school to home."

95

J. SACCO 2:99

Some kids weren't bothering to make the trip at all.

This 17 year old, a refugee from Rudo, lived with his brother and two sisters in one room of a burned-out house.

His mother had been killed by a shell out front two and a half years ago.

MY SISTERS STILL GO TO SCHOOL, BUT I SPEND MY TIME WITH FRIENDS.

Other kids were only nominally in school.

On one occasion, a student stopped by Edin's place with an older man.

The man explained that he'd been close friends with the boy's father, who'd been killed in the war.

COULD YOU PLEASE PASS THE BOY WITH A GOOD GRADE?

Edin told him the boy was hopeless at his studies.

The man insisted...

THE BOY HAS WORKED WITH THE ARMY FOR TWO YEARS. HE DELIVERS BREAD AND SUPPLIES BY HORSE TO THE FRONT.

THE SOLDIERS LOVE HIM.

Edin offered to speak to the boy's commander to get him released from duty for a few weeks. Then the boy could learn one subject well. (He was also flunking history and chemistry.)

But the boy didn't want that.

I WANT TO KEEP DELIVERING BREAD TO THE SOLDIERS.

After they'd left...

THE MAN SAID THE BOY IS A HARDSHIP CASE.

IS HE A HARDSHIP CASE?

EVERYONE HERE IS A HARDSHIP CASE.

J. SACCO 2·99

The hardship cases who actually went to school were served by a system teetering under wartime strain.

The facilities had not fared well.

This secondary school, one of three in Gorazde, had been gutted.

Other school buildings were damaged or were being used to house refugees.

Gorazde was jammed with people, and kids went to school in shifts. One girl told me she was going only three times a week, taking 13 subjects in 35-minute periods.

IT'S NOT ENOUGH. YOU CAN'T LEARN ANYTHING.

Classes were without heat and light, and children scrounged for basic supplies.

PENCIL?

PENCIL?

Only seven of her 13 instructors were certified teachers, she said. The Serb teachers had left, and many Muslim teachers had escaped before the war. Some new teachers had come in with the refugees, she said, but many instructors were university students, like Edin, who hadn't yet finished their studies.

EVEN MY DAD IS TEACHING.

HE'S AN ENGINEER BUT HE'S TEACHING MINERALOGY.

SORRY, GUYS.

J. SACCO 2-99

For every 10 of his students, only one or two had a book, Edin told me. He was spending a lot of class time copying lessons from the book to the blackboard.

Without any equipment and with his gym a ruin, this physical ed instructor was mainly teaching theory to his classes.

I DON'T EVEN HAVE A TRACK SUIT FOR MYSELF.

This computer instructor, who had no computers, also was teaching theory.

MY STUDENTS HAVEN'T HAD A CHANCE TO SWITCH ON A COMPUTER.

SOME OF THEM HAVE NEVER EVEN SEEN A COMPUTER.

And Edin?

He was one of a few score students already enrolled at the university.

He'd done five years at the mechanical engineering school in Sarajevo.

He'd completed all his courses, taken all his written exams.

All that was left was to orally defend his thesis before his professors, about 15 minutes' worth of talking, he told me.

Meanwhile, for students who had finished secondary school during the war, the university in Sarajevo may as well have been a million miles away.

WE MISS EDUCATION. WE'RE AFRAID WE'RE LOSING TIME.

But he was stranded in Gorazde.

He'd been 15 minutes from his degree for the past three and a half years.

TWO OUT OF FIVE. VERY STUPID.

J. SACCO 2-99

It was a night before Riki was due back at the front, his mom had laid out the usual spread, and he and Edin were asking about America, which was out there, they believed, over an ocean and mountains and the Serb lines.

RIKI
PART II

Then, somewhere between one pot of Turkish coffee and another,

Riki stood up,

cleared his throat,

and informed us that—

"PAULA JONES, WHO WAS 24 THEN, SUED PRESIDENT CLINTON FOR $700,000 FOR ALLEGEDLY VIOLATING HER CIVIL RIGHTS BY MAKING UNWELCOMED SEXUAL ADVANCES TOWARD HER IN A LITTLE ROCK HOTEL.

"PAULA JONES CHARGES THAT PRESIDENT CLINTON SPOTTED HER IN THE HOTEL, SUMMONED HER TO HIS ROOM, AND MADE A BLUNT SEXUAL PROPOSITION."

I HAVE MEMORIZED IT FROM 'TIME' MAGAZINE WHEN I WAS ON THE BATTLE-LINE.

It was boring in the mountains, he said, cold in the trenches and boring.

Generally, the cease-fire was holding.

He and his comrades played cards, he said, they traded insults with the Serbs 200 meters away...

and Riki read and reread his old copy of 'Time.'

J. SACCO 2-99

99

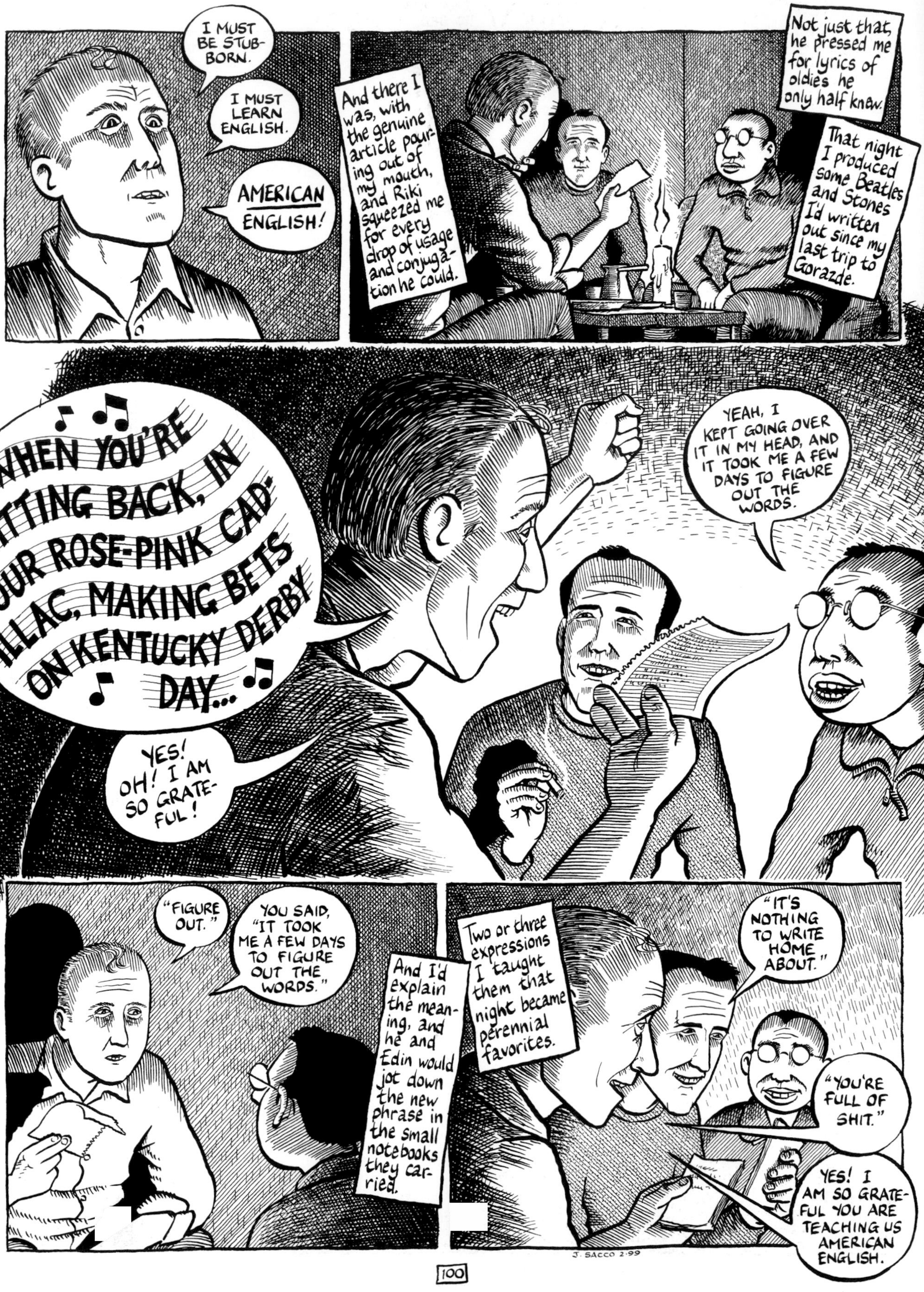
I MUST BE STUBBORN.
I MUST LEARN ENGLISH.
AMERICAN ENGLISH!
And there I was, with the genuine article pouring out of my mouth, and Riki squeezed me for every drop of usage and conjugation he could.
Not just that, he pressed me for lyrics of oldies he only half knew.
That night I produced some Beatles and Stones I'd written out since my last trip to Gorazde.
WHEN YOU'RE SITTING BACK, IN YOUR ROSE-PINK CADILLAC, MAKING BETS ON KENTUCKY DERBY DAY...
YEAH, I KEPT GOING OVER IT IN MY HEAD, AND IT TOOK ME A FEW DAYS TO FIGURE OUT THE WORDS.
YES! OH! I AM SO GRATEFUL!
"FIGURE OUT."
YOU SAID, "IT TOOK ME A FEW DAYS TO FIGURE OUT THE WORDS."
And I'd explain the meaning, and he and Edin would jot down the new phrase in the small notebooks they carried.
Two or three expressions I taught them that night became perennial favorites.
"IT'S NOTHING TO WRITE HOME ABOUT."
"YOU'RE FULL OF SHIT."
YES! I AM SO GRATEFUL YOU ARE TEACHING US AMERICAN ENGLISH.
J. SACCO 2·99

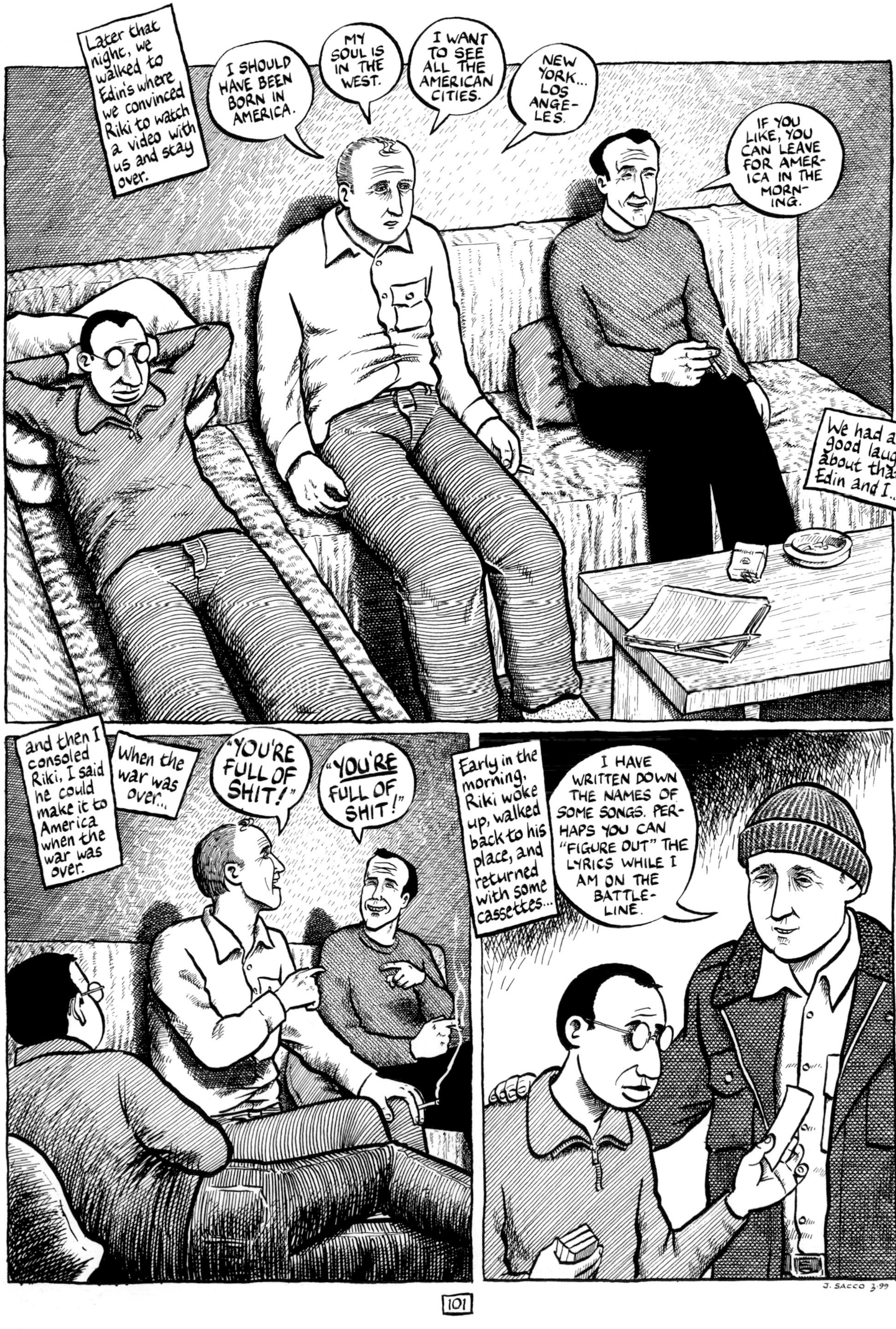

Later that night, we walked to Edin's where we convinced Riki to watch a video with us and stay over.
I SHOULD HAVE BEEN BORN IN AMERICA.
MY SOUL IS IN THE WEST.
I WANT TO SEE ALL THE AMERICAN CITIES.
NEW YORK... LOS ANGELES.
IF YOU LIKE, YOU CAN LEAVE FOR AMERICA IN THE MORNING.
We had a good laugh about that, Edin and I...
and then I consoled Riki, I said he could make it to America when the war was over.
When the war was over...
"YOU'RE FULL OF SHIT!"
"YOU'RE FULL OF SHIT!"
Early in the morning, Riki woke up, walked back to his place, and returned with some cassettes...
I HAVE WRITTEN DOWN THE NAMES OF SOME SONGS. PERHAPS YOU CAN "FIGURE OUT" THE LYRICS WHILE I AM ON THE BATTLE-LINE.
J. SACCO 3·99

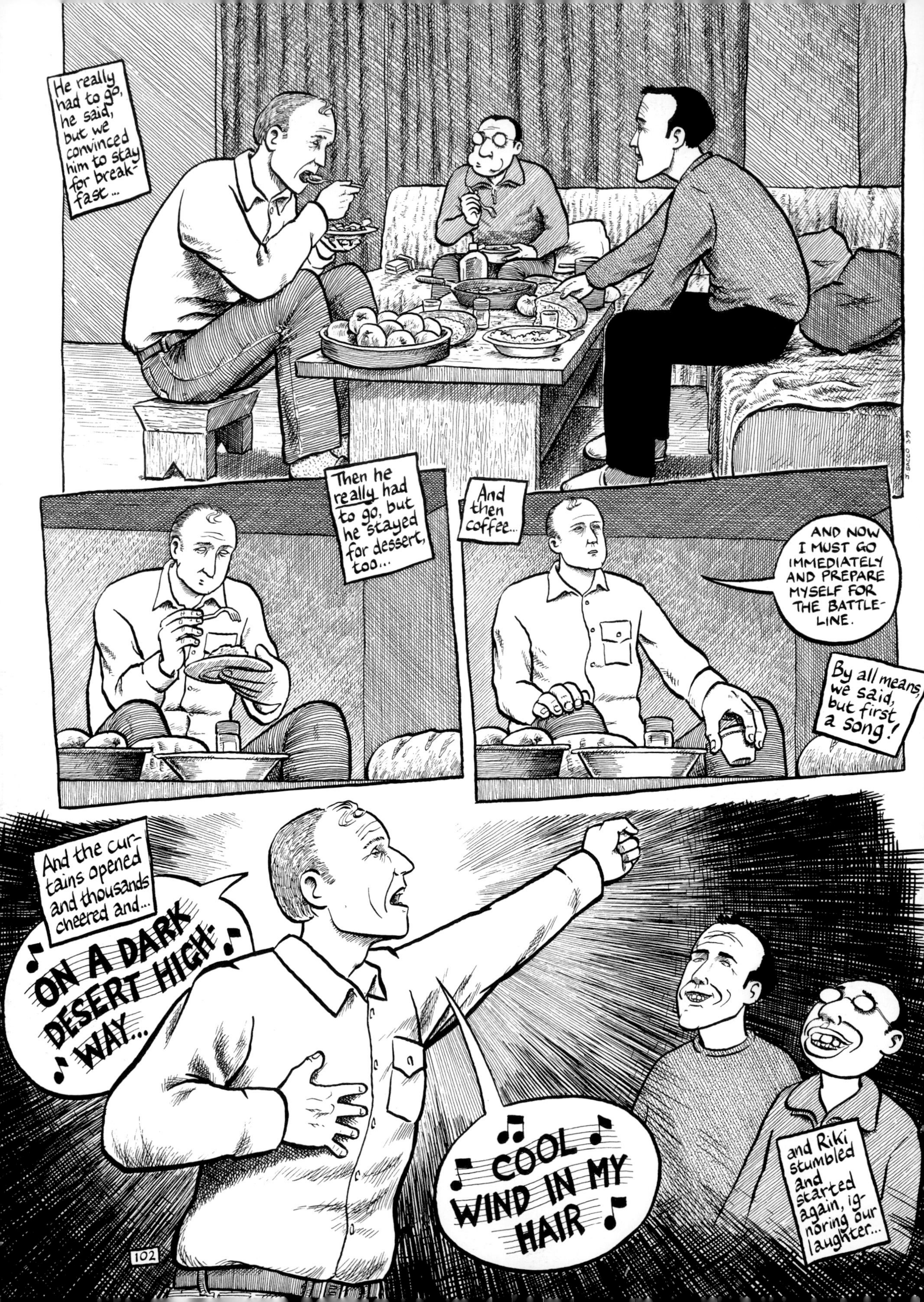
He really had to go, he said, but we convinced him to stay for break-fast...
Then he really had to go, but he stayed for dessert, too...
And then coffee...
AND NOW I MUST GO IMMEDIATELY AND PREPARE MYSELF FOR THE BATTLE-LINE.
By all means, we said, but first a song!
And the cur-tains opened and thousands cheered and...
ON A DARK DESERT HIGH-WAY...
COOL WIND IN MY HAIR
and Riki stumbled and started again, ig-noring our laughter...

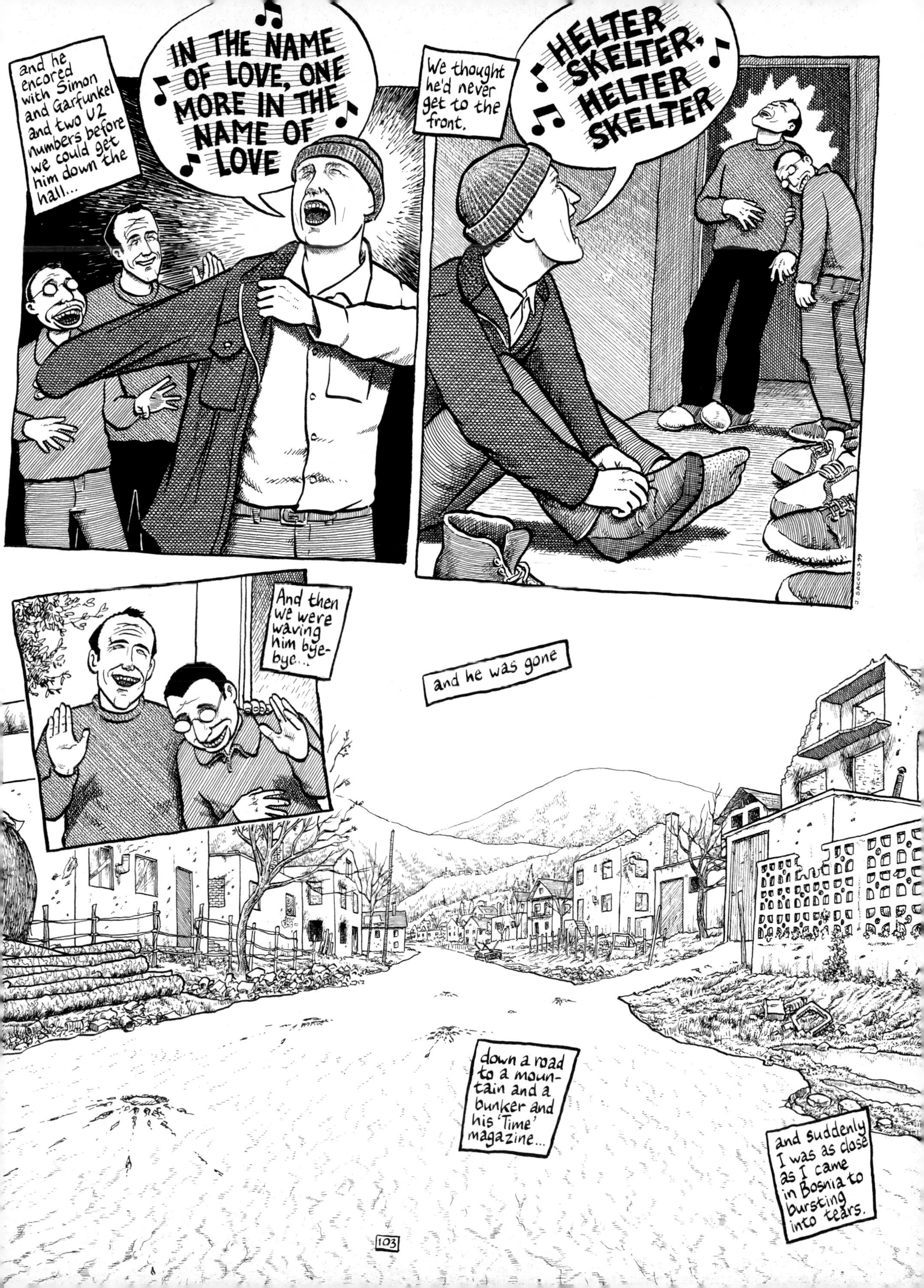

and he encored with Simon and Garfunkel and two U2 numbers before we could get him down the hall...
IN THE NAME OF LOVE, ONE MORE IN THE NAME OF LOVE
We thought he'd never get to the front.
HELTER SKELTER, HELTER SKELTER
And then we were waving him bye-bye...
and he was gone
down a road to a mountain and a bunker and his 'Time' magazine...
and suddenly I was as close as I came in Bosnia to bursting into tears.

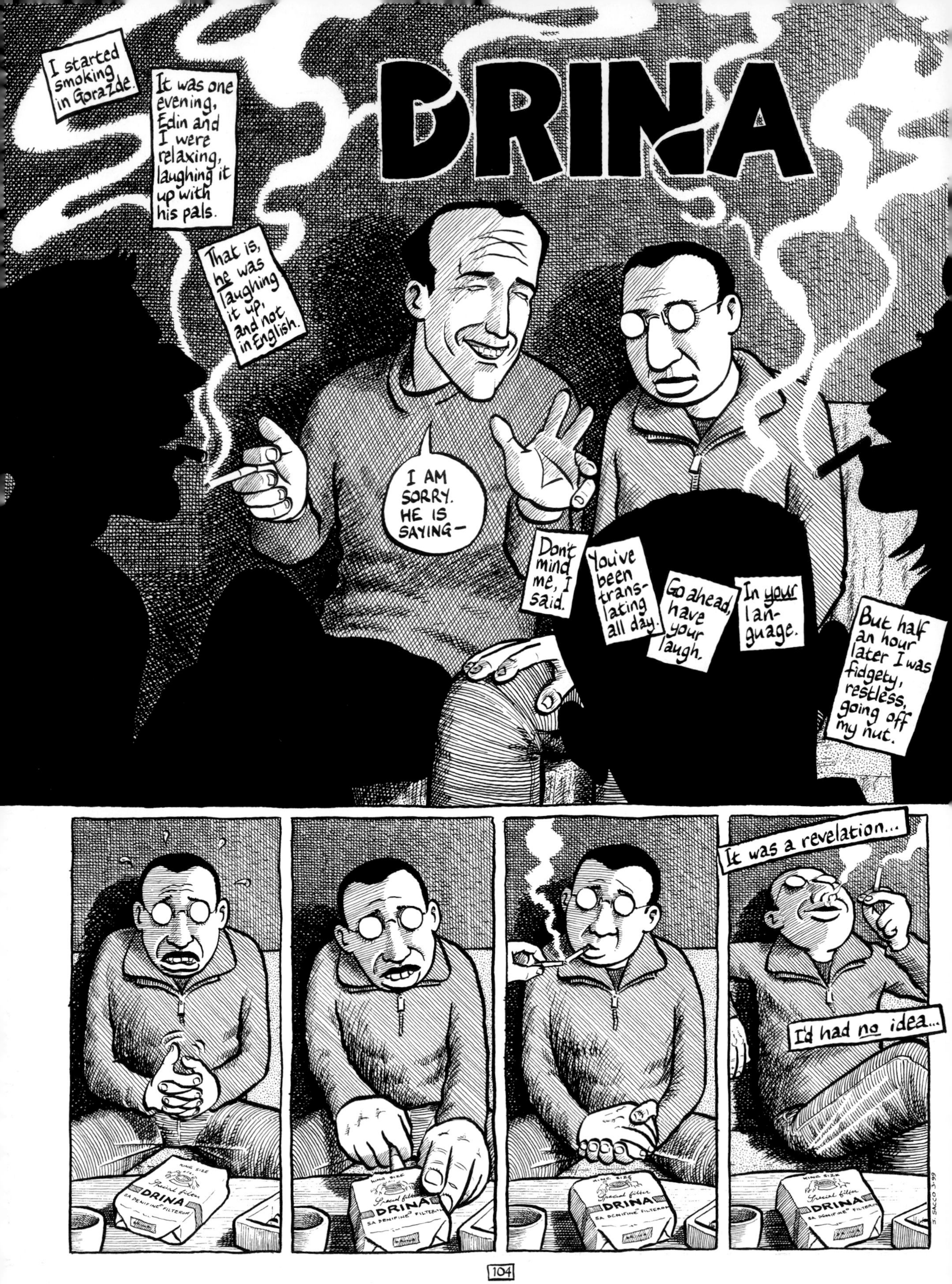
DRINA
I started smoking in Gorazde.
It was one evening, Edin and I were relaxing, laughing it up with his pals.
That is, he was laughing it up, and not in English.
I AM SORRY. HE IS SAYING—
Don't mind me, I said.
You've been translating all day.
Go ahead, have your laugh.
In your language.
But half an hour later I was fidgety, restless, going off my nut.
KING SIZE
Special filter
DRINA
SA DENIFINE FILTEROM
It was a revelation...
I'd had no idea...
S. SACCO 3·99

Those Drinas I started on, gotta say, they were nasty work.

Most Bosnians much preferred Marlboros or Lucky Strikes, but convoys were bringing in Drinas and no one was complaining.

In its own way, the Drina was special.

It had been manufactured in Sarajevo throughout the war. It was the national smoke.

KING SIZE
Special filter
DRINA
SA DENIFINE FILTEROM

The Drina cigarette is named for the famous river that runs along the border with Serbia and also through the Bosnian towns of Visegrad, Gorazde, and Foca. Visegrad and Foca had been ethnically cleansed in 1992 and were now in Serb hands...

Gorazde was full of refugees from those two towns, and I asked Edin to translate some of their stories for me...

It wore him out, visiting refugees, seeing how they lived. He'd had his own problems, he said, and the whole war thusfar he'd avoided theirs...

I ONLY KNEW WHERE THEY CAME FROM. FROM HERE, FROM THERE.

This woman didn't want to tell us what happened to her husband in Visegrad...

Reluctantly, this woman let us in from the rain to describe what she'd seen there, but only to a point...

I HAVEN'T TOLD YOU EVERYTHING. I'VE SEEN PEOPLE WITH THEIR EYES CUT OUT.

When this woman told us about her experiences in Foca, she started shaking so hard she had to sit down against the wall...

At the beginning of the war, bodies of Muslims massacred in Foca floated down the Drina river and through Gorazde...

Now, the Gorazde pocket was the only remaining Bosnian government territory on the Drina...

Soldiers defending Gorazde were paid in Drinas, 30 packs a month while I was there. (Getting paid at all was a recent development.)

School teachers had just started earning Drinas, too. On pay day they'd get their wages in a plastic bag and smoke some up in the staff room.

J. SACCO 11-96

They were also lighting up in the nurses' lounge at the hospital...

They had stories for Edin to translate there, too...

The head nurse of surgery had been the only medically trained person tending to thousands of Muslims retreating from Visegrad in 1992...

IN THOSE DAYS I DIDN'T SLEEP, I DIDN'T EAT ANYTHING, I ALWAYS HAD BLOODY HANDS.

She'd had no supplies, no gauze or bandages, and during the operations she improvised, the only pain killer she had to offer was 'rakija' — brandy.

And there was no tobacco, she said. She'd had to smoke nettles and grape leaves.

Now she had Drinas.

THANK GOD FOR THESE CIGA-RETTES.

J. SACCO 11-96

Drina

Drina

In Sarajevo, many urban people droned on about the "primitivism" of the eastern Bosnian refugees filling their proudly cosmopolitan city...

They smoked Drinas there, too, and some local hipsters told me they weren't so concerned about the fate of Gorazde and its "country" people.

Meanwhile, Edin had put two and two together.

GORAZDE NEEDS SARAJEVO, BUT SARAJEVO DOESN'T NEED GORAZDE.

I used to joke that if his government traded away Gorazde in a peace deal, Bosnia would have no territory left on the Drina and would have to change the name of its cigarette.

108

I SPENT SIX DAYS IN GORAZDE BEFORE RETURNING TO VISEGRAD.

A LOT OF SOLDIERS HAD COME FROM SERBIA, THE UZICKI CORPS, AND WE WERE THINKING, IT'S OUR ARMY, THEY'VE LIBERATED VISEGRAD FROM THE CHETNIKS, AND THAT'S WHY WE WENT BACK.

EVERYTHING STARTED TO SEEM LIKE NORMAL AGAIN.

In the spring of 1992, many Muslims still trusted the Serbian-dominated Yugoslav People's Army (JNA) to protect them from the Serb nationalist militias.

Around Gorazde
PART I

Rasim

In April Muslims had begun to leave Visegrad, a town made famous by Ivo Andric's Nobel Prize-winning novel, 'The Bridge on the Drina,' for Gorazde, which was 30 kilometers upriver and was not yet under attack.

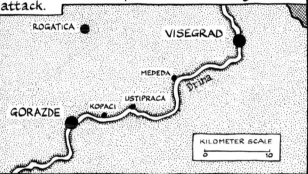

Many Muslims returned to Visegrad when the JNA promised them security in their own homes.

"The Uzicki Corps spent one month in Visegrad. They took the weapons from the Muslims and gave weapons to the Serbs. Guys from the Uzicki Corps told us—

WHILE WE'RE HERE, EVERYTHING WILL BE OKAY...

BUT WHEN WE LEAVE, DON'T EXPECT GOOD THINGS.

"The Uzicki Corps left Visegrad on May 18... and the Serbs started to burn villages... to kill people around Visegrad, and they put the town under siege."

I WAS AN EYEWITNESS WHEN SERBS BROUGHT MUSLIMS TO THE BRIDGE ON THE DRINA AND PUSHED THEM INTO THE RIVER AND SHOT THEM.

"They did that by night. The Serbs took my neighbors from their flats, even without shoes. They said to them—

YOU DON'T NEED SHOES.

YOU'RE GOING TO BE KILLED IN A FEW MINUTES.

"I was in Visegrad until June 17 and I saw almost everything. My home was between two bridges and I watched what happened.

"All night the Chetniks were taking people, even children, women, and you could hear splashing in the river.

"Sometimes they shot them, but they preferred to cut their throats.

I WAS AN EYE-WITNESS.

"In only three days and three nights I saw 2-300 killed."

J. SACCO J-99

"The worst things happened on June 8. If the Chetniks caught someone, they killed them on the spot."

WERE PEOPLE RESISTING? WERE THEY SCREAMING?

IF SOMEBODY STARTED TO RUN, THEY JUST SHOT THEM.

THEY WERE SCREAMING BUT NOBODY COULD HELP THEM.

THEY WERE UNARMED.

NO WEAPONS.

NOTHING.

WERE THEY TIED?

YES. BUT ONLY THE MALES. NOT WOMEN AND CHILDREN.

BUT DID THEY STILL KILL WOMEN AND CHILDREN?

YES. OF COURSE.

"On June 10 I was an eyewitness when the Chetniks brought two families—both families had three kids—and killed them behind the bridge.

"They cut their throats and pushed them in the river... The Guso and Sabanovic families. First they killed the children...

"And I was an eyewitness when a Chetnik cut off the breast of one of the mothers, who was trying to protect her kids.

"I was scared and two neighbors and I spent some nights in the forest because the worst things were happening at night...

"On June 16 three Chetniks came to my house. People from Visegrad. I knew them all.

WHERE ARE YOUR WEAPONS?

WHERE ARE YOUR WEAPONS?

"They broke 12 of my teeth and my nose. One of them took a picture from the wall and smashed it over my head.

WE'RE GOING STRAIGHT TO THE BRIDGE TO CUT YOUR THROAT!

"They put me in a vehicle. I wanted to escape but I couldn't walk. I felt a terrible pain in my leg.

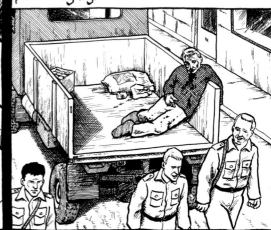

"I watched while they robbed a shop.

"Another 10 Chetniks came to rob things, and they brought three other Muslims who'd been beaten and put them with me.

"The Serbs were playing the accordion and drinking and singing.

"A Serb neighbor saw me all bloody and came over.

WHAT'S GOING ON?

IF YOU CAN, SAVE ME.

KEEP YOUR MOUTH SHUT.

I'M GOING TO SAVE YOU.

BUT IF YOU WANT TO STAY ALIVE, YOU HAVE TO HELP LOAD THE TRUCK.

"I couldn't because of my leg, but I received things while the other Muslims brought them...

WHEN YOU'RE FINISHED WITH THIS JOB, WE'RE GOING TO TAKE YOU TO THE BRIDGE AND KILL YOU.

"Then the Chetnik commander ordered me to his office and my neighbor helped me down.

THANKS TO YOUR NEIGHBOR, YOU CAN GO HOME, BUT STAY THERE.

CAN YOU GIVE ME SOME KIND OF PERMISSION SO I CAN CROSS THE BRIDGE? I'M SCARED SOMEONE WILL STOP ME.

IF I GIVE YOU SUCH A THING WITH MY NAME ON IT, IT'S SUICIDE FOR ME.

JUST TRUST IN GOD.

"He said I should report to the Red Cross building at 5:30 the next morning for evacuation.

"The Chetniks put the other Muslims back on the truck and I didn't see them again. I suppose they were killed.

"I went home.

"At 11 p.m., the neighbor who saved me came to my house. He bandaged my throat.

I'LL TRY TO HELP YOU ESCAPE TONIGHT.

I THINK THERE ARE TWO PLACES YOU CAN PASS THROUGH.

"We tried those places, but we couldn't pass. We came directly where the Chetniks were bringing a lot of people and killing them. Mostly women and children.

"I returned home.

"At 5a.m., I left to cross to the other side of the Drina.

"I met a Serb guy I'd known before the war. I told him where I was going.

DON'T YOU SEE WHAT THAT GUY LAKIC IS DOING ON THE BRIDGE?

DON'T GO THERE.

"Mirko Lakic was a butcher before the war, and I was an eye-

witness when some Chetniks took two guys from Lakic's car, and

Lakic cut their throats and pushed them in the river.

"All together I saw ten people killed in the same place.

"After Lakic killed his last victim he left for the other side. I made the decision to cross...

"and when I got to the middle of the bridge...

"I saw a lot of blood, maybe ten meters around and two centimeters deep...

"and I saw three pairs of shoes, a man's, a woman's, and a child's, full of blood.

"and I was walking through the blood.

"And when I crossed the bridge I saw one of the Chetniks who'd beaten me the day before... crossing in the opposite direction...

"And this Chetnik saw me.

"He stopped in the middle of the bridge, and someone helped him put 11 bodies in the Drina, and one of those bodies had no head.

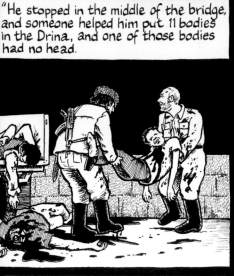

"I went to the Red Cross to put my name on the list for the convoy

"The woman who was making the list was a Serb friend of my daughter's. They'd gone to school together.

I CAN'T PUT YOUR NAME ON THE LIST. I KNOW WHAT WILL HAPPEN TO YOU.

TRY TO FIND SOME OTHER WAY TO LEAVE VISEGRAD.

"I asked her for some suggestion.

I CAN'T.

I'M AFRAID.

IF SOME-BODY EVEN SEES ME TALK-ING TO YOU, I'M GOING TO HAVE TROUBLE.

"I didn't know what to do. I thought maybe I'd cross the bridge again, but I saw two more bodies I hadn't seen before, and I changed my mind.

"I went back to the Serb woman.

TRY TO FIND A SECRET PLACE.

ARKAN AND HIS TROOPS ARE COMING.

"And I knew that Arkan's troops killed Serbs, too, if they helped Muslims.

"I waited for the convoy of three buses and three trucks. Then a woman read names and people got on the buses.

"And she put my name on the list.

"She found a place for me on the second truck.

"There were 75 people in this truck, all women and children except for me and another man."

Rasim and the others were taken close to Bosnian lines and released. He was lucky. On previous convoys, men had been routinely separated en route and killed.

I CAME TO GORAZDE FROM THE VILLAGE OF KAPOV HAN JUST BEFORE THE WAR, AND ON 24 APRIL I WAS SENT TO THE SPECIAL DEPARTMENT FOR PREGNANT WOMEN AT FOCA.

I HAD ONE MONTH TO GO.

Munira

Foca is less than 25 kilometers upriver from Gorazde and had the nearest hospital. Gorazde had only a large clinic before the war. Muslim patients like Munira were trapped in Foca after Serb forces took control of the town.

"For one month nobody touched us, and then Chetnik soldiers visited us. They took all our gold and took two women from our room at 3 a.m.

"One of those women had given birth to a dead baby before that and the other was three months pregnant.

"They brought them back at 9 a.m.

"The next night they came back and took four women, the two from before and another two, who had newborn babies...

"It happened every night. They came and took those four women all the time..."

"When I noticed someone was coming in the evening hours... I hid under a sink in a cupboard.

"Everything else was like normal. We got food for the children. A Serb doctor told us the soldiers wouldn't touch us...

"and we didn't tell the doctors or nurses anything."

I GAVE BIRTH TO MY DAUGHTER AIDA THERE.

After some months, Munira and the other women were told they would be freed in a prisoner exchange.

ONE EVENING, SOME SOLDIERS CAME WITH VEHICLES TO TAKE US. I THOUGHT WE WOULD BE KILLED. DR. CANCAR SAVED US.

DON'T WORRY, MY CHILDREN. WHILE I'M HERE NOTHING WILL HAPPEN TO YOU.

"And at that moment, one of the soldiers took away A., the woman who had had the still-born baby.

THAT WON'T HAPPEN TO THE REST OF YOU.

"A. was exchanged later, after her father-in-law paid the Serbs 10,000 dm.

J. SACCO 4·99

"We spent two more nights in the hospital, and then we were driven to the front lines."

"We were sent on our own down a road.

"Our soldiers picked us up...and we were taken to Gorazde."

I'D SPENT EIGHT MONTHS IN FOCA. I DIDN'T KNOW ANYTHING ABOUT MY HUSBAND AND OTHER CHILDREN.

I TOLD MYSELF, IF I DON'T FIND MY FAMILY, I'LL KILL MY CHILD AND MY-SELF.

Munira was reunited with her family in Gorazde.

The story of the women in the pregnancy ward was not unusual. Scores of Muslim women were held for months in Foca and raped repeatedly by Serb soldiers and para-militaries.

By the end of 1992, Gorazde's population had swollen to 60,000 by refugees. Many brought with them stories like Rasim's and Munira's.

The Gorazde pocket, which still included a narrow swath of the Drina Valley, tied down Serb forces and blocked the main road between Serbia proper and a large area captured by Bosnian Serbs in the south. As the Serbs made preparations to eliminate it, Gorazde's Muslims were under few illusions about their likely fate should their town fall.

J. SACCO 9-99

TOTAL WAR

There were tapes in town of unspeakable things. Goražde's own Most Horrifying Home Videos, amateur footage of shells coming in, animals split open, children sheared in two by anti-aircraft cannon, legs getting sawn off without anesthetic...

YOU MUST LOOK! YOU MUST LOOK! SHE WAS A SERB!

A Serb killed by a Serb shell!

Half her face sliced off!

An eyeball dangling on her cheek!

A few minutes of that and my Turkish colleague Šerif had enough, she was resisting our host's best efforts to smear her with more intestines and brains...

YOU MUST SEE THIS!

LOOK! LOOK!

He claimed the footage was his...

he'd been first on the scene after the shells had come in, he said...

he said he'd had unlimited access to operating rooms...

Šerif, overcoming her queasiness, told him she could use such a tape for Turkish television...

What was his price?

LOOK!

YOU MUST LOOK!

A close-up!

All that was left after a direct hit!

Toes!

Pulp!

That's all!

J·SACO 4·99

And in that way he beat around the bush for half an hour...

an hour...

an hour and a half...

while the video procession of dead children and shrieking parents went on and on...

He himself had been wounded seven, eight times!

And look at that!

Not even Serif's abundant charm could withstand the barrage!

and the heat in there!

the heat!

the wood stove roaring all out,

melting what remained of Serif's pleasant disposition!

LOOK!

and only when we'd finally forced our way out the door and into the outside chill did he name his price—

a figure so outrageous that it seemed to disgust Serif as much as all those full-color images of the dismembered and the disemboweled.

J. SACCO 4·99

PART II

That wasn't the first time I'd seen that footage (after which my curiosity had been exhausted) nor the last...

...but the next time 'round I was in a much cooler setting, the office of Dr. Alija Begovic, the director of Gorazde's hospital.

He put on the video...

we did our interview...

...and every once in a while he'd look up and recall an operation we were watching.

THIS ONE DIED.

And this girl— fully conscious and getting a bullet removed from her brain without anesthetic— had been evacuated.

I THINK SHE RECOVERED.

I'M NOT SURE.

I REMEMBER ONE GIRL, SHE WAS HIT BY AN ANTI-AIRCRAFT CANNON...

SHE WAS TWO YEARS OLD OR A LITTLE OLDER.

THERE WAS NO ANESTHETIC.

SHE HAD PROLAPSED INTESTINES— THEY WERE SPILLING OUT.

SHE'D JUST LEARNED TOILET TRAINING.

SHE WAS IN SHOCK, ASKING FOR A PAN TO GO TO THE TOILET IN DURING THE OPERATION.

SHE DIED ONE HOUR LATER.

He estimated that during hostilities he and his staff had performed 3-4,000 major operations— almost all war injuries— and tended to 10,000 or so other wounds.

From 78 doctors before the war, the institution was currently functioning with fewer than 20. It was still without running water.

I WOULD SEPARATE THE FIRST FIVE MONTHS BECAUSE THAT WAS THE WORST PERIOD FOR THE HOSPITAL.

J. SACCO 4·99

122

"In that period there was shelling, sniper fire."

"Patients were in the corridors and basement."

"There weren't enough bandages."

"We had to use bed sheets."

"We didn't have plaster."

"The main problem was we didn't have surgeons..."

"anesthetists or anesthetic drugs..."

"or even enough pain killers."

Begovic cut off his first leg with kitchen knives. He could dull the patient's pain only with a little morphine and brandy...

"We had to learn very quickly in that time."

"We had to become surgeons."

"Fortunately we had books on war surgery."

"Of course, nobody had any kind of experience with that,

"and we were faced with terrible wounds."

Nurse Sadija Demir, who had escaped from Visegrad (where she last saw her husband being taken away by the notorious White Eagles) and arrived in Gorazde in September '92, was put to work right away in the intensive care department. Four of her patients died that night.

WE WERE OPERATING ON PERSONS WITH OLD WOUNDS, ABDOMINAL WOUNDS. SOME OF THEM HAD BEEN WOUNDED 10 DAYS BEFORE...

THERE WEREN'T ENOUGH NURSES...

WE DIDN'T PAY ATTENTION TO WHAT WAS A WORKING DAY.

WE WORKED IN EVERY PLACE, IN EVERY DEPARTMENT.

IT WASN'T POSSIBLE TO ORGANIZE WELL AT THAT MOMENT.

J. SACCO 4-99

123

In the fall of 1992 a couple of trained surgeons walked over mountains through Serb lines to reach Gorazde, and over the next few months, before this route was cut, a few more medical personnel made it in with a limited amount of supplies.

NOW IT'S NOT VERY GOOD, BUT IT'S BETTER...

ONLY IN THE LAST FEW WEEKS, WITH THE OPENING OF THE BLUE ROAD, CAN WE BREATHE A LITTLE EASIER.

I CAN EVEN OFFER YOU A JUICE.

He watched the video absently.

There were plenty of distractions.

Staff, patients, others popped in...

Someone investigating war crimes plopped into a chair and began leafing through evidence...

He needed to go over a few incidents with the doctor.

His wife, also a physician, stopped by to whisper into his ear.

Even I had a visitor, and Dr. Begovic was good enough to translate.

YOU ARE TO MEET EDIN AT HIS COUSIN'S COFFEE BAR AT 11 O'CLOCK.

J. SACCO 4·99

As I got up to leave, the doctor seemed genuinely bewildered by the broader implications of the video we'd just watched.

I CAN'T UNDERSTAND WHY THE REST OF THE WORLD HASN'T INTERVENED MORE FORCEFULLY. THE U.N. IS ALWAYS POINTING OUT ITS NEUTRALITY, EVEN NOW.

NEUTRAL IN WHAT?

IN A SLAUGHTER OF LAMBS BY THE WOLVES?

I SIMPLY CAN'T BELIEVE SUCH PEOPLE EXIST —SOMEONE WHO WOULD FORCE A GRANDFATHER TO EAT THE LIVER OF HIS GRAND-SON.

I wasn't sure what he was referring to, and I didn't ask. Maybe it was one of those apocryphal stories going around about the enemy, remarkably far fetched even in a war like this...

or maybe not.

I let the doctor gather his thoughts, and I went away to dissipate my own.

PART III

DO YOU WANT TO MEET ONE OF GORAZDE'S BIGGEST WAR CRIMINALS?

He said he'd been an inductee in the Yugoslav People's Army in 1991 when his artillery unit was sent to intervene on behalf of Serbs fighting to remove themselves from newly independent Croatia.

He and his unit had taken part in the notorious bombardment of Vukovar, which killed hundreds.

J. SACCO 4-99

When his unit began flying the Serbian flag, he realized he was no longer fighting to preserve Yugoslavia.

He was a Muslim.

He deserted.

Back in his hometown, Gorazde, he found himself on the receiving end of bombardments more devastating than the ones he'd helped administer on Vukovar.

Many towns got pasted in the Balkan wars of the early and mid '90's.

Dubrovnik and Sarajevo endured their maulings in the living rooms of all those with a T.V. set.

But Gorazde had been cut off from cameras.

Its suffering was the sole property of those who had experienced it.

I could see only the scars so once a municipality worker tried to give me some idea of the scale of what had happened here.

On one day in July '92, he said, 2,500 shells landed in an area 600 meters square.

I asked him how they'd kept track of artillery bursts on Gorazde.

IT'S NOT A PROBLEM.

THE CHILDREN CAN COUNT THEM.

At one point in the '94 offensive, U.N. Military Observers, who were trained to do such things, reported impacts at a rate of eight per minute.

J. SACCO 4.99

126

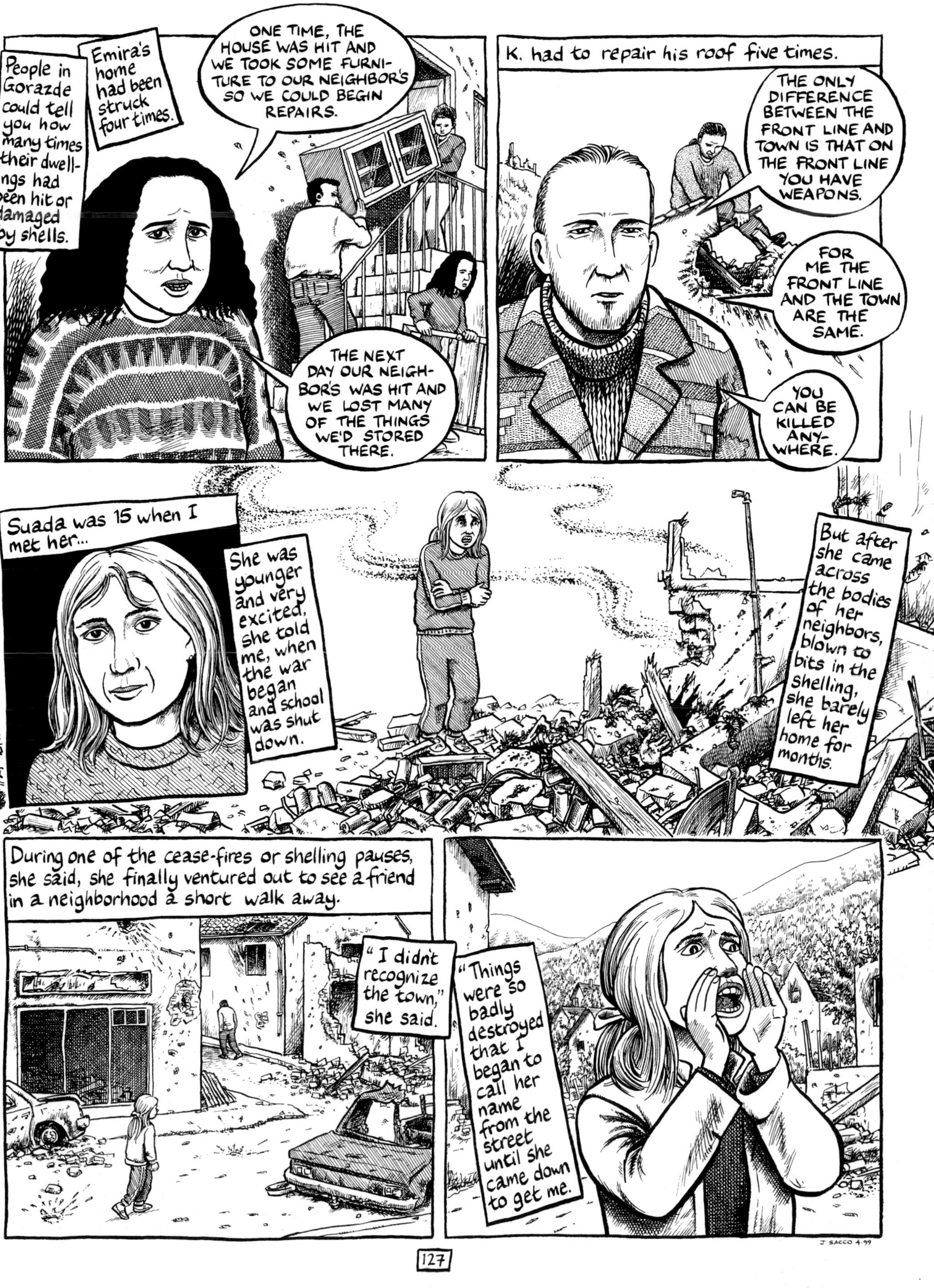
People in Gorazde could tell you how many times their dwellings had been hit or damaged by shells.
Emira's home had been struck four times.
ONE TIME, THE HOUSE WAS HIT AND WE TOOK SOME FURNITURE TO OUR NEIGHBOR'S SO WE COULD BEGIN REPAIRS.
THE NEXT DAY OUR NEIGHBOR'S WAS HIT AND WE LOST MANY OF THE THINGS WE'D STORED THERE.
K. had to repair his roof five times.
THE ONLY DIFFERENCE BETWEEN THE FRONT LINE AND TOWN IS THAT ON THE FRONT LINE YOU HAVE WEAPONS.
FOR ME THE FRONT LINE AND THE TOWN ARE THE SAME.
YOU CAN BE KILLED ANYWHERE.
Suada was 15 when I met her...
She was younger and very excited, she told me, when the war began and school was shut down.
But after she came across the bodies of her neighbors, blown to bits in the shelling, she barely left her home for months.
During one of the cease-fires or shelling pauses, she said, she finally ventured out to see a friend in a neighborhood a short walk away.
"I didn't recognize the town," she said.
"Things were so badly destroyed that I began to call her name from the street until she came down to get me.
J. SACCO 4.99

"I didn't know exactly where I was."

PART IV

S. had an idea... a way of getting out.

AN OPHTHAL-MOLOGIST SAYS MY GRAND-MOTHER'S EYE PROBLEMS ARE VERY SER-IOUS.

Since the beginning of 1995, U.N. forces had intermittently evacuated scores of the worst wounded and other critical medical cases from Gorazde.

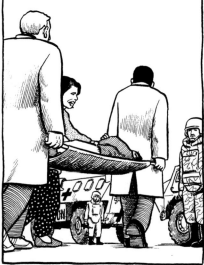

PERHAPS I CAN CONVINCE THE AUTHORITIES THAT MY GRAND-MOTHER SHOULDN'T TRAVEL ALONE...

THAT I SHOULD GO WITH HER.

Medivac! That was the ticket!

J. SACCO S 99

That's how her brother got out. He'd been taken to Britain to recover from his wounds.

HE JUST WROTE TO SAY HIS LEG WAS AMPUTATED.

At the Piramida one night a woman approached me to tell me "the truth about the medical situation in Gorazde."

I NEED TO BE MEDIVAC'D.

I NEED TO GO TO A HOSPITAL IN SARAJEVO FOR A BRAIN SCAN.

THERE IS SOMETHING WRONG WITH MY BRAIN.

I AM 25, I HAVE A TWO YEAR OLD, MY HUSBAND WAS KILLED.

SOMETHING IS WRONG... I LOSE MYSELF. I GO INTO A STATE.

SOMETIMES I BEGIN TO TAKE MY CLOTHES OFF AT COFFEE BARS. I THROW MY DAUGHTER TO THE GROUND.

BUT THE DOCTORS HERE DON'T WANT TO MEDIVAC ME.

I told her maybe civilians would be traveling the Blue Road to Sarajevo soon.

Then she could get treated.

WE DON'T BELIEVE IN THE BLUE ROAD.

WE DON'T BELIEVE IT WILL BE OPEN TO CIVILIANS.

I KNOW HEALTHY PEOPLE WHO'VE BEEN MEDIVAC'D.

IT'S ALL ABOUT MONEY.

WITH MONEY YOU CAN GET TO NEW YORK.

J. SACCO 5-99

I told this story to Dr. Begovic next time I saw him. It was difficult, he told me with a sigh, deciding who should be Medivac'd, and the number of evacuations was at the discretion of the Serbs.

THE CHETNIKS ARE ALLOWING CASUALTIES OUT...

BUT IF THERE ARE 100 WORTHY CASES, THEY MIGHT ALLOW TEN OUT.

Of course, he said, there were those who thought money changed hands, that he or someone else was wheeling and dealing with Medivac places.

SUCH TALK IS HUMILIATING.

Still, I heard money might get you out of Gorazde.

U.N.-mandated no-fly zone or not, the Bosnian army occasionally had flown helicopters into the pocket.

A guy I knew thought he could get a seat on a helicopter out for 2,000 d.m.

In my world there were certain privileges.

I was a guest of the Bosnian war.

I could get out of Gorazde gratis.

No one ever asked me for money or a limb.

J. SACCO 5.99

PART V

In those days, most journalists blew in with the U.N. convoy in the morning,

hit the hospital for some English-language quotes from Dr. Begovic,

noted the mini-centrales on the Drina,

did some man-in-the-street and/or a quickie stand-up on the second bridge,

and blew out with the U.N. convoy in the afternoon...

They needed their journalism now, for the top of the hour, and a few weren't above inducing some quickie action themselves.

Angry townsfolk told stories of photographers throwing candy at kids to capture the predictable mad scramble.

Sure the children liked the new taste of sweets, and they weren't shy asking strangers for 'em.

MISTER, BON-BONS? MISTER, BON-BONS?

They'd take no for an answer, though, and, anyway, some of them had graduated to other things.

I was giving directions to a British photographer once when a boy approached us for a smoke.

I DON'T KNOW IF IT'S A GOOD THING TO GIVE HIM A CIGARETTE.

HE'S TOO YOUNG.

HERE'S A BON-BON.

Poor kid, he didn't want no stinking bon-bon.

But I suppose we had to set a good example.

J. SACCO 5-99

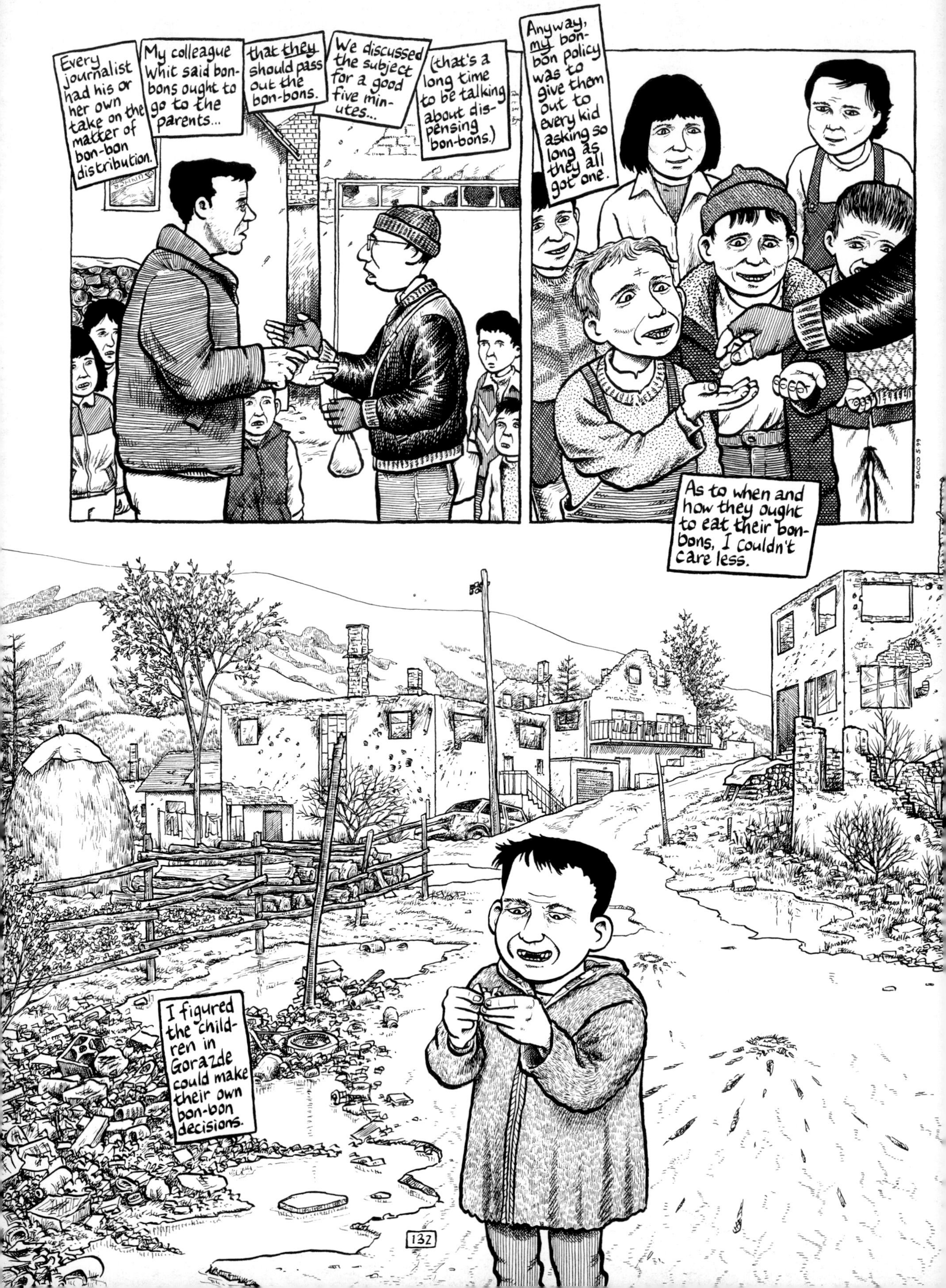
Every journalist had his or her own take on the matter of bon-bon distribution.
My colleague Whit said bon-bons ought to go to the parents...
that they should pass out the bon-bons.
We discussed the subject for a good five minutes...
(that's a long time to be talking about dispensing bon-bons.)
Anyway, my bon-bon policy was to give them out to every kid asking so long as they all got one.
As to when and how they ought to eat their bon-bons, I couldn't care less.
I figured the children in Gorazde could make their own bon-bon decisions.

White Death

WE MADE A MISTAKE. WE WERE LOOKING FOR CEMENT, LIME, CONSTRUCTION MATERIALS TO REPAIR THE HOUSE.

OTHERS WERE LOOKING FOR FOOD.

"People found food in Serb homes. I took some, maybe 100 kg of corn, and from that corn we could make flour. But 100 kg doesn't last when that's the main thing you have.

"We ran out of flour in November.

"We had planted potatoes before the war, but you have to tend to potatoes, you have to dig around them two or three times, and after the war started, we didn't do anything in the garden, we had escaped to Kopaci. When we returned, I dug up the potatoes and they were very small.

"My mother didn't bother to take off the skin. when she was preparing potato pie.

"That year we had plenty of fruit, very nice fruit, in our garden. We didn't have any sugar, but my mother heard how you could make jam without sugar... by cooking overripe fruit for a long time.

"We had milk and cheese from the cow...

"We ate jelly over bread with some cow's cream.

"Plenty of refugees were coming from villages, and they brought cows and sheep. They couldn't do anything with their sheep. We asked for the prices. 15 d m. each. Before the war the price of a sheep was 150-200 d m. They were satisfied if you gave them flour or cigarettes.

"I gave two packets of cigarettes and got three sheep.

"We slaughtered two of the sheep and had meat until the end of January."

IT WAS VERY CRITICAL IN DECEMBER AND JANUARY. NO MORE FLOUR, NO MORE POTATOES. WE COULDN'T EAT FRUIT ONLY... AND YOUR ORGANISM CANNOT EAT MEAT EVERY DAY...

MY FAMILY, MY RELATIVES AND SO ON, HELPED EACH OTHER AS MUCH AS POSSIBLE REGARDING FOOD. SOME PEOPLE TOOK CARE ONLY OF THEMSELVES, THEY DIDN'T CARE ABOUT THEIR RELATIVES.

U.N. attempts to deliver food to the enclave were a failure. A convoy in July '92 had been ambushed. The first relief convoy arrived in August with 46 tons of food. (The U.N. estimated Gorazde needed 35 tons per day.) Convoys got through only sporadically thereafter. Serbs turned back or delayed convoys with impunity despite a U.N. Security Council resolution authorizing the use of force to deliver food and medicine to besieged Bosnian civilians.

By the end of 1992, the food situation in Gorazde had become desperate. Some people were making soup and pie from nettles.

"Nobody had enough food. Children were coming very often, old people, poor people, on the main road, they knocked, looking for food. Every day, ten children.

J. SACCO 5·99

"They were satisfied with a piece of bread. You couldn't give to everyone. The bread wouldn't last.

"Down in town, apartments were well furnished, and people had taken whatever they wanted out of the shops. People from the villages in the area where there was no fighting were growing corn, potatoes, tomatoes...they were coming with eggs, and they were exchanging for what people in apartments had.

"At the end of '92, for a T.V. you could get 10 kg of flour. People in villages couldn't watch T.V. There was no electricity. But they wanted to have a T.V.

"A new T.V. You enjoy it. That's great.

"There were people who didn't have anything to trade. Refugees from Visegrad, for example, didn't bring anything with them, they didn't have money, they didn't have apartments, they lived with others.

"They were the first ones going to Grebak."

Grebak was a Bosnian army mountain post west of the Gorazde pocket that could be reached by a precarious route through Serb-controlled territory. The Bosnian military had been using the path to inject some weapons and personnel into the enclave.

THE ROUTE TO GREBAK WITH SELECT ELEVATIONS SHOWN IN METERS

KILOMETER SCALE
0 2 4 6 8 10

THE GORAZDE ENCLAVE

TRNOVO
GREBAK
1090
1315
1311
1333
845
1750
1674
1395
ZOROVICI
GORAZDE
Drina

It now trucked food supplies from Trnovo to Grebak for the people of Gorazde. But the people of Gorazde had to come and get the food themselves.

WE DIDN'T HAVE ANY CHOICE.

MY FATHER WENT THREE TIMES TO GREBAK, MY BROTHER AND I TWO TIMES EACH.

"That trip was very dangerous. It wasn't possible to use the path over the day, only at night. It was the middle of winter ...storms, snow... through the mountains... On one trip there was a snowstorm and my father fell unconscious. The son of a neighbor saved his life. He had frostbitten fingers and toes. On that trip, many persons froze to death."

Scores died of exposure —known to Gorazdans as White Death —on the Grebak path. Others were killed by landmines and in ambushes.

Edin described one of his trips to Grebak.

I PREPARED A LITTLE FOOD, DRIED PLUMS, WALNUTS, WITH MY NEIGHBOR.

"We went downtown to wait for a vehicle. There was shelling at that moment.

"I think I paid two kg of flour for the ride to Zorovici, which was very dangerous and cold. This was February or March.

"Once, on the same road, my brother was in a truck that slid out and turned over...He wasn't badly injured...but three or four died.

"It wasn't possible to go all the way to Zorovici because of the snow. We had to go two or three kilometers on foot.

"We waited in Zorovici two or three hours for the evening, and when the whole group had gathered, about 200 people, we went.

J. SACCO 5-99

"In front of our group was a guide who knew the way. It was deep dark. If you stray, maybe three or four meters, you can lose the group. And lots of times we had to stand and wait for everyone to gather. And then, again, 'Let's go!'"

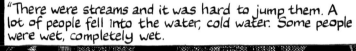

"We stopped at two or three springs to take water. We were thirsty, the whole time walking.

"There were streams and it was hard to jump them. A lot of people fell into the water, cold water. Some people were wet, completely wet.

"When we got close to Grebak, a group going back to Gorazde passed us. They had loads, and they were tired, very tired.

"I got there about 4 o'clock, 4:30 in the morning.

"It wasn't possible to sleep anywhere... Maybe I slept for half an hour, 15 minutes, an hour near a fire, without blankets. We waited for the distribution of food. We tried to keep warm... Sitting around, eating, drinking something. All day in that way."

"At Grebak there was a black market. People from Trnovo brought products like coffee, tobacco, cigarettes, salt, sugar, batteries, for which people from Gorazde had to pay plenty of money. Trnovo was cheaper if you had the papers to continue to there. Some people went to find tobacco, sugar..."

"It was better to bring five kg of tobacco to Gorazde...because you could very easily exchange it for food...it could get you maybe 100 kg of other stuff... There was a control of what you carried out. They didn't allow someone to take a full rucksack of tobacco, sugar, coffee, but for some people with good connections, with friends in the military...they closed their eyes."

"In the afternoon we got the free food. You carried as much as you could. I took 28 kg. It was a lot for me. Mostly flour and some oil, sugar, pasta, and two cans of fish. I wanted some yeast and salt, but there wasn't any... Some people were taking hand grenades back. I took two clips of bullets.

"Again we waited for the evening hours. We formed a line and came back in the same way.

"It was harder.

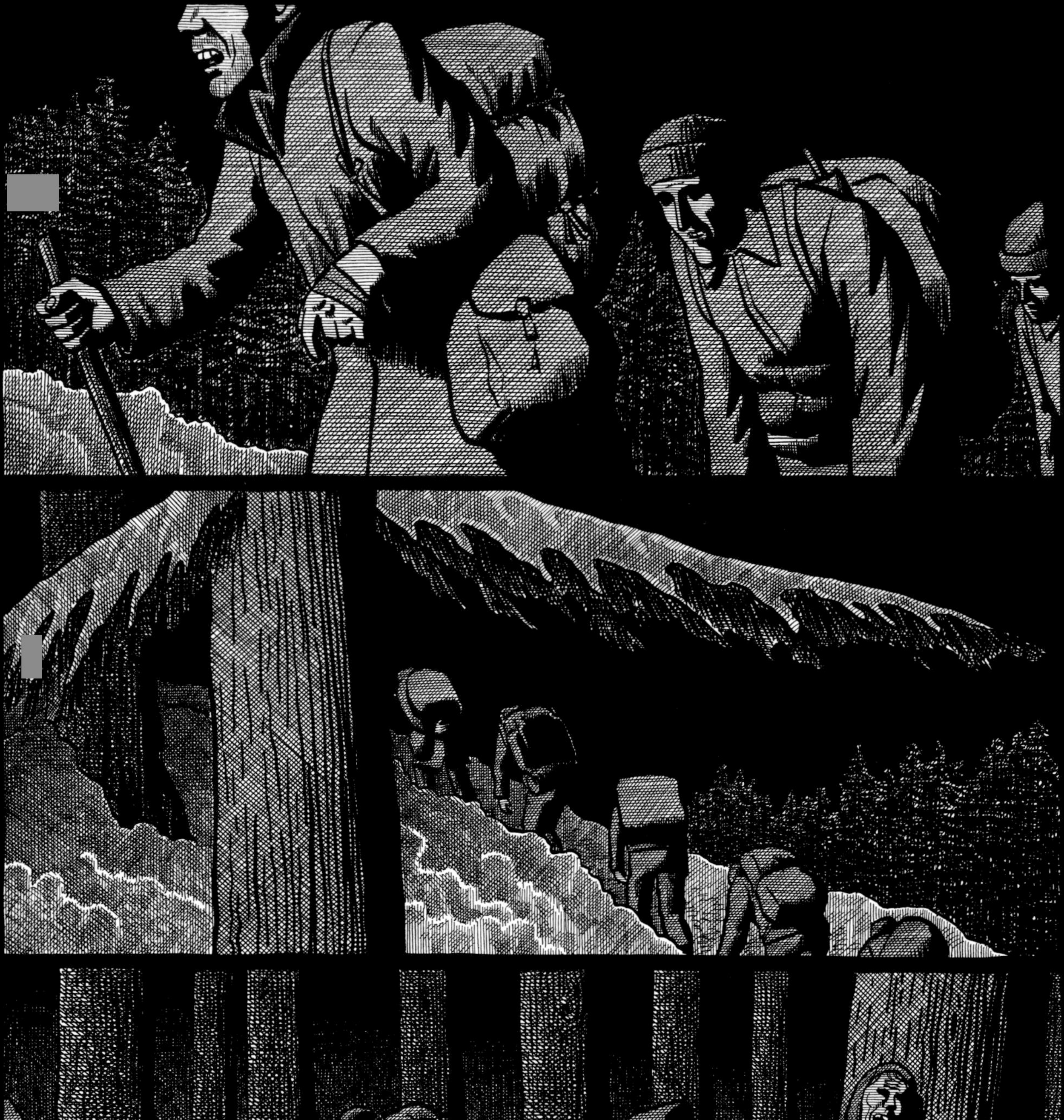

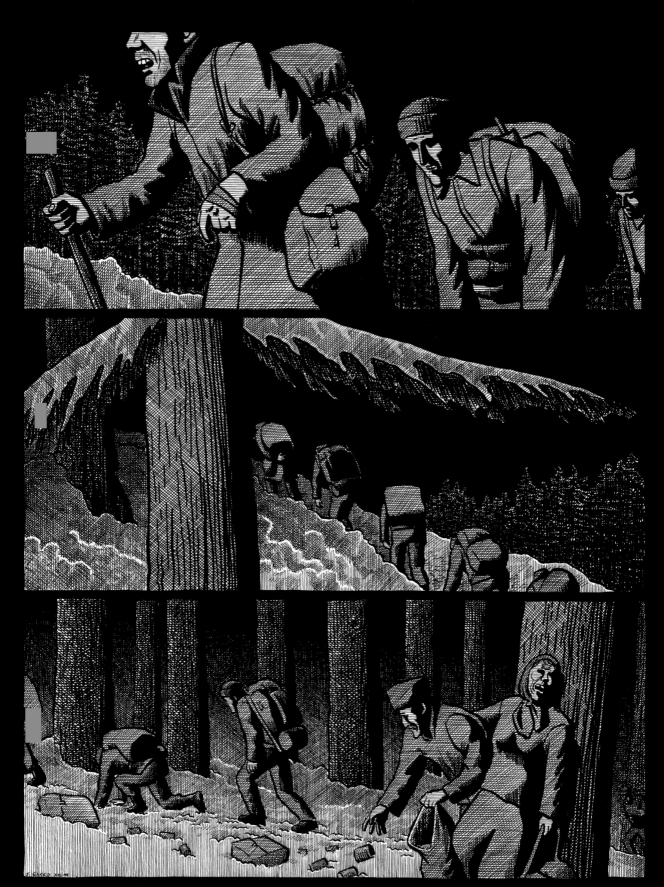

"The line didn't stay together...

"My neighbor knew the way. He had been four or five times."

"I trusted him... If something would happen to me, he would help...

"We came across people who couldn't go on.

"Alone. Without anybody.

"They had their eyes closed or were sleeping.

"We saw two or three people like that.

"I was tired. I didn't know who they were... I wasn't interested.

"My main thought was to stay alive,

"to be strong.

"You can't think about anything, only about the way,

"how long the walk is,

"will you see your family again?

"your friends? girlfriends?

"We got to our territory early, about three.

"We found a damaged old house. My neighbor slept at once, but it was so cold I couldn't sleep.

"In the morning we left that village, and that was the hardest, walking again, about one hour, three or four kilometers.

"After that we waited three or four hours for the vehicles. They came with a new group from town and picked up our group.

"Again we paid two kg of flour for the ride."

AFTER THAT TRIP I SLEPT TWO OR THREE DAYS.

I'D BROUGHT FOOD FOR MY FAMILY, FOR FOUR PEOPLE, FOR 20-25 DAYS.

BUT THAT'S ONLY IF WE ATE A LITTLE.

OTHERWISE IT WAS ONLY ENOUGH FOR TEN DAYS.

In early March 1993, the situation in Gorazde was still desperate. Only 12 U.N. relief convoys had arrived since the beginning of the war. Those who couldn't make the trip to Grebak or had no other source of food had to survive on a ration that was sometimes less than one slice of bread per day.

The Bosnian government induced action by refusing U.N. aid deliveries to media magnet Sarajevo unless food and medicine were brought through Serb blockades and into Gorazde and the other eastern enclaves as well. Over the objections of the top U.N. military commander in Bosnia, U.S. President Bill Clinton ordered airdrops on the enclaves.

U.S. aircraft, flying out of Germany, first dropped supplies on the Gorazde pocket in the early morning of March 9, 1993.

AT FIRST THE CIVIL POLICE TRIED TO CONTROL THE AIR-DROPS.

Mesa

"But they couldn't stop the people. They went around the checkpoints.

J. SACCO 6-95

"It went from civilian to army control.

"People fought over the pallets. Soldiers fired in the air but people still went for it.

"They gave up controlling."

SOMETIMES WE WERE WAITING IN ONE PLACE BUT THEY DROPPED FAR AWAY.

"We chatted about where they might drop, whether we'd found food the day before, how often we'd been lucky. There were plenty of jokes.

I'VE LOST MY WIFE...

NEXT TIME SHE'LL STAY HOME.

SHE CAN DO ANYTHING IN THE DARK.

"Then the aircraft would come.

"Sometimes we'd see lights in the sky...and the sound of the airplanes changed when they lost their weight."

I HEAR THE PALLETS—BANG! BANG!

I SAY, 'OKAY, LET'S GO!'

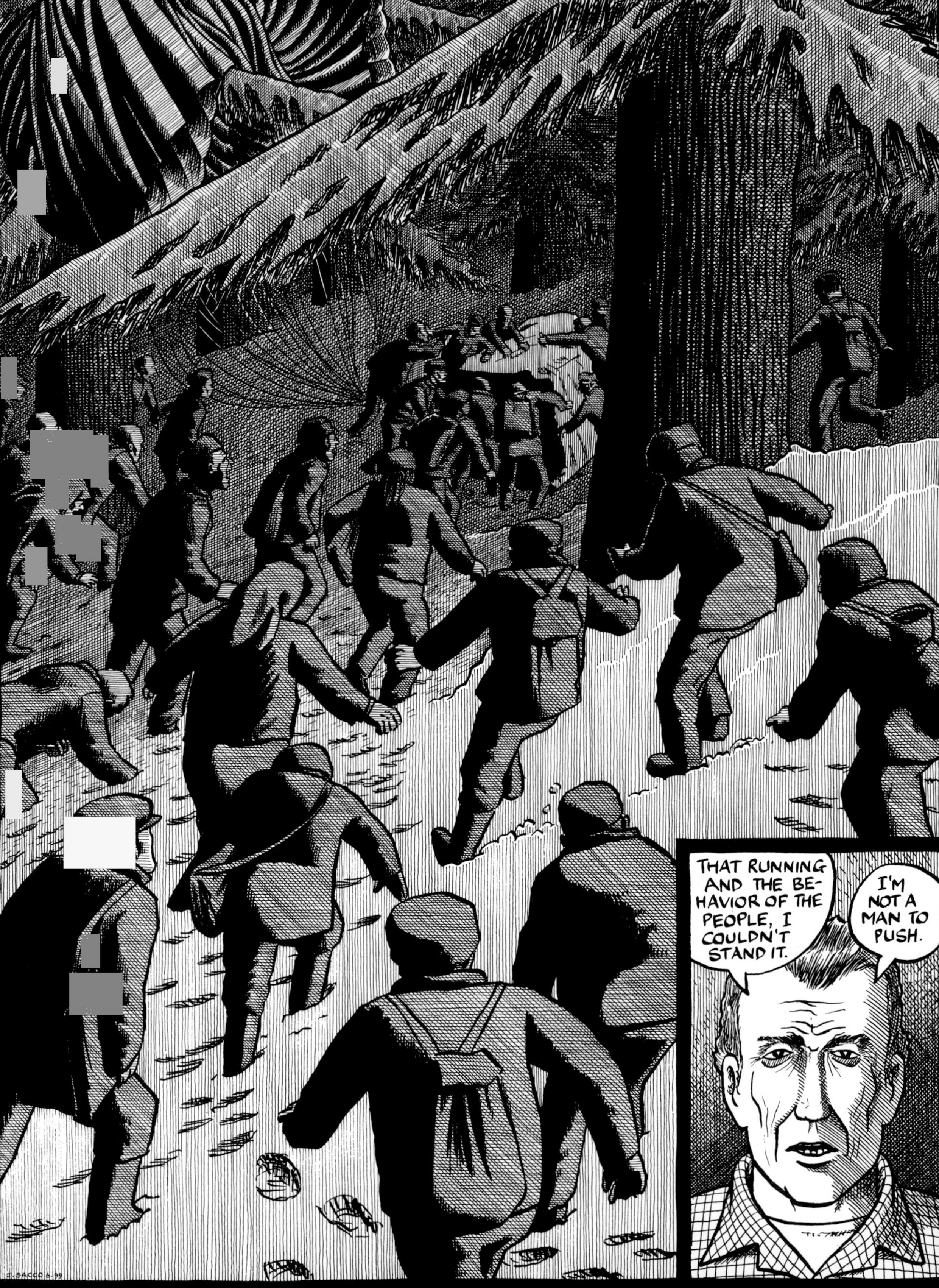
THAT RUNNING AND THE BEHAVIOR OF THE PEOPLE, I COULDN'T STAND IT.
I'M NOT A MAN TO PUSH.

WHEN YOU FIND A PALLET, AT ONCE YOU TAKE YOUR KNIFE, YOU CUT THE PLASTIC.

"Inside there are packs, cardboard boxes. Some periods there was only flour and beans. After 15 days, maybe rice... Sometimes cans.

"Sometimes they dropped food near the front line, and if we were already there... we'd carry food home over the night and then return to the line.

"One time there was an armed group that didn't allow anyone to get close to the food. Robbers... No one could regulate that.

"Stronger people found more food and brought much more back than older or younger people. At the most, I'd take 50 kg. I waited a lot of times. Maybe 30 times. I brought back food maybe 20 times. I was very lucky, almost the luckiest man in town. But I was ready, you know, in good condition, young, a good runner."

THE BEHAVIOR OF THE PEOPLE WASN'T ACCEPTABLE, BUT, ON THE OTHER HAND, THE AIRDROPS SAVED US.

IT WAS THE MOST IMPORTANT THING AT THAT MOMENT, THE MOST—

FOOD.

The airdrops staved off starvation, but the eastern Bosnian enclaves now faced a military catastrophe. In April 1993, northeast of Gorazde, attacking Serb forces were set to overrun the Srebrenica enclave. Seeking to prevent a new refugee crisis — or worse — especially while the doomed Vance-Owen peace plan was still on the table, the U.N. Security Council declared Srebrenica a "safe area."

Meanwhile, a surrender of sorts had been worked out whereby the Serbs would keep their positions around Srebrenica and a small U.N. force would be inserted to "demilitarize" the town's defenders.

CROATIA

SERBIA

BIHAC

BOSNIA

TUZLA

SREBRENICA

ZEPA

SARAJEVO

GORAZDE

MONTE-NEGRO

THE SIX SAFE AREAS
MID 1993

BOSNIAN GOVERNMENT-CONTROLLED TERRITORY

REBEL SERB- OR REBEL CROAT-CONTROLLED TERRITORY

KILOMETER SCALE
0 — 50

In early May the U.N. extended safe area status to other Bosnian enclaves, including Gorazde. But the U.N. had yet to work out what the concept meant. On the one hand, the U.N. was obligating itself, presumably, to keep the safe areas safe; on the other, the safe areas implicitly formalized Serb gains and the concentration of Muslims into what President Clinton warned would become "shooting galleries." (Which didn't stop the U.S. from supporting the plan.)

Not waiting for further clarification, the Serbs launched an offensive that conquered all government territory in the Drina Valley from Mededa to Ustipraca. Refugees streamed into Gorazde while the Serbs began a relentless bombardment of the town.

J. SACCO 9.99

148

In early June, the U.N. acted again, mandating that U.N. forces "deter attacks on the safe areas," but only, it seemed, if U.N. forces themselves came under attack. In Gorazde's case, the point was moot; no U.N. troops were stationed there. True, the Security Council also called for further troop deployments to the safe areas, but member states balked at the number of extra troops—originally 34,000—the U.N. deemed necessary to protect the safe areas.

A total of eight U.N. military personnel—observers*—eventually got to Gorazde after being blocked by the Serbs for weeks.

The attack on Gorazde continued from multiple directions and carried on into July. Hundreds were killed in the shelling.

Sadako Ogato, U.N. High Commissioner for Refugees, proposed that Gorazde and the other eastern safe areas, Srebrenica and Zepa, be evacuated of civilians. That was the "only life-saving alternative," she said.

The attack paused. Meanwhile, further west, Trnovo fell to the Serbs and the base at Grebak was lost.

The mountain path that connected Gorazde to central Bosnia, however tenuously, was severed. Gorazde was completely cut off.

*THE OBSERVERS WERE PART OF A SEPARATE MISSION UNRELATED TO THE DEPLOYMENT CALLED FOR BY THE SECURITY COUNCIL.

SILLY GIRLS

PART II

Ah, those convoys.

Infusing Goražde with stacks of sacks of flour and sugar!

Putting Goražde's women back into their kitchens again!

in particular putting Kimeta back into hers.

and in the annals of wartime cookery, Kimeta merited a chapter unto herself.

mmmhmm...

When it came to desserts she was Queen of the Enclave!

Riki was sweet on Kimeta, I think—and who could blame him?

and everyone was astonished by how loudly he was regaling her with 'The Sound of Silence.'

HELLO, DARKNESS, MY OLD FRIEND...

Tonight we were over at Kimeta and Sabina's, their second home since escaping from Čajniče in May '92. The first house their family had squatted had been burned down by the Serbs in the '94 offensive. This place was only half gutted.

150

SOME DANCE TO REMEMBER ♪ ... TO FORGET...

Sabina and Dalila jumped up!

They started MTVing Riki!

They were dancing and clowning as usual!

Sabina clowning the most!

And where was poet-boyfriend Dude?

Woo!

(Her "main task" was to take care of him, she'd once told me.)

Well, tonight Mister "Main Task" was at the front...

taking care of her.

Sabina was 18.

AIR VIDEO CAMERA

AIR MICRO-PHONE

I took her aside. I was International Press. Suddenly I'd remembered. And the Real Truth was I hadn't come to Gorazde to record the antics of some silly girls.

but she grinned about the time the cannon fired at her while she hung the wash...

and giggled about how bad posture saved her and Kimeta from shrapnel.

IT'S A GOOD THING WE WERE SLOUCHING.

Amusing? One could say. But I had my obligations, you understand, and let me add that I wasn't getting paid to sample Kimeta's desserts or listen to Riki sing, either...

WHAT WAS YOUR WORST MOMENT?

J. SACCO 7·99

Two months ago, she said. one of her best friends —a cousin— also 18 two months ago killed by a sniper.

And her brother-in-law he had escorted his wife, Sabina's sister, out of Bosnia all the way to Sweden then returned to Gorazde to fight the Serbs.

HE LIVED WITH US FOR FIVE MONTHS.

HE WAS KILLED IN ACTION IN 1993.

THAT WAS THE WORST MOMENT, WHEN I FOUND OUT.

WE WANTED TO TELL MY SISTER ON THE HAM RADIO, BUT WE COULDN'T.

WE DIDN'T HAVE THE HEART.

SHE FOUND OUT, THOUGH.

PROBABLY THE RADIO OPERATOR TOLD HER.

WELL SHAKE IT UP, BABY, TWIST AND SHOUT! ♪

J. SACCO 7. 99

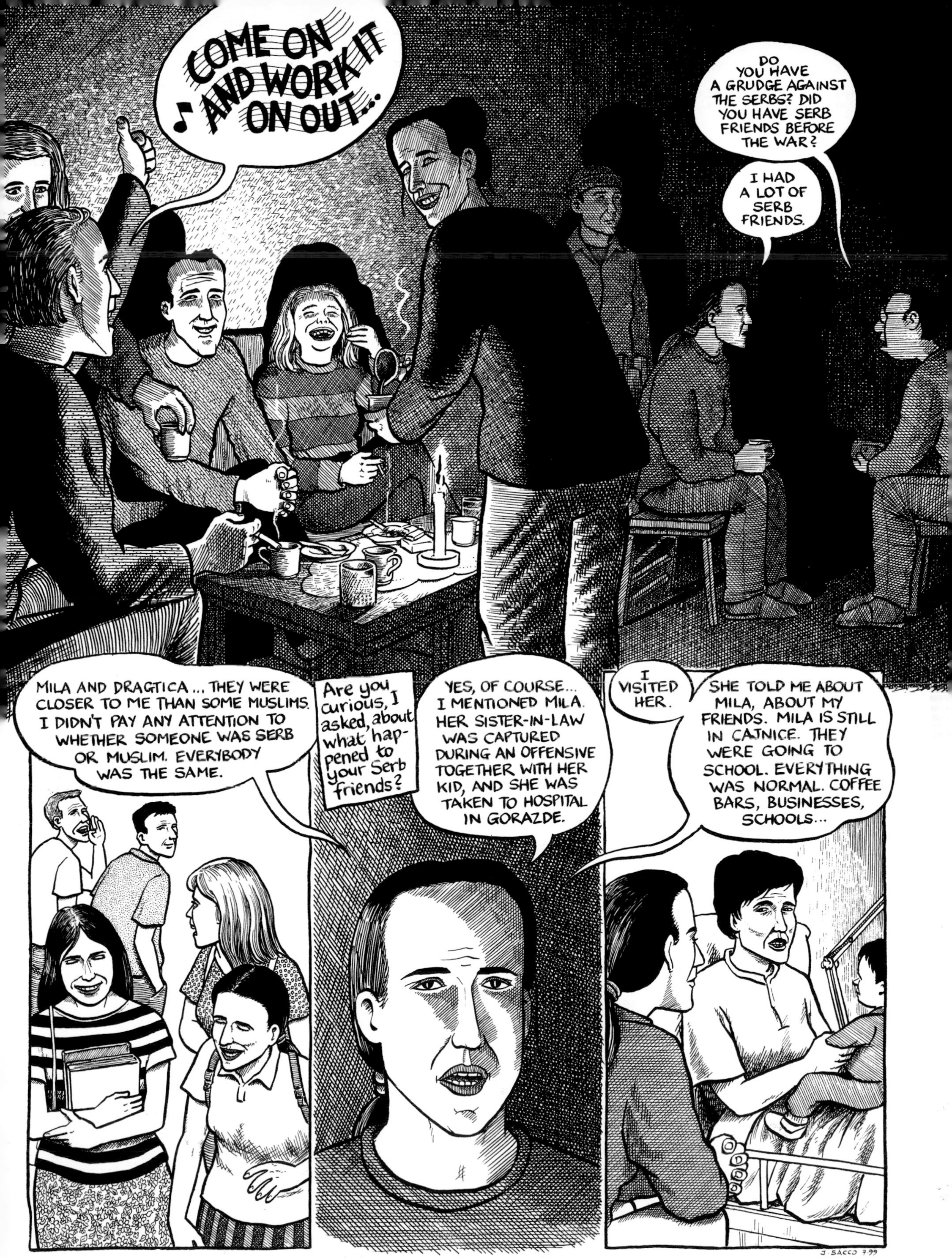

COME ON AND WORK IT ON OUT...
DO YOU HAVE A GRUDGE AGAINST THE SERBS? DID YOU HAVE SERB FRIENDS BEFORE THE WAR?
I HAD A LOT OF SERB FRIENDS.
MILA AND DRAGTICA... THEY WERE CLOSER TO ME THAN SOME MUSLIMS. I DIDN'T PAY ANY ATTENTION TO WHETHER SOMEONE WAS SERB OR MUSLIM. EVERYBODY WAS THE SAME.
Are you curious, I asked, about what happened to your Serb friends?
YES, OF COURSE... I MENTIONED MILA. HER SISTER-IN-LAW WAS CAPTURED DURING AN OFFENSIVE TOGETHER WITH HER KID, AND SHE WAS TAKEN TO HOSPITAL IN GORAZDE.
I VISITED HER.
SHE TOLD ME ABOUT MILA, ABOUT MY FRIENDS. MILA IS STILL IN CAJNICE. THEY WERE GOING TO SCHOOL. EVERYTHING WAS NORMAL. COFFEE BARS, BUSINESSES, SCHOOLS...
J. SACCO 7.99

EVERYTHING WAS NORMAL EXCEPT WE WERE NOT THERE.

HOW DID YOU FEEL TOWARD YOUR FRIEND'S SISTER-IN-LAW?

SHE WASN'T GUILTY FOR WHAT HAPPENED TO US. SHE WASN'T ABLE TO STOP THIS WAR.

I DON'T ACCUSE ANYONE.

MY FRIENDS AREN'T GUILTY OF THIS.

A moment after I finished talking with Sabina, I asked Dalila about her Serb friends.

I NEVER HAD ANY SERB FRIENDS.

HOW COULD THEY HAVE BEEN YOUR FRIENDS IF THEN THEY TRIED TO KILL YOU?

154

THE SERBS

By the end of 1995, the beautiful idea of a multi-ethnic Bosnia was finished. True, Serbs, Muslims, and Croats continued to live together in enlightened pockets like Sarajevo and Tuzla, but these were exceptional cases.

In eastern Bosnia, the situation was black and white. Towns and villages had been cleansed of Muslims.

What had been a majority Muslim region was now almost entirely Serb and part of break-away Republika Srpska. Only Gorazde remained under government control, and its ethnic mix, too, had undergone a fundamental change.

Most of Gorazde's Serbs had left in the pre-war exodus or in the overnight disappearance in May 1992.

Of 5,600 Serbs, only a few score now remained.

Veljko was one who stayed.

I DIDN'T BEHAVE LIKE A NATIONALIST. I WAS ALWAYS A YUGO-SLAV AND NOW I'M A BOSNIAN MAN. I HAD STRAINED RELATIONS WITH OTHER SERBS BECAUSE OF MY VIEWS.

He said Serbs who hadn't left had nowhere else to go, didn't believe there would be war, or, like him, had no interest in Serb nationalism.

ALL TROUBLES ARE FROM THE CHETNIKS... I'VE FELT MORE TERROR FROM THAT SIDE — BEFORE THE WAR AND DURING THE WAR AS WELL.

J. SACCO 7-99

155

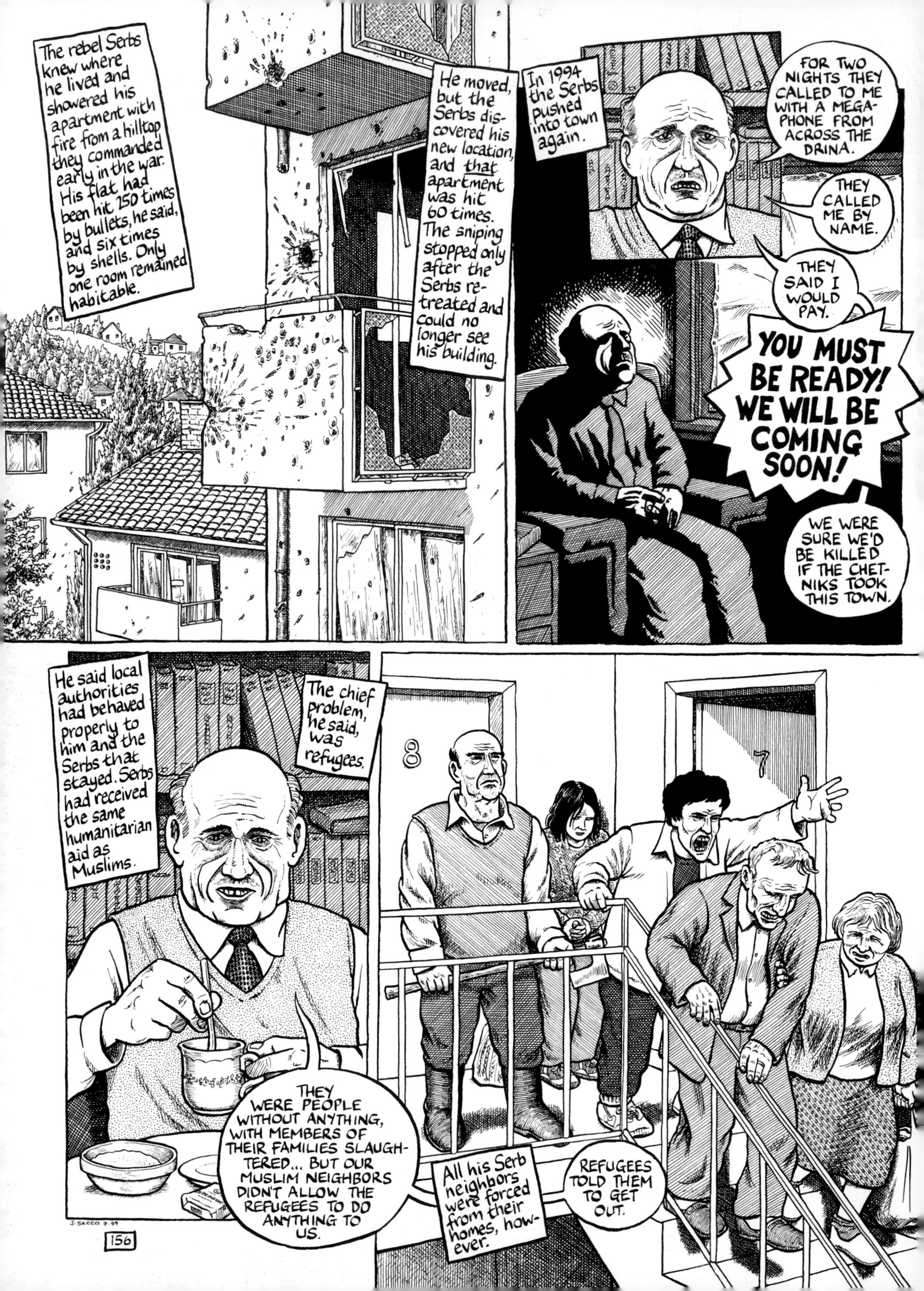

The rebel Serbs knew where he lived and showered his apartment with fire from a hilltop they commanded early in the war. His flat had been hit 250 times by bullets, he said, and six times by shells. Only one room remained habitable.
He moved, but the Serbs discovered his new location, and that apartment was hit 60 times. The sniping stopped only after the Serbs retreated and could no longer see his building.
In 1994 the Serbs pushed into town again.
FOR TWO NIGHTS THEY CALLED TO ME WITH A MEGAPHONE FROM ACROSS THE DRINA.
THEY CALLED ME BY NAME.
THEY SAID I WOULD PAY.
YOU MUST BE READY! WE WILL BE COMING SOON!
WE WERE SURE WE'D BE KILLED IF THE CHETNIKS TOOK THIS TOWN.
He said local authorities had behaved properly to him and the Serbs that stayed. Serbs had received the same humanitarian aid as Muslims.
The chief problem, he said, was refugees.
THEY WERE PEOPLE WITHOUT ANYTHING, WITH MEMBERS OF THEIR FAMILIES SLAUGHTERED... BUT OUR MUSLIM NEIGHBORS DIDN'T ALLOW THE REFUGEES TO DO ANYTHING TO US.
All his Serb neighbors were forced from their homes, however.
REFUGEES TOLD THEM TO GET OUT.
8
7
J. SACCO 7-99

Anger at the Serbs often was directed at their property.

The Serb neighborhood of Jabucko Sedlo was behind a ridge-line from where Serb fire terrorized Gorazde in 1992.

When the Serbs withdrew, their homes were destroyed.

In the mixed neighborhood of Kokino Selo, the graffiti on this structure identified it as Muslim for those looking for something Serb to burn down.

MUSLIMAN. KUČA BAVČIĆ AHMO

One soldier explained what happened here...

IN 1992 THIS AREA WAS OCCUPIED BY THE CHETNIKS. MY SERB NEIGHBORS HAD KEPT MY HOME FROM BEING BURNED. THEIR HOMES WERE ON EITHER SIDE OF MINE.

AFTER THE SERBS WITHDREW THERE WERE TWO OR THREE DAYS WHEN ANGRY REFUGEES FROM PLACES LIKE FOCA AND VISEGRAD WERE BURNING DOWN SERB HOMES, BUT I TOLD THEM TO GET AWAY.

I WOULDN'T LET THEM BURN THE HOMES OF MY SERB NEIGHBORS.

OUR AREA WAS OVERRUN AGAIN IN '94 BY THE ILIDZA BRIGADE, SERBS FROM SARAJEVO, AND THEY DIDN'T KNOW WHICH HOMES BELONGED TO MUSLIMS OR SERBS.

THEY BURNED DOWN EVERYTHING, 60 HOMES ALL AT ONCE, MY HOME, MY SERB NEIGHBORS'...

J. SACCO 7.99

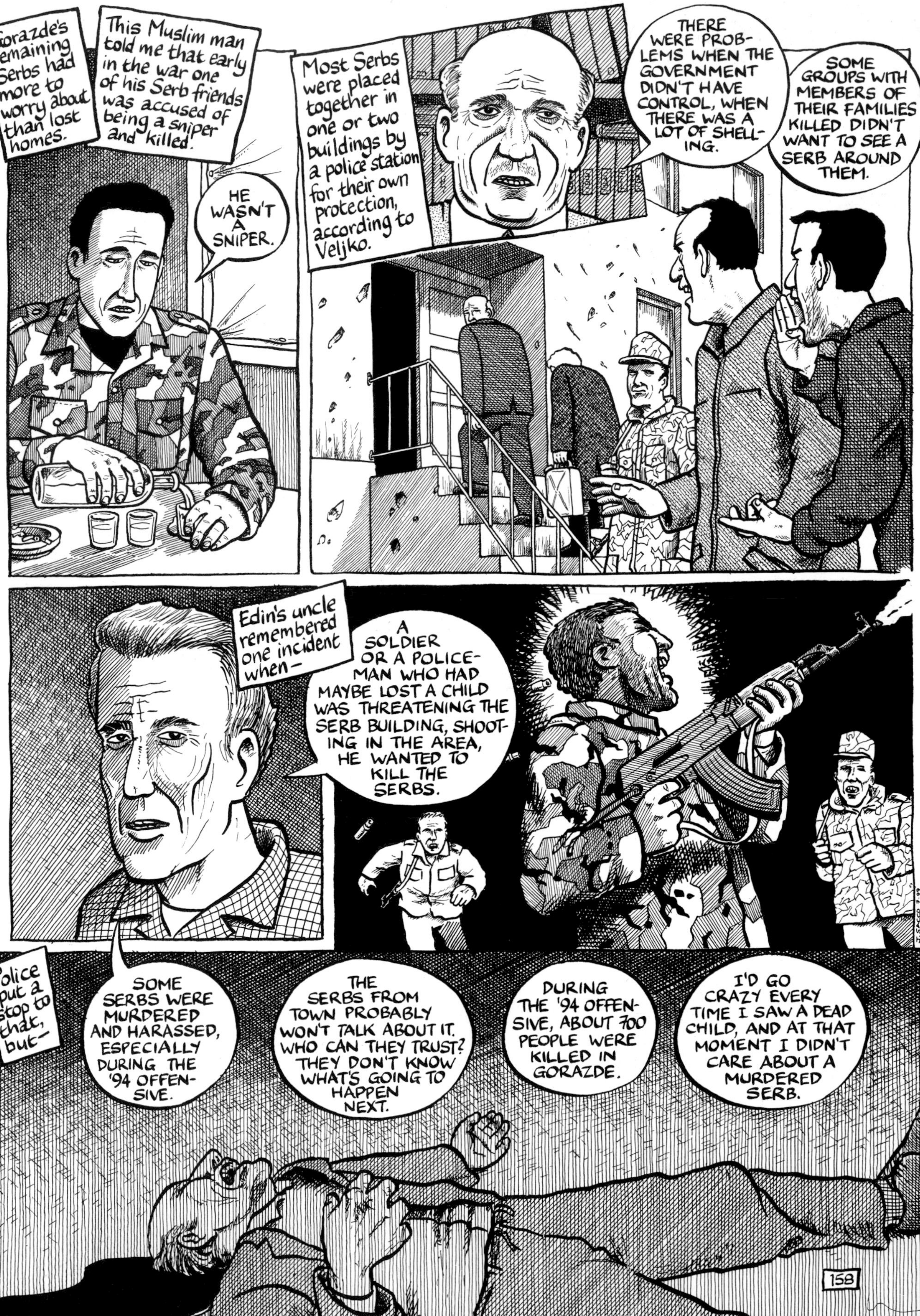

Gorazde's remaining Serbs had more to worry about than lost homes.
This Muslim man told me that early in the war one of his Serb friends was accused of being a sniper and killed.
HE WASN'T A SNIPER.
Most Serbs were placed together in one or two buildings by a police station for their own protection, according to Veljko.
THERE WERE PROBLEMS WHEN THE GOVERNMENT DIDN'T HAVE CONTROL, WHEN THERE WAS A LOT OF SHELLING.
SOME GROUPS WITH MEMBERS OF THEIR FAMILIES KILLED DIDN'T WANT TO SEE A SERB AROUND THEM.
Edin's uncle remembered one incident when—
A SOLDIER OR A POLICEMAN WHO HAD MAYBE LOST A CHILD WAS THREATENING THE SERB BUILDING, SHOOTING IN THE AREA, HE WANTED TO KILL THE SERBS.
Police put a stop to that, but—
SOME SERBS WERE MURDERED AND HARASSED, ESPECIALLY DURING THE '94 OFFENSIVE.
THE SERBS FROM TOWN PROBABLY WON'T TALK ABOUT IT. WHO CAN THEY TRUST? THEY DON'T KNOW WHAT'S GOING TO HAPPEN NEXT.
DURING THE '94 OFFENSIVE, ABOUT 700 PEOPLE WERE KILLED IN GORAZDE.
I'D GO CRAZY EVERY TIME I SAW A DEAD CHILD, AND AT THAT MOMENT I DIDN'T CARE ABOUT A MURDERED SERB.
J. SACCO

OF COURSE, THAT THINKING IS ABSOLUTELY WRONG BUT WHEN YOU WEIGH IT AGAINST 700 OTHERS KILLED —THE CHILDREN—

AT THAT MOMENT YOU SIMPLY DON'T CARE.

Many Serbs took the opportunity to cross to the other side when the U.N. organized medical evacuations from Gorazde. Basically Serbs were exchanged for severely wounded Muslims being allowed to pass through Serb territory and get to Sarajevo.

Veljko insisted that "nobody pushed them out of Gorazde."

MOST OF THE SERBS WHO LEFT HAD BEEN SEPARATED FROM THEIR FAMILIES... OR HAD LOST THEIR FLATS... ABOUT 150 SERBS WERE PUSHED FROM THEIR HOMES BY REFUGEES IN THE '94 ATTACK, AND MOST WERE EXCHANGED FOR MEDIVAC.

At the hospital, Dr. Begovic told me—

I'M SURE MANY WOULD NOT HAVE GONE IF THEY HAD FOOD...

IF THERE WAS NO SHELLING...

IF THEY DIDN'T HAVE TO LIVE IN THESE CONDITIONS.

But given those conditions... given their greatly reduced number... given the tense atmosphere... and the future uncertainty...

Veljko's daughter Liljana:

I WOULD HAVE GONE, NOT TO SERBIA, BUT OUT, IF I HAD KNOWN IT WOULD BE LIKE THIS.

J. SACCO 7-99

159

CAN YOU LIVE WITH

TOO MUCH HAS HAPPENED, TOO MANY FAMILY MEMBERS KILLED. I USED TO HAVE MANY SERB FRIENDS... I HAD A CLOSE FRIEND NAMED MIRO, AND IT'S POSSIBLE HE WAS A SNIPER SHOOTING AT MY DAUGHTER, THAT HE WAS ONE OF THOSE PEOPLE WHO RAPED AND SLAUGHTERED...

I CAN NEVER TRUST THOSE SERBS AGAIN, THAT'S OBVIOUS, AND NOT ONLY THAT, MY RELATIONSHIP WITH SERBS WHO REMAINED IN GORAZDE HAS CHANGED, TOO...

THINGS CAN NEVER BE THE SAME.

I DON'T WANT TO HEAR ANYTHING ABOUT THEM. I THINK MY FORMER SERB FRIENDS ARE DEAD, METAPHORICALLY. WE HAD A GOOD PAST. THIS WAR HAS LASTED ALMOST FOUR YEARS AND MANY THINGS HAVE CHANGED... OF COURSE BOSNIA CAN ONLY BE A SINGLE STATE WITH SERBS AND CROATS, BUT I WOULD LIKE TO LIVE WITHOUT THEM...

MY ROOMMATE IN THE DORMITORY IN ZENICA WAS A SERB, A GOOD GUY. HE WENT TO BELGRADE, HE DIDN'T WANT TO FIGHT FOR KARADZIC. I COULD LIVE WITH SOMEONE LIKE HIM, BUT HE LEFT. IN SARAJEVO, IT'S OKAY TO LIVE TOGETHER WITH SERBS, BUT IN EASTERN BOSNIA IT'S IMPOSSIBLE. WE ARE UNABLE TO DISTINGUISH BETWEEN NORMAL SERBS AND THE KILLERS.

THE SERBS CAN'T BE TRUSTED, THEY LIE. THE ONLY REASON SOME SERBS REMAINED IN GORAZDE WAS BECAUSE THEY WERE AFRAID OF LOSING THEIR HOMES.

I CAN LIVE WITH THE SERBS AGAIN, BUT NOT THOSE GUILTY OF CRIMES. I'M QUITE AWARE OF THE LOYAL SERBS LIVING IN SARAJEVO...

I CAN'T UNDERSTAND IT. ABOUT 90 PERCENT OF MY FRIENDS WERE SERBS. OLDER PEOPLE SAID THAT SERBS HATED MUSLIMS, BUT WE DIDN'T BELIEVE THEM.

I UNDERSTAND SERBS LIVED WITH US DURING THE WAR, ESPECIALLY IN SARAJEVO, BUT I'M SUSPICIOUS OF THEM. I CAN'T HELP IT. I DON'T HAVE THE SAME FEELINGS FOR THEM I HAD BEFORE...THEY CAN VISIT ME IF THEY WANT, BUT I CAN'T FEEL COMFORTABLE WITH THEM AGAIN.

J. SACCO 8-99

THE SERBS AGAIN?

BEFORE THE WAR, EVERYONE HAD EVERYTHING, CARS, FOOD, JOBS. THEY HAD A GOOD LIFE... AND THEN THEY STARTED SHOOTING. NEVER IN MY LIFE WILL I UNDERSTAND WHY. THEY DESTROYED OUR LIVES, THE SERBS, BUT ALSO THEY DESTROYED THEIR OWN LIVES.

BUT MOST IMPORTANT TO ME IS THAT EVERY SERB IS NOT A CHETNIK. THE SERBS WHO STAYED GOT THE SAME FOOD, THEY CARRIED WATER AND GOT WOOD... THEY WERE IN THE SAME SITUATION...

I THINK THEY ALWAYS HATED US.

THEY'RE NOT ALL CHETNIKS, THERE ARE GOOD PEOPLE THERE, TOO.

OUR NEIGHBORS... WE THOUGHT WE COULD TRUST THEM. BECAUSE OF THAT WE HAVE A TRAGIC STORY. I DON'T WANT TO LIVE WITH THE SERBS BECAUSE I LOST MY DAUGHTER... SERB NEIGHBORS CAN LIVE HERE AGAIN, BUT I DON'T WANT TO HAVE CONTACT WITH THEM. I DON'T WANT TO CHAT WITH THEM.

WE DIDN'T DO THE SAME THING TO THEIR CHILDREN, THEIR DAUGHTERS, THEIR WIVES. IN '92 AND '93 SERBS LIVED AROUND HERE, BUT WE DIDN'T TOUCH THEM. THEY ATE LIKE ME, THE SAME FOOD. THEY HAD THE SAME CONDITIONS. I CHOPPED WOOD FOR A SERB HERE, A 70-YEAR-OLD MAN.

I BELIEVE IN A MULTI-ETHNIC BOSNIA. NOT ALL SERB SOLDIERS ARE WAR CRIMINALS. MAYBE A SMALL PERCENTAGE ARE BAD, THOSE WHO DID THE SLAUGHTERING AND THOSE WHO FIRED ARTILLERY INTO CIVILIAN AREAS...

THEIR PROBLEM IS THEY'RE ALWAYS TALKING ABOUT THEIR HISTORY. THEY'RE ALWAYS LOOKING AT THE PAST, NEVER THEIR FUTURE.

I HAD A SERB FRIEND IN FOCA I WOULDN'T MIND SPEAKING TO AGAIN, JUST TO GET HIS SIDE OF THINGS, BUT GENERALLY I DON'T WANT TO SEE THE PEOPLE WHO'VE DONE THIS FOR ANOTHER 20 OR 40 YEARS. THEY SHATTERED MY LIFE AND I CAN'T PUT THE PIECES TOGETHER AGAIN.

J. SACCO 8-99

The 94 Offensive

IN 1993 I WAS ON JABUKA TVICIJAK, STRATEGICALLY AN IMPORTANT MOUNTAIN FOR DEFENDING THE TOWN.

MY DUTY WAS FOUR DAYS THERE, EIGHT DAYS AT HOME.

"The director of schools didn't have enough teachers of mathematics. For all the secondary schools there were only two. They looked for people. And finally they asked me.

"I started teaching in February '94.

"I'd worked for about one and a half months when the Serbs started to attack our positions. We thought it wasn't serious, just the usual. After about a week, the director decided to close the schools, and all teachers were sent back to the front line.

J. SACCO 8-99

"I was back in the same place. It was awful...

"The Serbs attacked us every day, first with shelling...

"after with patrols to check if we were still in our positions.

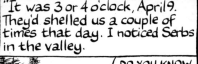

"It was 3 or 4 o'clock, April 9. They'd shelled us a couple of times that day. I noticed Serbs in the valley.

DO YOU KNOW WHERE THE SNIPER RIFLE IS?

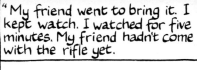

"My friend went to bring it. I kept watch. I watched for five minutes. My friend hadn't come with the rifle yet.

HAS THE BULLET GONE THROUGH MY EYE?

I DON'T KNOW. THERE'S TOO MUCH BLOOD.

"I lost consciousness. The guy with me bandaged me well. Maybe he saved my life.

"They took 30 to 40 minutes to carry me to the car.

"My cousin was the driver on duty and he drove fast. I heard the sound of tires taking curves and I regained consciousness.

DON'T DRIVE SO FAST!

WE'LL ALL BE KILLED!

"Then I lost consciousness again.

"I don't know what happened... I heard the screaming of a nurse, a close friend.

DOCTOR, DOCTOR, YOU DIDN'T CONNECT HIS ARTERIES PROPERLY!

YES! CHECK AGAIN.

"I was becoming conscious... I had pain... I didn't get any injection... there was no anesthetic.

"My face was completely swollen. I had an ache in my head and a sound like an unlimited number of bees. Zzzzzzzzz."

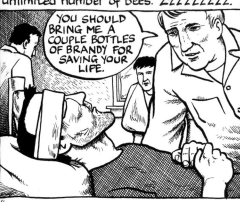

YOU SHOULD BRING ME A COUPLE BOTTLES OF BRANDY FOR SAVING YOUR LIFE.

"He said I was going to be fine, but he wasn't sure about my eyesight."

"I spent one day and night in hospital. It was full, crowded... Wounded, from every part of the front... A lot of persons were much more heavily wounded than me, much heavier."

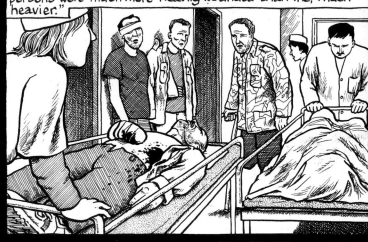

In February 1994, the U.N. had threatened air-strikes on Serb tanks and artillery units bombarding Sarajevo. The Serbs suspended those attacks, switched many of their heavy weapons to the Gorazde front, and launched a major offensive against the enclave.

U.S. Secretary of Defense William Perry ruled out U.S. intervention to prevent the fall of Gorazde.

WE WILL NOT ENTER THE WAR TO STOP THAT FROM HAPPENING.

President Clinton, frustrated that the offensive was endangering a U.S.-Russian peace initiative, told the combatants to—

—NEGOTIATE A PEACE AND GET IT OVER WITH.

He denied that his administration's utterances had given the Serbs a "green light."

But the next day, Joint Chiefs-of-Staff Chairman General John Shalikashvili publicly doubted that air-strikes, threatened against the Serbs to protect Sarajevo, would be effective in Gorazde's case because, he said, heavy weapons were not "the principal cause of death and destruction" there.

However, one U.N. doctor on the scene protested that "all the bodies I saw had been killed by artillery fire."

Meanwhile, Lt. General Sir Michael Rose, the U.N.'s military commander in Bosnia, feared that air-strikes on the Serbs would compromise the U.N.'s neutral peace-keeping role. He continually downplayed the Serb offensive, calling it a "tactical operation" and claiming the Serbs had not advanced far into the enclave.

But his own military observers in Gorazde reported, "The death toll continues to rise and serious losses of territory are occurring... It is very disquieting to hear radio reports from the international media reiterate that the situation is not serious ... It is a grave situation."

The attack on Gorazde was clearly intensifying. The U.N. was facing the embarrassing and grim prospect of one of its designated safe areas being overrun. The U.S. administration changed tack. The U.S. had not ruled out air power to stop the attack, said National Security Adviser Anthony Lake.

SERB OFFENSIVE ON GORAZDE, SPRING 1994

0   5   10 km

USTIPRACA
KOPACI
Drina
GORAZDE
ZUPCICI
GRADINA
CAJNICE
SERBIA

On April 9 the Serbs captured the Gradina mountaintop above the east bank of Gorazde and now had direct line-of-sight into the town.

I CAME HOME, I LAY THERE... BUT THERE WAS ALWAYS A DISTURBANCE...

"Refugees, friends came here... They were always asking the same questions...women...stupid... always with the wrong information...

THEY'VE TAKEN THE OTHER SIDE!

THEY'RE CLOSE TO THE HOSPITAL!

OUR LINES HAVE COLLAPSED!

"I went to hospital to change my bandages twice a day... every day for injections. Among the patients there was panic. Always women, children, older persons panicked. But the doctors did their jobs."

With words out of Washington now implying firm backing, the U.N. demanded the offensive stop and warned the Serbs of air-strikes by NATO, which was acting as the U.N.'s air arm. Technically, a continued attack on the enclave would be considered an attack on the handful of U.N. personnel there—which would invoke the previous year's Security Council resolution authorizing "the use of force" to protect them.

The attack didn't stop.

On April 10 and 11 NATO carried out its first bombing raids ever, dropping six bombs on Serb positions and vehicles near Gorazde.

THIS IS A CLEAR EXPRESSION OF THE WILL OF NATO AND THE WILL OF THE UNITED NATIONS.

Bosnian Serb leader Radovan Karadzic told the U.N.:

THE GOOD MANNERS WHICH WE DISPLAYED OUT OF OUR TRUST FOR YOU ARE NOW A THING OF THE PAST.

The Bosnian Serb military commander, General Ratko Mladic, cut off routes into Sarajevo and took hostage scores of U.N. personnel throughout Bosnia.

His defiant troops advanced into the outskirts of Gorazde's east bank and rained tank, artillery, and small arms fire into the town center.

MUNICIPALITY BUILDING

HOSPITAL

SECOND BRIDGE

FIRST BRIDGE

Thousands of civilians crossed the river to escape the onslaught.

J. SACCO 8-99

Clinton's resolve slackened. He sought to re-assure the Serbs that NATO and the U.N. were not taking sides, that the air-strikes were designed —

—TO GET THEM TO HONOR THE U.N. RULES, AND TO ENCOURAGE THEM TO DO WHAT THEY SAY THEY WISH TO DO, WHICH IS TO ENGAGE IN NE-GOTIATIONS.

But it seemed the Serbs would be ready to return to the negotiating table only to consolidate their gains after eliminating Gorazde or rendering it untenable.

On April 15, two U.N. Military Observers — who were actually British commandos coordin-ating air operations over Gorazde — were wounded, one fatally.

The next day a NATO jet called in to destroy tanks firing into the town was shot down by a Serb missile.

Yasushi Akashi, the top U.N. official in the former Yugoslavia, buckled. He openly wondered whether the U.N.'s peace-keeping mandate in Bosnia was now "meaningless."

One of his senior aides said, "We are close to the end of what we can do."

In Gorazde's case, President Clinton was beginning to concur. He revived the earlier sentiments of General Shalikashvili. Clinton now believed—

—IT WOULDN'T NECESSARILY BE POSSIBLE FOR CLOSE AIR SUPPORT TO HAVE THE DESIRED MILITARY EFFECT...

The threat of air power had been tabled.

I WAS HOME FOR SEVEN DAYS...

AND THEY HAD BROKEN OUR LINES... AND PUSHED ALL OUR FIGHTERS INTO TOWN.

"People from Kopaci were coming into Gorazde... passing in front of my house. Seven or ten families brought their stuff here. Clothes, food, T.V.'s. They knew me or my father.

IT ISN'T SAFE HERE. THERE'S NO FRONT LINE.

"But if I tell you, no, no, don't leave your things here, you're going to be angry.

"In one day the Serbs took all the territory from Ustipraca to Kopaci ... and we moved to my cousin's place. I thought Serb soldiers would take the town, kill a lot of people. Because of that I didn't want to carry any goods from my house.

WE WON'T BE NEEDING ANYTHING.

"We took whatever we could in my father's car. He had gas. He always had five liters in the car just in case.

"I left by bicycle to my cousin's place and then returned home.

There was disorganization. You could do what you wanted—go to the front line, stay in a basement. There were no units. Collapse. Everything.

"Commander Sejdic from Visegrad, he was trying to organize a front line between Kopaci and Gorazde. He was in front of my house ordering our soldiers to pull back from a church up the road and make a line about 2-300 meters in front of my house.

"I told them I was going with them. With my brother.

"There was the same amount of shelling on the line as in the center of town... It was better to be killed on the line.

"Nobody ordered me back.

"Some of the guys I knew, some of them I didn't. We didn't need orders. Somebody said:

LET'S SET UP IN THAT HOUSE.

THAT HOUSE.

THAT HOUSE.

"...two, three, four of us in each house, ten houses.

"I was in a house on the hill. I could see the Serbs coming, walking in a line, a long line.

"When the NATO airplanes came, the tanks hid, under trees, under roofs, and when they left, the Serbs were coming again, using the main road.

"Some guys had brought brandy. We were sitting, one of us watching. We were talking, introducing ourselves...

"and in that way, it became dark.

"Next morning. They didn't hurry. Around 11 they started shooting. Three tanks, all firing, plus artillery, guns. We'd lost the territory across the river, and they were shooting from there as well.

"It wasn't possible to move over the day.

"We were trying to hide in the basement where tank fire couldn't reach us, but sometimes it didn't work. A shell is coming through all the walls and destroying everything.

"One guy was wounded, another killed by a tank.

"The Serbs could have passed very easily with their tanks. They didn't know we didn't have anything to destroy tanks. We didn't have anything.

"Perhaps there were 30, 40 of us. Some of us on the front, some further behind trying to find food, brandy in houses.

"I thought everything was going to collapse, the whole town. We didn't speak about that, we tried to encourage each other, but I could see the faces.

"Their infantry came closer to the church and onto a hill higher than ours. They passed the church.

J. SACCO 11-99

"We decided to fall back. I was against that, I wanted to stay in the same position. But they decided — a number of refugees from Visegrad. They didn't know me, I didn't know them.

WE ALREADY LOST TWO MEN TODAY. WE'LL GO BACK AND WAIT. MAYBE SUPPORT WILL COME.

"We fell back 200 meters.

"We established a line... just in front of my house. We didn't get any support from town.

"There was no discussion about what we could do. What can you discuss?

"The Serbs were coming from every side. Our people had left the other side of the river. It was empty except for the hospital. They didn't know what to do with the wounded people. Where could they move hundreds of people?

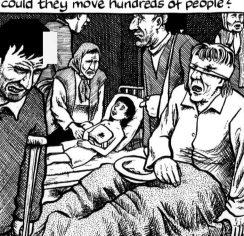

"The next morning, peaceful again until 11, 12, and then the Serbs started like the day before.

J. SACO 8.99

171

"They came closer. Their commander was ordering them with a whistle. You could hear a whistle and instruments... And they were singing Montenegrin songs, Chetnik songs. A lot of voices. They were drunk, drugged, who knows? They were singing when they attacked.

"It has a very big effect on you.

"We were silent. We didn't shoot too much. We didn't have enough ammunition. You can imagine how awful it was for us. They were enjoying themselves. They had everything. Power. Tanks.

"Ever coming.

"I thought, if I can just kill three of them before I die. I wouldn't allow myself to be captured I saw what happened to my friends who were captured in the first attack.

"Our only hope was the support of the world. We'd expected that for months and years. We thought they would stop it... But they didn't do anything.

"Again, two or three of us were killed. By tank fire, artillery, shelling...

"That night one guy said we should fall back, behind my house, closer to town.

LOOK, THERE'S A CEMETERY HERE, A CLEAR AREA, NO HOUSES. THEY CAN'T CROSS THAT FIELD.

"I spent the night at my cousin's home because my head ached, the wound wasn't better. I had to change the bandages at the hospital... crossing the bridge in the first dark and the early morning... with my cousin or a car from the hospital.

"Okay, we decided to stay...

"Then back to the line...

"We were in my place, my grandmother's place, and across the main road in four or five houses further up the hill.

"I whistled to those refugees when it was peaceful to see if they were still there. I was afraid they'd leave their positions so I wanted one of them with us.

"We were my father, my brother, and me... all day together.

"You can trust the most in your father and brother. If you're wounded, they'd help you, but someone else might leave you.

"There was a big attack... The Serbs came into the house just in front of where the checkpoint is now... 18 of them, we counted, my father and I.

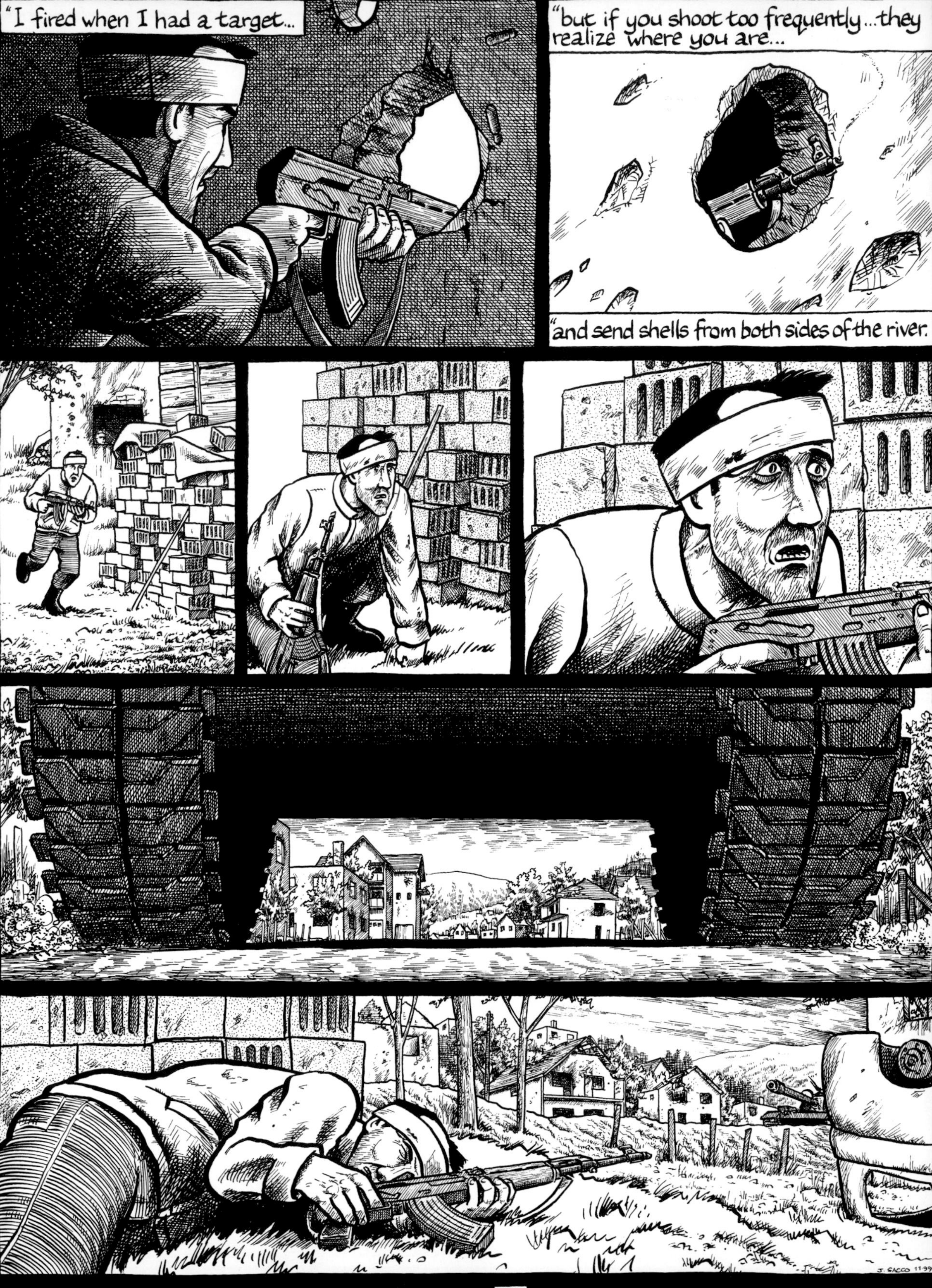
"I fired when I had a target...
"but if you shoot too frequently... they realize where you are...
"and send shells from both sides of the river.
J. SACCO 11-99

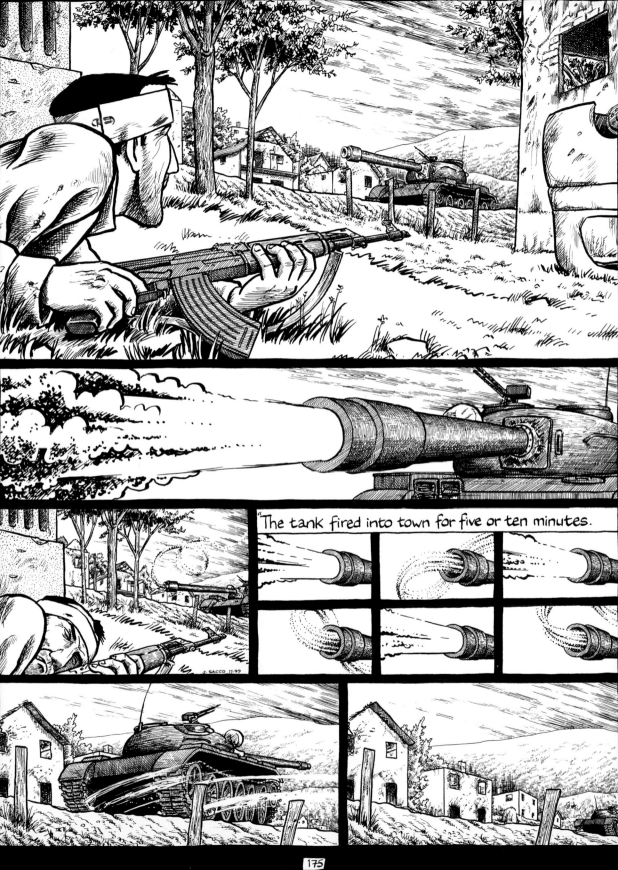

"The tank fired into town for five or ten minutes.

"Two were wounded that day, I don't know if anyone was killed.

"That night 36 refugees from Kopaci organized a unit and came to help us. The front line was in my house, and I explained where the Serbs were, approximately how many, where the tank was...

I'M GOING TO SLEEP AT MY COUSIN'S PLACE. I'LL COME BACK TO-MORROW. THEY WON'T ATTACK BEFORE 11.

"My mother had been coming every night to milk the cow.

"That night we moved the cow and the two sheep.

"In the morning I went to the hospital to change my bandages... and then I tried to reach my house with one of my neighbors. It was already 11 o'clock. They occupied the other side of the river and a sniper could shoot you.

"We were running between houses.

"A couple of hundred meters from my house we met a guy who had slaughtered a sheep, and he invited us to eat...

"And we thought, why not, the line is peaceful and we have more soldiers there than yesterday.

"12... one o'clock... shooting...

"Then — silence.

THEY'RE ABOUT TO OCCUPY THE HILL ABOVE US!

THEY'LL CAPTURE ALL OF US!

"The Serbs had come, tanks were shooting, my house had been hit by a tank.

"I realized the line was broken. Nobody on the line. Panic.

"I didn't know what was happening on the main road, where the tanks were, nothing. Everything was empty.

"There were seven of us, maybe more, and we moved forward. I wanted to get closer to my home.

J. SACCO 9-99

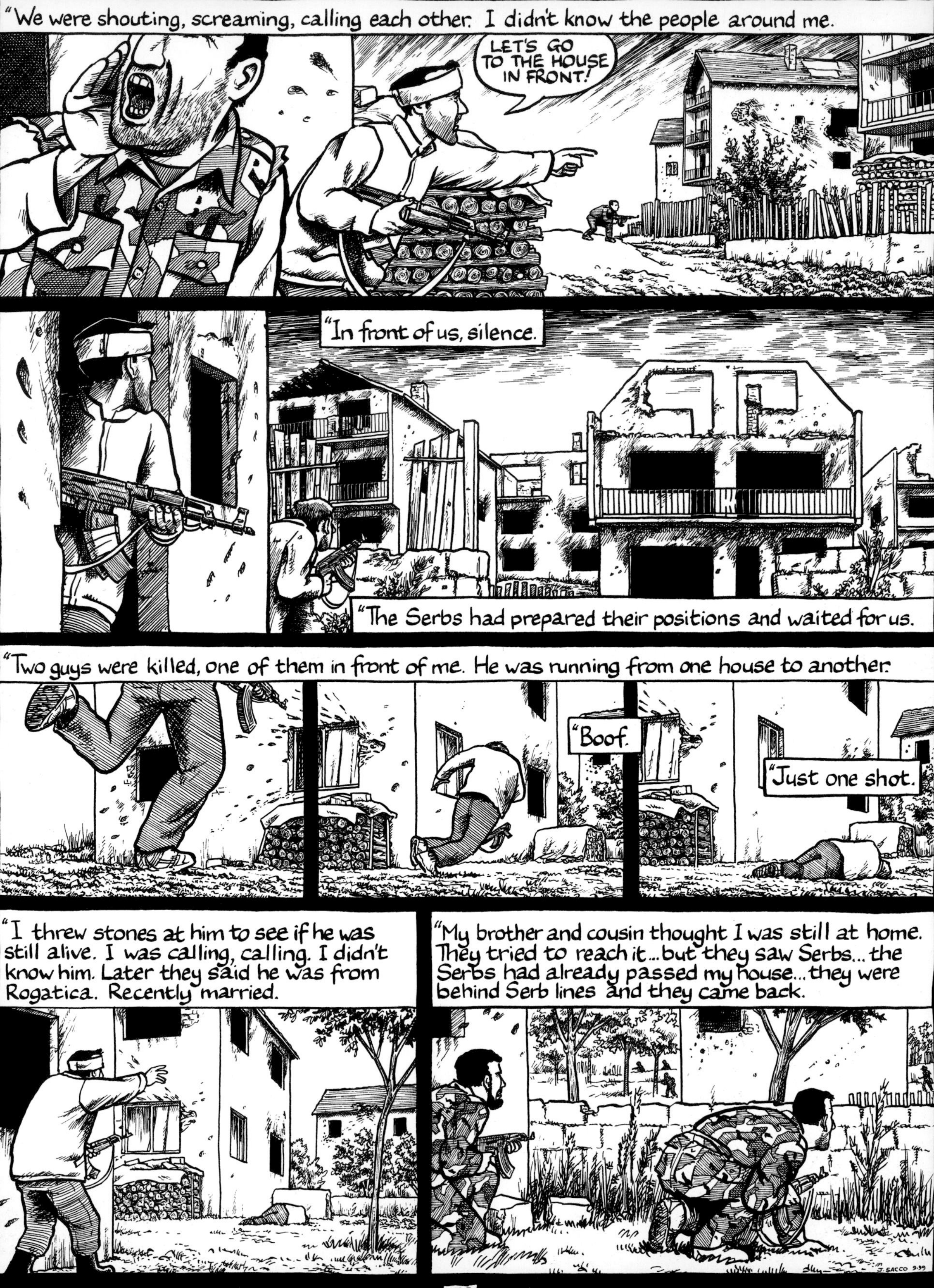
"We were shouting, screaming, calling each other. I didn't know the people around me.
LET'S GO TO THE HOUSE IN FRONT!
"In front of us, silence.
"The Serbs had prepared their positions and waited for us.
"Two guys were killed, one of them in front of me. He was running from one house to another.
"Boof.
"Just one shot.
"I threw stones at him to see if he was still alive. I was calling, calling. I didn't know him. Later they said he was from Rogatica. Recently married.
"My brother and cousin thought I was still at home. They tried to reach it... but they saw Serbs... the Serbs had already passed my house... they were behind Serb lines and they came back.
J. SACCO 9.99

"I stayed alone in a house until dark...My cousin and brother found me there. They were in a house behind me, but I couldn't speak to them.

"When the dark got deeper... soldiers came and organized a line. About 40 or 50 of them. And my brother told me my father had been wounded."

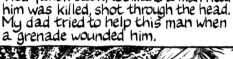

"He'd fallen back, too...and a man near him was killed, shot through the head. My dad tried to help this man when a grenade wounded him.

"Two men carried him back... He was in the hospital, but his wound wasn't life-threatening...

"We had our new positions.

"It was spring and there were a lot of trees...

"I could no longer see my house."

On April 17, a U.N. spokesman had announced that "Bosnian army defenses around Gorazde have collapsed—they are non-existent."

U.N. Lt. General Rose admitted, "We are on the brink of a humanitarian disaster there," and ordered the secret evacuation of the U.N. Military Observers.

The Serbs agreed to and broke one cease-fire after another. U.S. Secretary of State Warren Christopher blamed them for a "tangle of lies and misleading statements that have seldom been equaled."

The Russians saw a withdrawal pledge they had brokered side-stepped by Bosnian Serb leader Karadzic while Akashi, the compliant and non-confrontational U.N. regional chief, announced progress. A disgusted Russian Deputy Foreign Minister Vitaly Churkin said, "I've heard more broken promises in the last 24 hours than I have in my entire life." President Boris Yeltsin demanded, "Stop the attacks. Withdraw from Gorazde."

J. SACCO 11-99

Said Karadzic:

THE SERBIAN SIDE UNILATERALLY PROCLAIMS PEACE IN GORAZDE. WITH THIS, THE GORAZDE CRISIS COMES TO AN END.

But the Serb attack continued.

Meanwhile, Bosnian President Izetbegovic had written to U.N. Secretary General Boutros Boutros-Ghali, "The so-called safe area has become the most unsafe place in the world... Neither you nor your personnel have done anything to use the mandate of all those resolutions to protect the people of Gorazde or the credibility of the United Nations."

PATIENTS WERE IN THE BASEMENT, IN THE KITCHEN, THE LAUNDRY, WITH THE CHARCOAL.

70 TO 100 PATIENTS WERE COMING IN IN 24 HOURS.

Dr. Alija Begovic

"What can you do with them? Ten patients were waiting to go into the theater at one time.

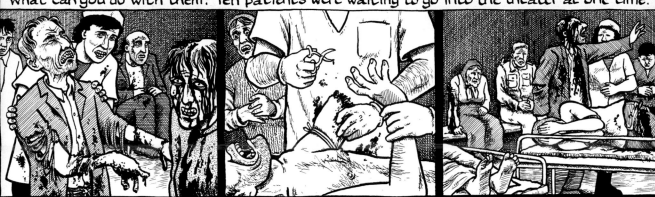

"A surgeon doesn't have time to prioritize. Of course, we had no pain killers, people were

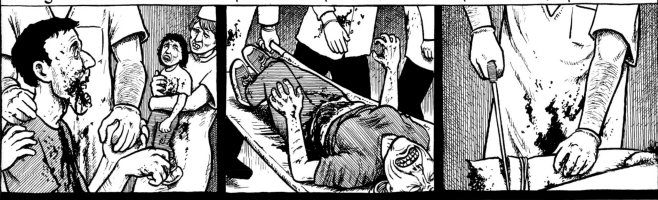

"suffering, dying... Relatives, friends, neighbors were everywhere. We couldn't stop them. We

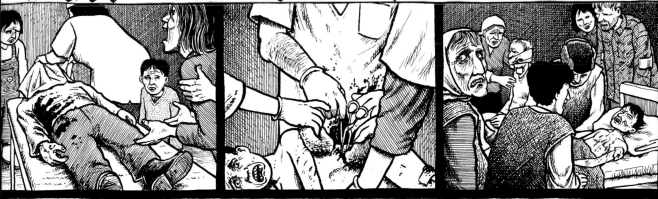

"didn't want to stop them... How could you? It might be the last minutes with their loved one."

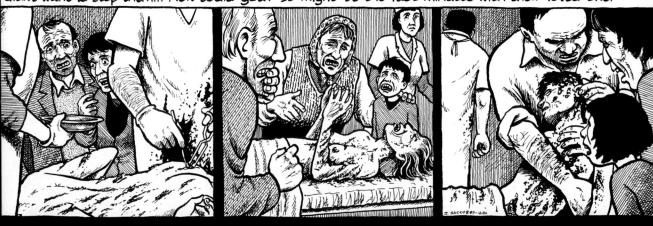

FOR ME IT WAS A SITUATION WITHOUT EXIT.

I WAS ON THE FRONTIER OF BEING PSYCHO-LOGICALLY BROKEN.

Nurse Sadija Demir

"A lot of children were wounded... dead children.

"In one day 97 wounded persons came in. From 10 p.m. till 5:30 a.m. there were 47...

"I thought it was the end, that they'd kill us all. On the way to my house, I didn't know if I'd survive.

"All the time they were shelling."

WE HAD A DEPARTMENT FOR DRESSING, FOR GIVING INJECTIONS, ON THE OPPO-SITE SIDE OF THE STREET.

WITH 28 BEDS.

J. SACCO 9-99

"A tank hit it.

"Ten patients and one nurse were killed, many wounded.

*RPG: ROCKET PROPELLED GRENADE

"NATO planes were always circling, flying above the town, but they didn't do anything. Only watching, taking pictures.

"I didn't understand. It seemed all the countries of the world were going to allow the Serbs to take this town although it was a protected town."

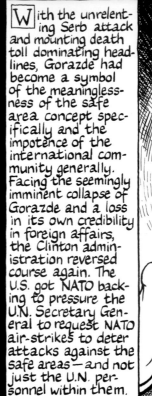

With the unrelenting Serb attack and mounting death toll dominating headlines, Gorazde had become a symbol of the meaninglessness of the safe area concept specifically and the impotence of the international community generally. Facing the seemingly imminent collapse of Gorazde and a loss in its own credibility in foreign affairs, the Clinton administration reversed course again. The U.S. got NATO backing to pressure the U.N. Secretary General to request NATO air-strikes to deter attacks against the safe areas—and not just the U.N. personnel within them.

The Serbs would have to pay—

—A HIGHER PRICE FOR CONTINUED VIOLENCE.

On April 22, NATO gave the Serbs an ultimatum demanding an immediate cease-fire and the withdrawal of their forces from Gorazde.

NATO DEMANDS OF SERB WITHDRAWALS

0   5   10 Km

ROGATICA

PULL-BACK TROOPS 3 KM BY APRIL 23

MEDEDA

KOPACI

PULL-BACK HEAVY WEAPONS 20 KM BY APRIL 26

GORAZDE

Drina

CAJNICE

FOCA

The Serb artillery barrage intensified.

The Russians, ostensibly sympathetic to the Serb cause, dropped their previous objections to air-strikes. Said Foreign Minister Andrei Kozyrev, "The Bosnian Serbs' military command has criminally defied the elementary norms of humanity."

As NATO pushed hard for air-strikes, the Serbs hinted at further reprisals against U.N. peacekeepers should they take place. U.N. representative Akashi declined to request air-strikes, saying he had assurances the Serbs would withdraw.

The Serbs recognized that they had played the game as far as it could go. NATO and the Russians were now arrayed against them, and only a command mechanism that kept the air-strike trigger in the hands of U.N. official Akashi had kept additional bombs from falling.

The Serbs allowed a convoy of U.N. peacekeepers into town and permitted British and French helicopters to take out Gorazde's most heavily wounded.

The Serbs began to pull-back from Gorazde, and as they left—

THEY WERE BURNING MOST OF THE HOMES

"Chetnik soldiers were 100 meters away...and just as they ran back I came to my house.

"I found three bottles of fuel in the corner ready for making a fire. But probably they were rushed and didn't have time.

"I saw my cousin Azra's house burning. Only two rooms were burning, but I couldn't do anything without water.

"The whole house burned down.

"In my house, part of the roof was completely destroyed, shot by a tank.

"I found their literature, food, shirts, cigarettes, hand grenades, bullets... They'd slept upstairs... They'd taken our two televisions, a stereo, videotapes...

"The toilet was destroyed, with shit everywhere. One of the rooms upstairs was full of shit... rubbish, shit... They used my room like a toilet...

"I cleaned up... My mother didn't come, she was scared to come. It was a mess here."

In the view of Lt. General Rose, the U.N.'s top military commander in Bosnia, the battle for Gorazde had endangered his peacekeepers and brought the U.N. perilously close to taking sides in the war.

Visiting British peacekeepers, who had just set up in Gorazde, he said that the Bosnians—

—THINK THAT WE SHOULD BE FIGHTING THE WAR FOR THEM...

Panel 1: HOW THE HELL DID THEY LET TANKS DOWN THAT ROUTE?

Panel 2: ONE BLOKE WITH A CROWBAR COULD HAVE STOPPED THAT TANK.

Panel 3: I THINK THEY BASICALLY TURNED AND RAN, AND LEFT US TO TRY AND PICK UP THE PIECES FOR THEM.

Said Rose: "The situation was a lot better than I had been led to believe... the town had not been destroyed to the level which I had expected."

Rose toured the hospital and claimed its director, Dr. Begovic, had admitted that casualty estimates "were indeed an exaggeration."

(Dr. Begovic told me he was greatly upset by Rose's representation of his remarks.)

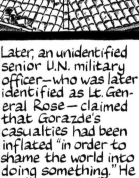

Later, an unidentified senior U.N. military officer—who was later identified as Lt. General Rose—claimed that Gorazde's casualties had been inflated "in order to shame the world into doing something." He said casualty figures had come from untrustworthy sources, among them the U.N. Military Observers, whom he said were of a low standard. The observers, whom Rose himself had ordered in, were, in fact, elite British troops.

In any case, the U.N. High Commission for Refugees stuck to its casualty figures for the '94 offensive against Gorazde— more than 700 killed, nearly 2,000 wounded.

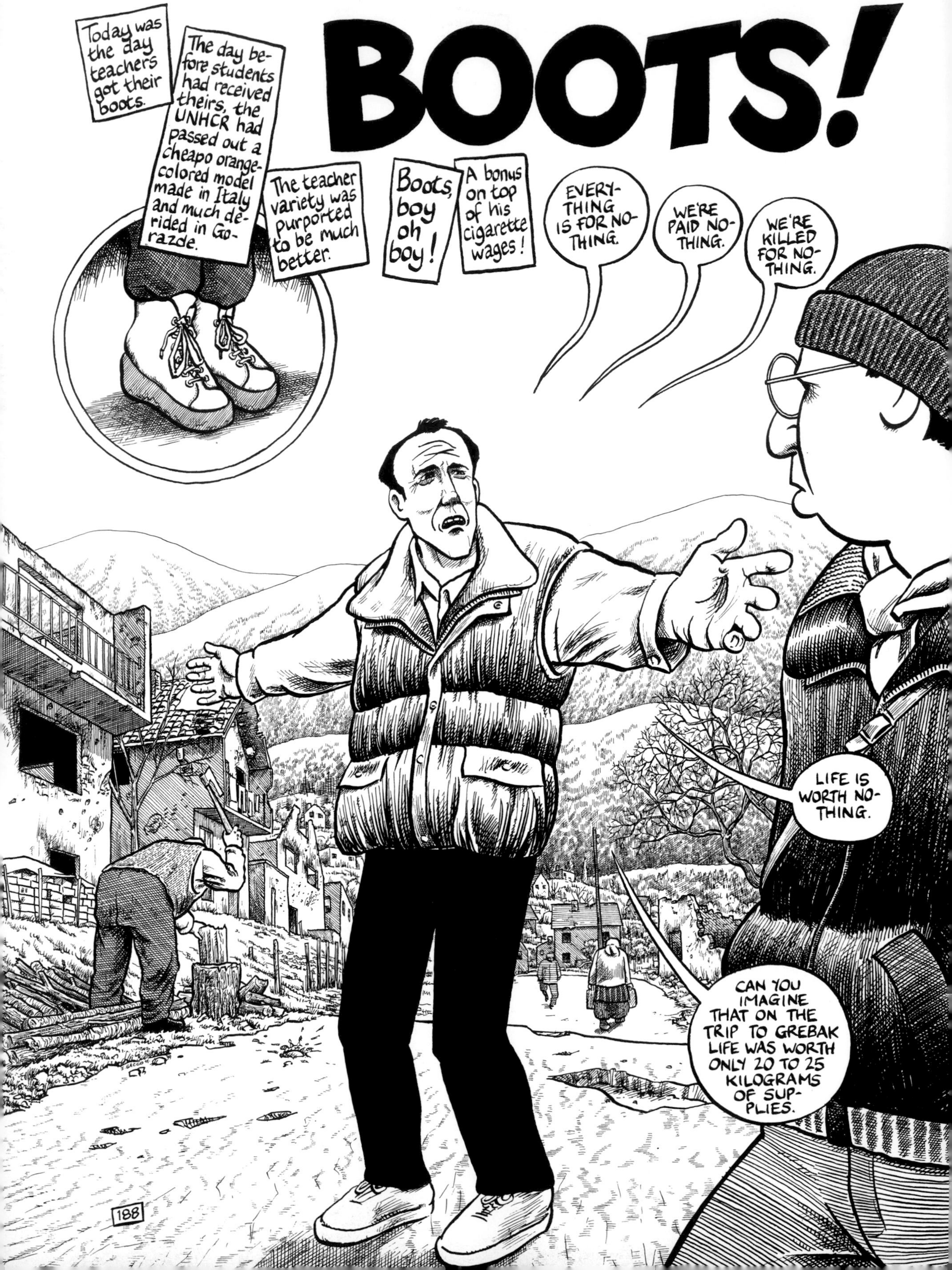
BOOTS!
Today was the day teachers got their boots.
The day before students had received theirs, the UNHCR had passed out a cheapo orange-colored model made in Italy and much derided in Gorazde.
The teacher variety was purported to be much better.
Boots, boy oh boy!
A bonus on top of his cigarette wages!
EVERYTHING IS FOR NOTHING.
WE'RE PAID NOTHING.
WE'RE KILLED FOR NOTHING.
LIFE IS WORTH NOTHING.
CAN YOU IMAGINE THAT ON THE TRIP TO GREBAK LIFE WAS WORTH ONLY 20 TO 25 KILOGRAMS OF SUPPLIES.

A young girl, a student of Edin's, got into step with us.

WHERE ARE YOU GOING?

To get boots!

YOU CAN HAVE MY BOOTS!

Ah, those orange monstrosities!

we laughed!

< I'VE GIVEN HER A BAD GRADE, BUT I DON'T WANT TO TELL HER. >

At the school Edin learned that the boots for teachers hadn't come in.

Every now and then I'd ask him if they'd arrived.

No, he'd say, not yet.

And Edin never got his boots.

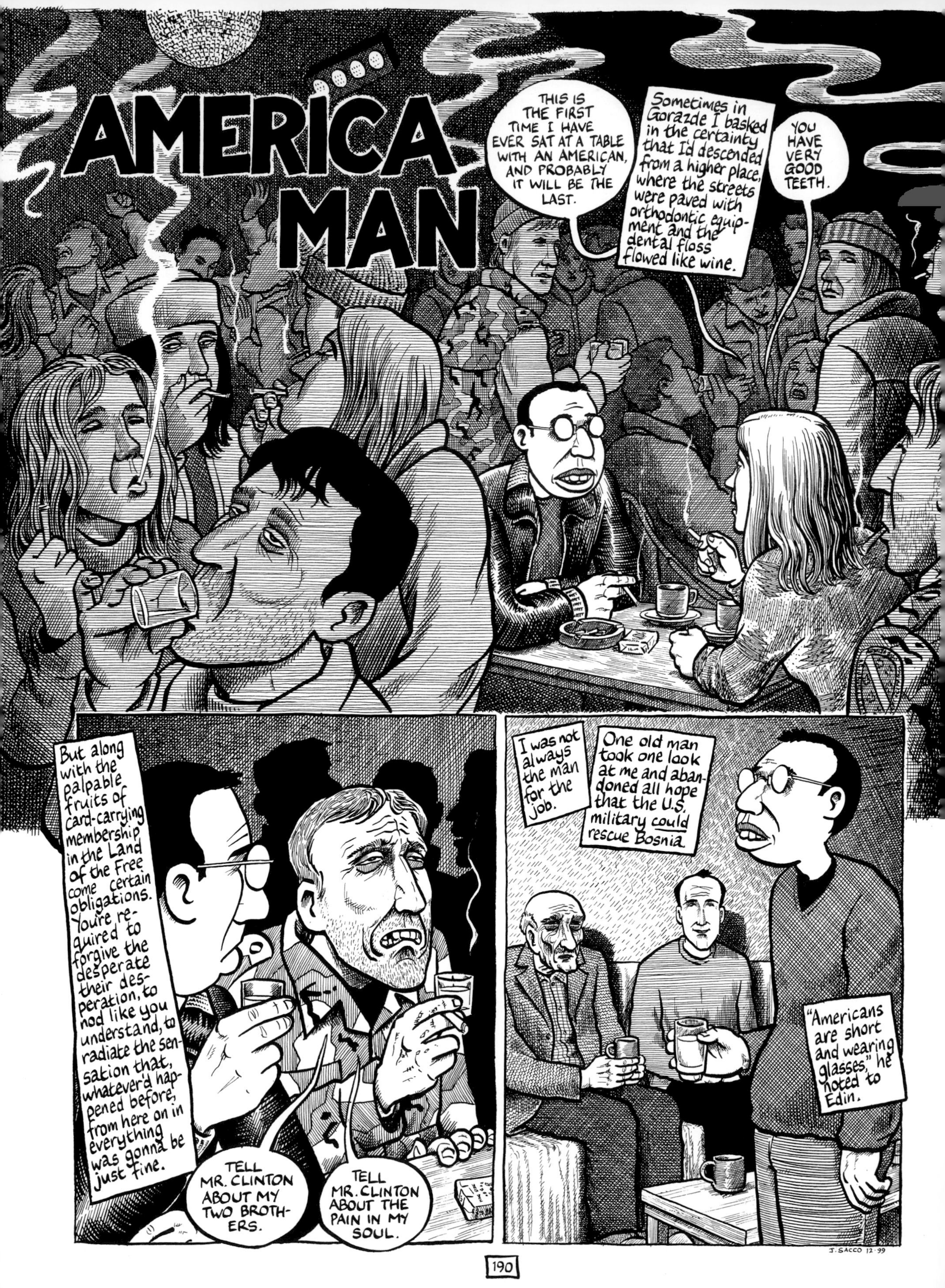
AMERICA MAN
THIS IS THE FIRST TIME I HAVE EVER SAT AT A TABLE WITH AN AMERICAN, AND PROBABLY IT WILL BE THE LAST.
Sometimes in Gorazde I basked in the certainty that I'd descended from a higher place, where the streets were paved with orthodontic equipment and the dental floss flowed like wine.
YOU HAVE VERY GOOD TEETH.
But along with the palpable fruits of card-carrying membership in the Land of the Free come certain obligations. You're required to forgive the desperate their desperation, to nod like you understand, to radiate the sensation that, whatever'd happened before, from here on in everything was gonna be just fine.
TELL MR. CLINTON ABOUT MY TWO BROTHERS.
TELL MR. CLINTON ABOUT THE PAIN IN MY SOUL.
I was not always the man for the job.
One old man took one look at me and abandoned all hope that the U.S. military could rescue Bosnia
"Americans are short and wearing glasses," he noted to Edin.
J. SACCO 12·99

One night, on my first trip to Gorazde, my colleague Whit and I were out relaxing over a bottle of home-made...

Whit was having an animated chat with Edin's uncle, an eloquent man who'd spent some years in America and whose English was fluent..

Meanwhile, I was sandwiched between the wall and F.

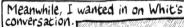

F. didn't know much English, but I understood that his wife was in Sarajevo, that he hadn't seen her in years...

Ask anyone who knows me, I am a very pleasant fellow. And I was being very pleasant to F.

I listened politely while he patched fragments of English together to tell the story of how he'd assisted a foreign journalist and been paid $100 for a day's work.

Meanwhile, I wanted in on Whit's conversation.

MISTER? MISTER?

AMERICA...

AMERICA MAN THINKS BOSNIA MAN PRIMITIVE.

JOURNALIST...

WHY YOU COME?

MONEY?

J. SACCO 12·99

I THINK— SREBRENICA. I BE-COME ANGRY.

VERY ANGRY.

SIX THOUSAND KILLED SREBRENICA. WHAT YOU THINK, MISTER? MISTER?

YOU DON'T WRITE FOR SREBRENICA.

I wanted Edin to intervene, Whit to notice... I wanted out, out of there... I wanted to put a hundred thousand miles between me and Bosnia,

between me and these horrible, disgusting people and their fucking wars and pathetic prospects...

And finally we were spilling into the street...

Air!

Air!

And F. started laying into Whit, too...

DON'T FUCK WITH ME!

And then we were walking, walking...

Whit, Edin, and I...

walking...

across the second bridge...

into the deep dark...

and when we got back to Edin's I threw up and felt much better, thank you.

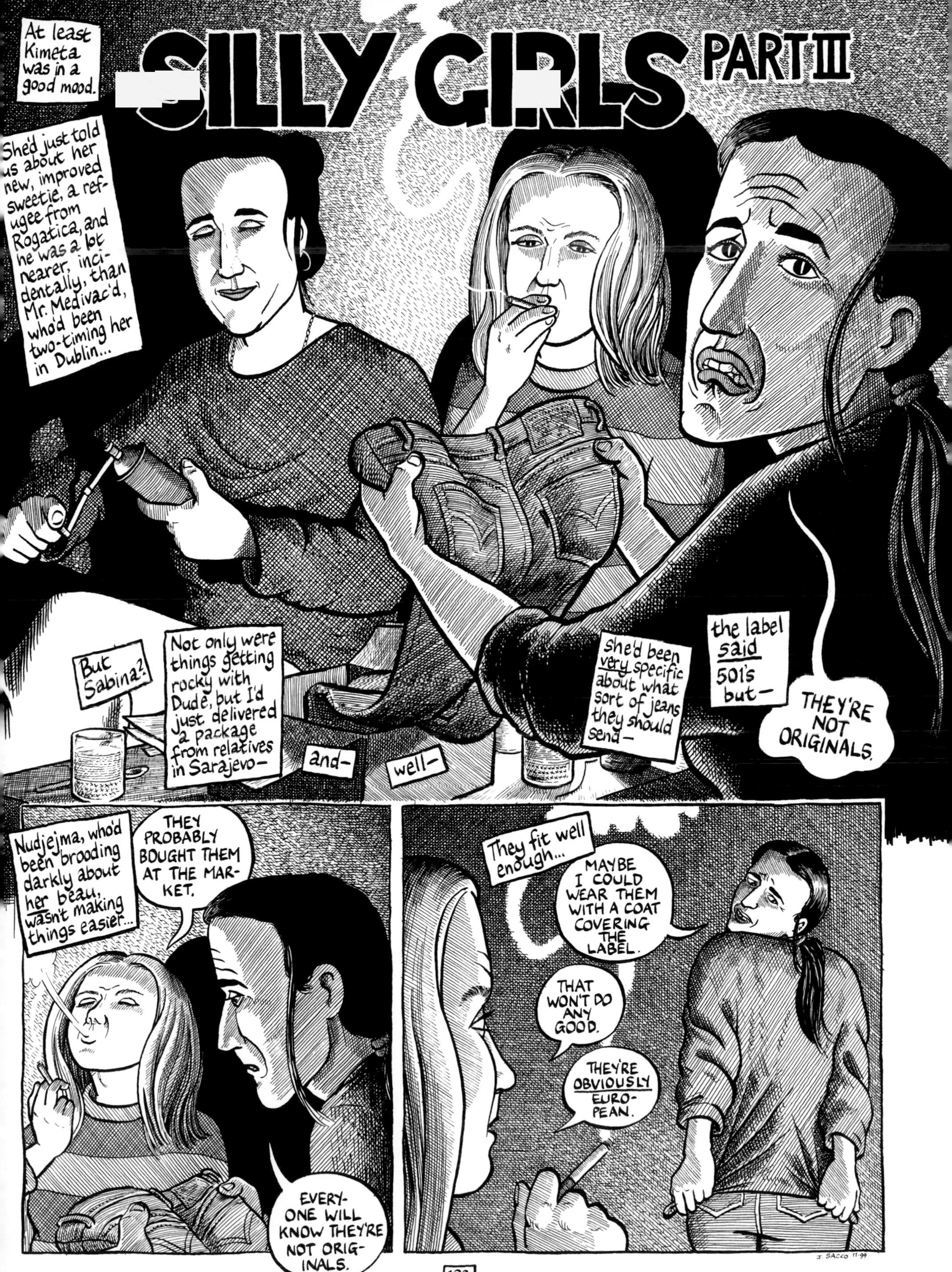

SILLY GIRLS PART III
At least Kimeta was in a good mood.
She'd just told us about her new, improved sweetie, a refugee from Rogatica, and he was a lot nearer, incidentally, than Mr. Medivac'd, who'd been two-timing her in Dublin...
But Sabina?
Not only were things getting rocky with Dude, but I'd just delivered a package from relatives in Sarajevo—
and—
well—
She'd been very specific about what sort of jeans they should send—
the label said 501's but—
THEY'RE NOT ORIGINALS.
Nudjejma, who'd been brooding darkly about her beau, wasn't making things easier...
THEY PROBABLY BOUGHT THEM AT THE MARKET.
EVERYONE WILL KNOW THEY'RE NOT ORIGINALS.
They fit well enough...
MAYBE I COULD WEAR THEM WITH A COAT COVERING THE LABEL.
THAT WON'T DO ANY GOOD.
THEY'RE OBVIOUSLY EUROPEAN.
J. SACCO 11·99

"I FEEL LIKE CRYING."

"JOE, ARE YOU "DESIROUS" OF SEEING YOUR PARENTS AGAIN?"

Ah, trust Riki to test drive a newly looked-up word...

to get in some practice no matter what...

So I conjugated a few verbs for him...

but that was hardly entertaining the multitude...

the evening was getting glum...

I decided to amuse everyone with tales of my visits to the *other* side, to Grbavica, a Serb-held area of Sarajevo...

I'd made some friends there.

The silly girls were curious about how the Serbs were getting along and whether the Serbs were curious about them...

"DO THEY ASK ABOUT THE PEOPLE IN GORAZDE?"

A couple of people had, I said.

Then I read from my interviews, and most Serbs hadn't minced words, they *didn't* want to live with Muslims, they accused the Muslims of starting the war, of all kinds of atrocities...

as for Serb atrocities, most Serbs I talked to denied they'd happened.

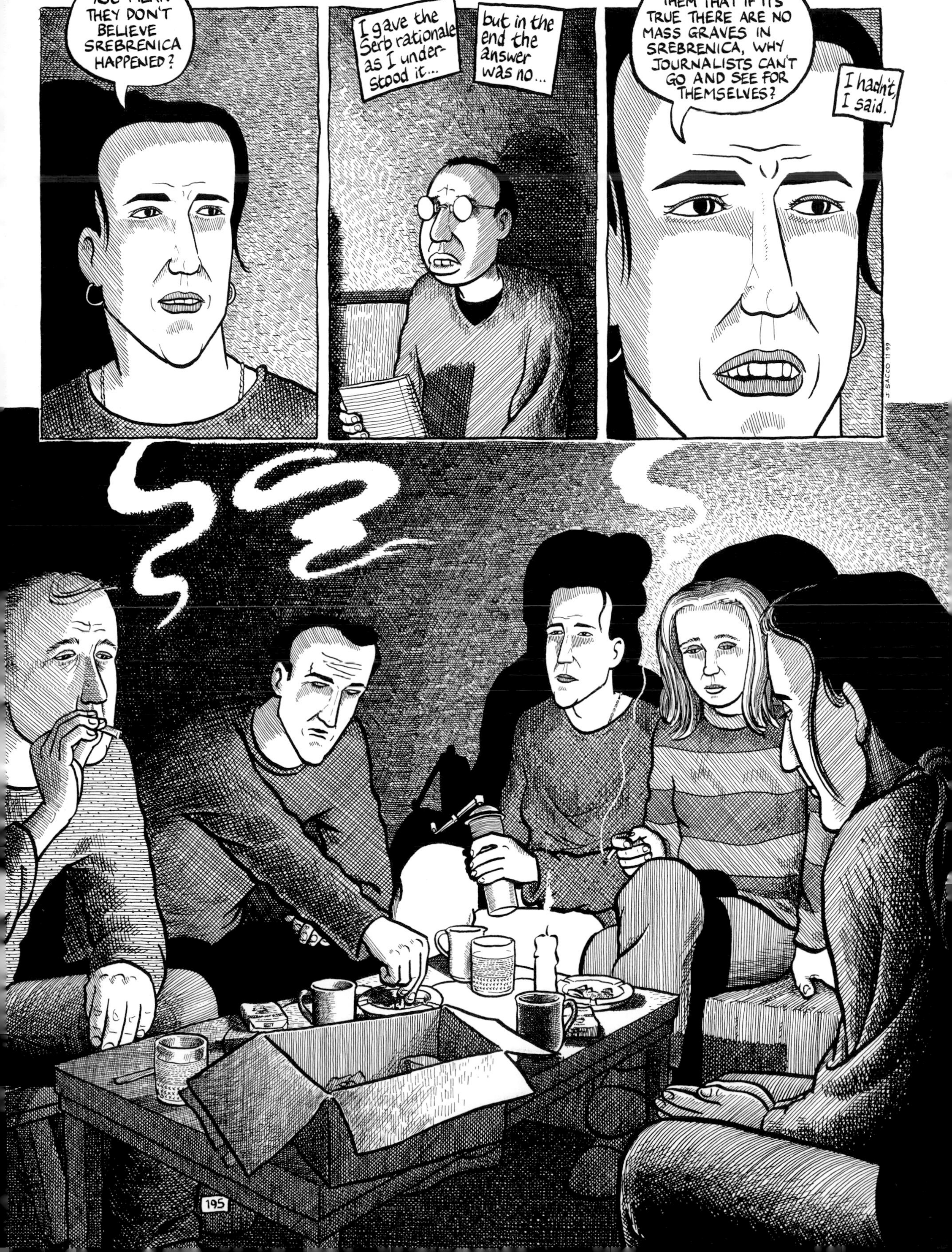

YOU MEAN THEY DON'T BELIEVE SREBRENICA HAPPENED?
I gave the Serb rationale as I understood it...
but in the end the answer was no...
DID YOU ASK THEM THAT IF IT'S TRUE THERE ARE NO MASS GRAVES IN SREBRENICA, WHY JOURNALISTS CAN'T GO AND SEE FOR THEMSELVES?
I hadn't, I said.
J. SACCO 11.99

Death and Deliverance

I STARTED WORKING FOR THE BRITISH PEACEKEEPERS IN MID JANUARY 1995.

I WAS WORKING AT SCHOOL, TOO, 24 HOURS A WEEK.

"I would go to Britbat* with my bicycle from the technical school over the pedestrian bridge.

"The Serbs could see the second bridge, the first bridge, everything."

"It was dangerous, especially because of snipers. They were shooting many times.

"At Britbat I worked with an engineering squadron. I built them a mini-centrale. They had generators, but they wanted it for emergency situations.

"I stayed on as a translator.

"I was part-time and they paid me with food. Sometimes eggs, flour, canned food. Sometimes coffee, sometimes Coke."

U.N. peacekeepers had retained their presence in Gorazde since the end of the Serb offensive of 1994. In 1995 mostly British and Ukranian peacekeepers were stationed there.

The Serbs were only intermittently allowing the resupply of the peacekeepers and relief convoys into the enclave.

Meanwhile, the Bosnian Serb military was preparing a decisive campaign to end the war that year. Its commander, General Ratko Mladic, would first test the resolve and unity of the international community on the Sarajevo front.

Mladic once referred to himself as a "super-general."

IF I'D BEEN A SURGEON, I'D HAVE BEEN A SUPER-SURGEON. IF I'D BEEN A LAWYER, I'D HAVE BEEN A SUPER-LAWYER.

BUT I'D NEVER MAKE FRANK SINATRA BECAUSE I DON'T HAVE A SUPER VOICE.

* BRITBAT: BRITISH BATTALION.

In May his forces seized back heavy weapons—previously turned over to the U.N. by agreement—and added them to a renewed bombardment of Sarajevo.

NATO retaliated with limited air strikes, and Mladic's men once again took hundreds of U.N. soldiers and personnel hostage, including 33 British peacekeepers from the Gorazde enclave.

Some of these hostages were chained to Serb military installations as human shields.

The Serbs further demonstrated the limits and dangers of air power to NATO and the U.N. by downing a U.S. fighter with a surface-to-air missile.

On June 4, the commander of U.N. military forces in the former Yugoslavia, Lt. General Bernard Janvier of France, secretly met Mladic to obtain the release of the hostages, more than half of whom were French. Mladic demanded that Janvier first promise there be no future air strikes.

Whether Mladic got an explicit guarantee from Janvier is still disputed, but three days later a phased release of the hostages began.

On June 9, the U.N.'s top civilian representative in the area, Yasushi Akashi, indicated the U.N. would back away from confrontation with the Serbs. It would now—

ABIDE STRICTLY BY PEACEKEEPING PRINCIPLES...

Satisfied the U.N. had been cowed, General Mladic now turned his attention to eastern Bosnia and its safe areas.

SREBRENICA

ZEPA

SARAJEVO

GORAZDE

THE THREE EASTERN SAFE AREAS, JULY 1995

For his part, U.N. Lt. General Janvier had already expressed his misgivings about the U.N.'s commitment to the eastern safe areas and the presence of its peacekeepers there. Defending those safe areas, he had argued, could contravene U.N. neutrality.

... ABOVE ALL LET US BE HONEST WITH OURSELVES AND THOSE WE ARE PLEDGED TO PROTECT.

ONE SHOULDN'T PLAY IN THE STORM IF ONE CANNOT THROW LIGHTNING BOLTS.

AT A CLOSED-DOOR U.N. SECURITY COUNCIL SESSION.

J. SACCO 3/01

Mladic's first target was Srebrenica, whose fighters had waged an aggressive war against neighboring Serb villages early in the conflict. Their attacks often were followed by a wave of desperate, hungry Muslim civilians—many of whom had been cleansed from their own communities—looting and burning homes and exacting vengeance on the Serbs they caught.

After an overwhelming Serb offensive in 1993, the enclave's defenders had agreed to a U.N.-monitored demilitarization,* and Srebrenica had become the first U.N. safe area.

Mladic launched his attack on Srebrenica in July 1995. His forces brushed aside the Dutch peacekeepers stationed there and took some of them hostage. The Dutch put up no resistance themselves but called for air support to halt the Serbs six times.

Their requests were turned down or postponed by top U.N. officers, including Janvier personally, even after the Dutch themselves came under attack.

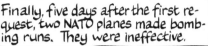

Finally, five days after the first request, two NATO planes made bombing runs. They were ineffective.

The Serbs threatened to kill their Dutch hostages and shell panicked civilians if NATO attacked again.

In any case, it was too late. Bosnian soldiers, who had believed the U.N. would defend the safe area, put up an ineffectual defense.

The Serbs entered Srebrenica.

THERE WAS A VERY BIG PANIC.

Nermin

"I left Srebrenica with other soldiers. The civilians went to Potocari, the main base of U.N. forces..."

*SEE P. 148. THE DEMILITARIZATION WAS ONLY PARTIALLY FULFILLED.

Most of Srebrenica's male population—including soldiers, boys, and older men—preferred running a Serb gantlet to surrendering. They formed a column and attempted to force their way toward Tuzla and Bosnian government lines.

I WAS WITH 12,500 MILITARY-AGED MEN. THE REST OF THE PEOPLE FROM SREBRENICA, THE OLD PEOPLE, CHILDREN, AND WOMEN... MY FATHER, MOTHER, AND SISTER, WE LEFT BEHIND.

Haso

WE WERE SURROUNDED BY CHETNIKS.

NERMIN: "The Chetniks started shelling. They were firing anti-aircraft cannon, heavy machine-guns...

"Nobody knew where to escape."

HASO: "We escaped from Konjevic Polje... We left wounded and dead people behind.

"I went back to pick up my friend. He'd been wounded beside me. I approached the village where my friend was wounded.

"The Chetniks had flashlights and they were killing the wounded one by one.

"I saw about 50 killed."

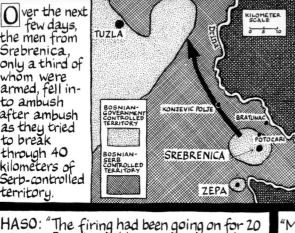

Over the next few days, the men from Srebrenica, only a third of whom were armed, fell into ambush after ambush as they tried to break through 40 kilometers of Serb-controlled territory.

TUZLA

Drina

KILOMETER SCALE
0 5 10

BOSNIAN-GOVERNMENT CONTROLLED TERRITORY

KONJEVIC POLJE

BRATUNAC

POTOCARI

BOSNIAN-SERB CONTROLLED TERRITORY

SREBRENICA

ZEPA

Both Nermin and Haso claimed the Serbs attacked the column with what they called "combat gas."

Perhaps the incapacitating chemical agent BZ, a benzilate compound, "combat gas" rendered its victims disoriented and hallucinatory, among other effects, they said.*

HASO: "The firing had been going on for 20 minutes. Bosnian soldiers were surrendering to the Serbs. They were not behaving normally—crazy because of the combat gas."

"My neighbor was captured with a large group...more than 3- or 400 soldiers. They were forced to say—

WE ARE SERB SOLDIERS.

WE ARE THE SERB ARMY.

"They were taken away, and I didn't see what happened to them."

NERMIN: "I was with a group of soldiers who'd survived those ambushes and mines. The Chetniks saw us.

SURRENDER! WE'LL MAKE YOU A CORRIDOR TO TUZLA!

"Some people started surrendering. Some started carrying the wounded toward the Chetniks. A lot of them were crazy from combat gas.

"I stayed there in the field... My brother and a couple of friends were with me...

"I wasn't feeling normal...I was suffering from combat gases.

"I didn't know what was happening around me.

"The Chetniks approached and started firing...

* DESPITE MANY EYEWITNESS ACCOUNTS, HUMAN RIGHTS WATCH FOUND EVIDENCE OF GAS ATTACKS "INCONCLUSIVE" THOUGH SUCH ATTACKS "CANNOT BE RULED OUT."

"Two guys approached me...I didn't know them.

"We were together all night.

"The Chetniks were moving around us.

"I heard crying and screaming in the field. And Chetnik voices. They were shouting—

WHY ARE YOU CRY-ING?

FUCKING ALIJA*!

"We stayed till early morning...The Chetniks called on us to go toward Tuzla.

YOU KNOW THE ROAD...

"The two guys agreed to go with some Serbs—they didn't know they were Serbs.

"I knew so I stayed hidden.

"The Chetniks discovered me.

"One Chetnik started shooting in the air. I pretended nothing was happening.

"They thought the combat gas had damaged my mind...so they left me.

"After 15 minutes I realized there wasn't anyone around...I started moving toward Žepa."

Nermin had given up on reaching Tuzla and joined other stragglers retracing their steps to get to the safe area directly south of Srebrenica.

"I found about 200 men searching for Chetniks to surrender to. I was in a group of 15 people, and they asked if we were surrendering.

"We saw what the Serbs had done. I tried to persuade them not to surrender...

*A REFERENCE TO THE PRESIDENT OF BOSNIA, ALIJA IZETBEGOVIC

"The 15 of us moved toward Zepa, but the rest of them started surrendering."

HASO: "We found another group in the forest and we stayed there for 12 days. I ate only apples for seven days.

"We made the decision to go back toward Srebrenica."

"We saw many dead people. They were soldiers, some old people...

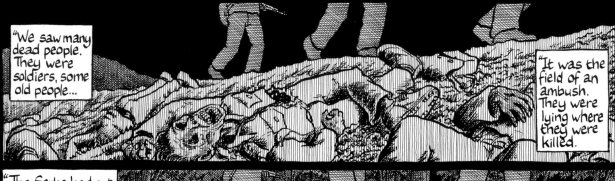

"It was the field of an ambush. They were lying where they were killed.

"The Serbs had put bodies in the forest. Probably they had captured them, killed them, and put them in the forest. One beside another. Some had been killed by gunfire, others by slaughtering."

Nermin and Haso reached Zepa separately after long and dangerous trips.

Back in the Srebrenica enclave, General Mladic and Serb soldiers had walked among Muslim civilians gathered for protection at the U.N. compound.

YOU HAVE NO REASON TO BE AFRAID.

His men dispensed sweets.

The Serbs transported the Muslim women and children to Bosnian government territory. However, while disarmed Dutch peacekeepers watched, hundreds of men in the civilian group were separated and led away.

J. SACCO 2-00

Together with thousands of men and boys captured by the Serbs in the break-out to Tuzla, they were exterminated.

It was the largest mass killing in Europe in 50 years.

All told, in the ambushes and executions, more than 7,000 Muslim men were killed.

At a briefing on July 14, while the Srebrenica calamity was still unfolding, Janvier seemed to unilaterally abandon the notion that the U.N. would defend any safe area other than Sarajevo. Gorazde, he said, was "perfectly capable" of defending itself. As for Zepa:

IT IS ABSO-LUTELY CLEAR THAT WE CAN'T REINFORCE ZEPA.

WE CAN'T DE-FEND ZEPA AS A RESULT.

J. SACCO 2-00

Within several days, Zepa would fall to the attacking Serbs with barely a murmur from those who had once proclaimed it a safe area.

203

Many of Zepa's men hid in caves around the town before trekking to Bosnian government territory or technically neutral Serbia.

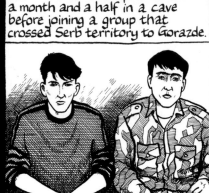

Nermin and Haso spent almost a month and a half in a cave before joining a group that crossed Serb territory to Gorazde.

That's where I met them.

I asked Nermin if he knew what happened to his brother, from whom he'd been separated in the break-out from Srebrenica.

I DON'T HAVE ANY INFORMATION ABOUT HIM.

I DON'T KNOW IF HE'S DEAD.

The Serbs trucked Haso's mother and sister from Srebrenica to Bosnian government lines, but—

MY FATHER WAS TAKEN FROM THE CONVOY IN BRATUNAC.

I DON'T KNOW WHAT'S HAPPENED TO HIM.

At the end of July 1995, Gorazde was the last remaining U.N.-designated safe area in eastern Bosnia. Said Mladic—

BY THE AUTUMN WE'LL TAKE GORAZDE, BIHAC, AND, IN THE END, SARAJEVO, AND WE'LL FINISH THE WAR IN BOSNIA.

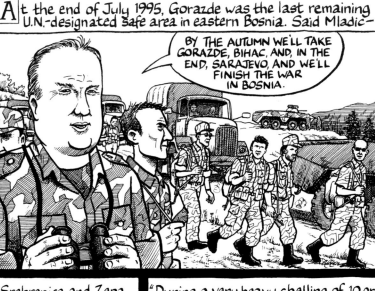

ALL OF US THOUGHT WE WERE NEXT.

"After Srebrenica and Zepa fell, we expected an attack from the other side. We knew what was going on. We were getting Radio Sarajevo and Voice of America.

"During a very heavy shelling of 10 or 15 days, the British soldiers left Gorazde and hid themselves in the deep forest...

"People realized. We didn't have any protection from them.

"Some of our soldiers wanted to take arms, weapons, whatever they could from the U.N. soldiers, because they were useless. The Dutch in Srebrenica hadn't done anything.

IF WE HAD THEIR WEAPONS AS WELL, WE COULD STOP THE SERBS.

"My mother was scared about my brother's destiny and mine. She told us many times—

TAKE CARE OF YOUR-SELVES.

LEAVE US.

WE ARE GETTING OLD.

YOU MUST TRY TO FIND A WAY TO REACH SARAJEVO, FREE TERRITORY.

"I'd had something packed for one and a half years."

The fall of the Srebrenica safe area and the liquidation of Muslim men from there was the nadir of the U.N.'s tenure in Bosnia.

The U.N.'s peace-keeping mission had failed.

Even before the Srebrenica disaster, the British and French had begun to prepare for the possible withdrawal of their large peacekeeping contingents from what had long been considered a quagmire.

J. SACCO 2-00

President Clinton had pledged a covering force of 20,000 in the event of such a U.N. withdrawal and he was now faced with the prospect of U.S. ground troop involvement in an escalating European war as he entered an election year.

But the U.S. now had an opening to fore-stall a U.N. pull-out by leading the allies into direct confrontation with the Serbs from the air. The allies had been outraged by the magnitude of the U.N.'s humiliation at Srebrenica, and at a conference convened in London on July 21, the U.S. galvanized them into issuing a warning to the Serbs that a final tripwire had been set—at Gorazde.*

Said U.S. Secretary of State Warren Christopher:

THE BOSNIAN SERBS ARE NOW ON NOTICE THAT AN ATTACK AGAINST GORAZDE WILL BE MET BY SUBSTANTIAL AND DECISIVE AIR POWER.

THERE WILL BE NO MORE PINPRICK STRIKES.

The united allied front pushed U.N. Secretary General Boutros-Ghali to prune the procedure for authorizing air attacks.

He removed the veto power of the the civilian area representative and hardcore neutralist, Yasushi Akashi.

*TINY ZEPA, WHICH WAS STILL HOLDING ON AT THIS POINT, WAS IGNORED AT LONDON.

On Aug. 19, the U.N. announced its peacekeepers would soon start withdrawing from Gorazde.

On Aug. 28, one Serb shell killed 38 people in Sarajevo, which earlier had been afforded the same protection guaranteed Gorazde at the London conference.

To many in Gorazde, it seemed they were about to be abandoned.

The next day, the U.N. essentially ceded its authority over air power to U.S.-dominated NATO, which now had a pretext it couldn't pass up.

I WAS IN THE CAMP. IT WAS AFTERNOON.

"The British had already prepared themselves for a fast evacuation. A captain came and ordered the soldiers to be ready to leave in two hours.

WE HAVE PERMISSION FROM THE SERB SIDE TO LEAVE THROUGH THEIR TERRITORY.

WHAT DOES THIS MEAN? IS THE SAME THING GOING TO HAPPEN TO US THAT HAPPENED TO SREBRENICA AND ZEPA?

NO. IT'S BETTER THIS WAY. NOW OUR AIRPLANES CAN HIT SERB LINES.

"I didn't believe him.

"The British left the camp.

"And people heard. They approached the camp. There was a mass of people. They wanted to take food, gasoline.

"And I told myself, 'The Serbs can see everything. They'll start shelling. They'll kill everyone...'

"I was the first one who could have taken sugar, salt, coffee, batteries for cars, fuel, but I didn't...

"because I thought everything was going to end for us.

"I took my portion of food and left.

"The people came in, started to grab. Behind them came our soldiers, military police, who pushed them away to keep everything for the military.

"It was only a couple of hundred meters to the Serb lines. But they didn't shell."

THE NEXT DAY THE AIR STRIKES STARTED.

On Aug. 30, with the Gorazde peacekeepers out of harm's way—and no longer potential hostages—NATO began a two-week bombing campaign against the Bosnian Serbs.

More than the damage they caused, the air attacks demonstrated to the Serbs that the NATO states had unambiguously lined up against them.

Suddenly the military balance in the former Yugoslavia was shifting. Earlier in August the Croatian army had overrun a separatist Serb statelet and chased tens of thousands of Serb refugees into a Serbia worn down by years of U.N. sanctions.

J. SACCO 1-00

Then, in September and October, a combined Croatian and Bosnian offensive recaptured large amounts of territory from the Serbs in northern Bosnia.

The Bosnian Serbs were reeling and came under pressure from Serbian President Slobodan Milosevic to make peace. A country-wide cease-fire went into effect on Oct. 12. Among its provisions, the Serbs were required to allow U.N. and relief-organization convoys unhindered access to Gorazde.

It was on one of these convoys that I first entered Gorazde.

Final peace talks were set for November in Dayton, Ohio, but the U.S. had already floated ideas for a settlement. The elimination of the Srebrenica and Zepa enclaves played into the hands of those who advocated simplifying the map, including National Security Adviser Anthony Lake. He wanted the Bosnian government to make the map even simpler by swapping Gorazde for Serb-controlled suburbs of Sarajevo.

EVERYONE WAS TALKING ABOUT IT.

"Were they going to trade us for Brcko? Or Banja Luka? Nobody knew exactly what would happen. It was a period when people were confused... nervous."

YOU WERE ASKING THOSE QUESTIONS.

"At that time, TV crews and everybody were coming with the same question: 'What do you think about that? About being traded?'"

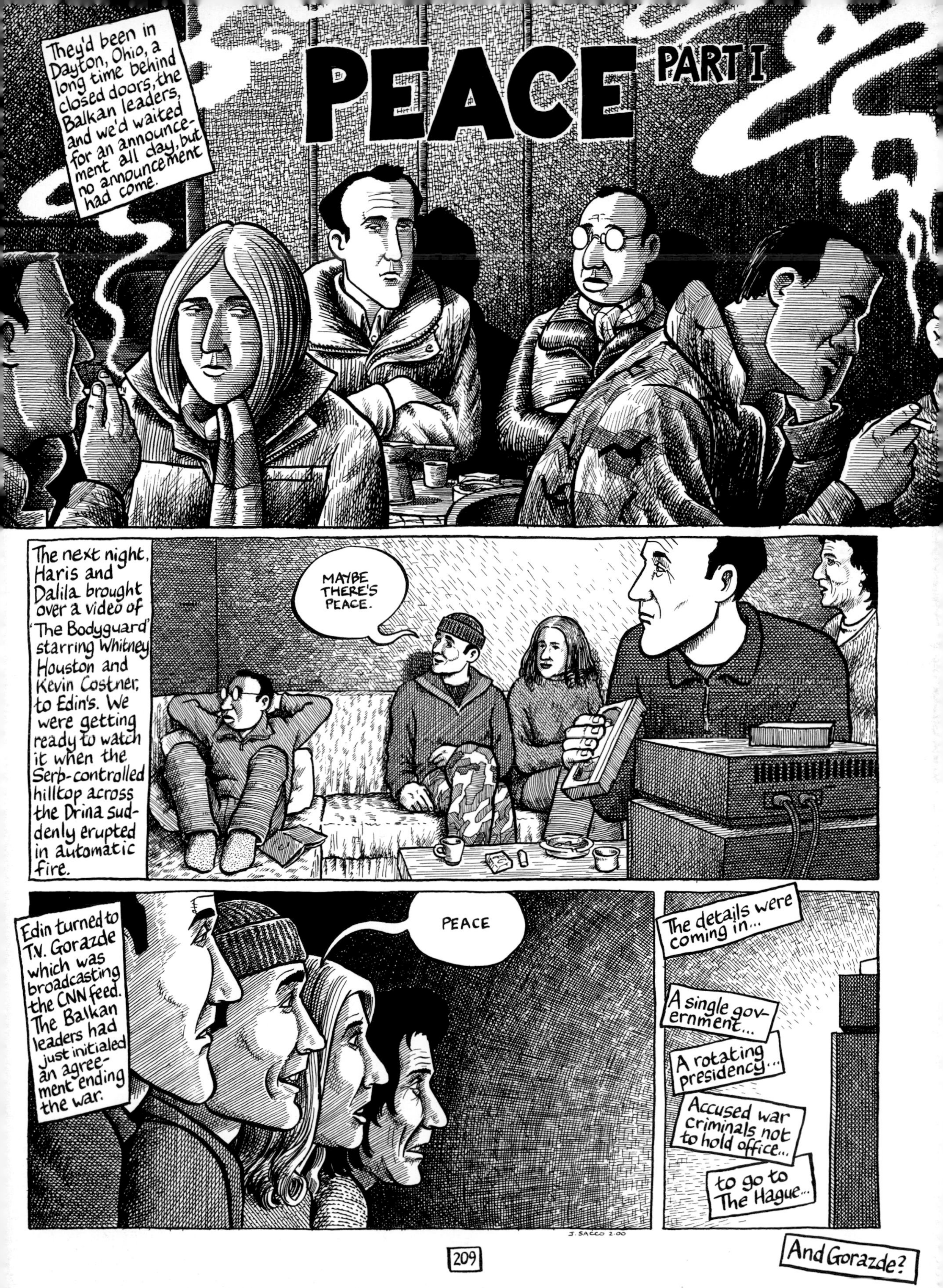

PEACE PART I
They'd been in Dayton, Ohio, a long time behind closed doors, the Balkan leaders, and we'd waited for an announcement all day, but no announcement had come.
The next night, Haris and Dalila brought over a video of 'The Bodyguard' starring Whitney Houston and Kevin Costner, to Edin's. We were getting ready to watch it when the Serb-controlled hilltop across the Drina suddenly erupted in automatic fire.
MAYBE THERE'S PEACE.
Edin turned to T.V. Gorazde which was broadcasting the CNN feed. The Balkan leaders had just initialed an agreement ending the war.
PEACE
The details were coming in...
A single government...
A rotating presidency...
Accused war criminals not to hold office...
to go to The Hague...
J. SACCO 2.00

And Gorazde?

would not be traded.

A narrow corridor would link Gorazde to Sarajevo...

There was another provision:

...DEMOBILIZATION...

DEMOBIL-IZATION.

DEMOBIL-IZATION.

I DON'T BELIEVE IT.

IT'S PEACE AND I DON'T KNOW HOW TO BEHAVE.

Half an hour later, we couldn't stand it any more.

We put in the video...

We couldn't stand that half way through...

We switched over to the news again...

more details, more announcements...

We switched back to the video...

then back to the news...

Dalila from Gorazde danced with the President of the United States.

After Haris and Dalila left, Edin's brother came home with another video, 'Slaughter in San Francisco.' It was late but we stayed up to watch Chuck Norris dropkick his way through the bad guys.

I DON'T BELIEVE IN IT.

But Edin decided to start reviewing his university thesis the next day. Just in case. After all, if there was peace, and if he could get to Sarajevo, he might as well be ready to finish up his degree right away.

J. SACCO 2.00

On Nov. 1, 1995, the Balkan leaders arrived in Dayton, Ohio, to settle the Balkan wars under the auspices of the United States.

Peace Part II

President Alija Izetbegovic of Bosnia had once acknowledged that the eastern enclaves, including Gorazde, would probably have to be sacrificed in a peace deal. But after the Srebrenica massacre and the fall of Zepa, the Bosnian government opposed an American proposal to trade Gorazde away. Despite Pentagon concerns that Gorazde was indefensible, a new chief U.S. negotiator, Richard Holbrooke, dropped the idea of a Gorazde swap.

J. SACCO 3.00

Gorazde would be linked to Sarajevo by a corridor. President Slobodan Milosevic of Serbia, who was representing Bosnia's sidelined Serbs, and Bosnian Prime Minister Haris Silajdzic initially haggled over the width of the corridor on napkins.

Milosevic and the Americans further refined the corridor while boozing on scotch.

The Gorazde safe area had been saved.

TERRITORY CONTROLLED BY THE BOSNIAN SERBS

SARAJEVO

The Corridor

GORAZDE

Drina

TERRITORY CONTROLLED BY THE MUSLIM-CROAT FEDERATION

KILOMETER SCALE
0   5   10

But the rest of Eastern Bosnia — including Visegrad and Foca; the fallen safe areas, Srebrenica and Zepa; and all the other towns and villages where Muslims had been expelled or slaughtered — would remain under the control of those who had cleansed it: the Bosnian Serbs.

On Nov. 21 the Balkan leaders initialed an overall peace settlement.

The war in Bosnia was over.

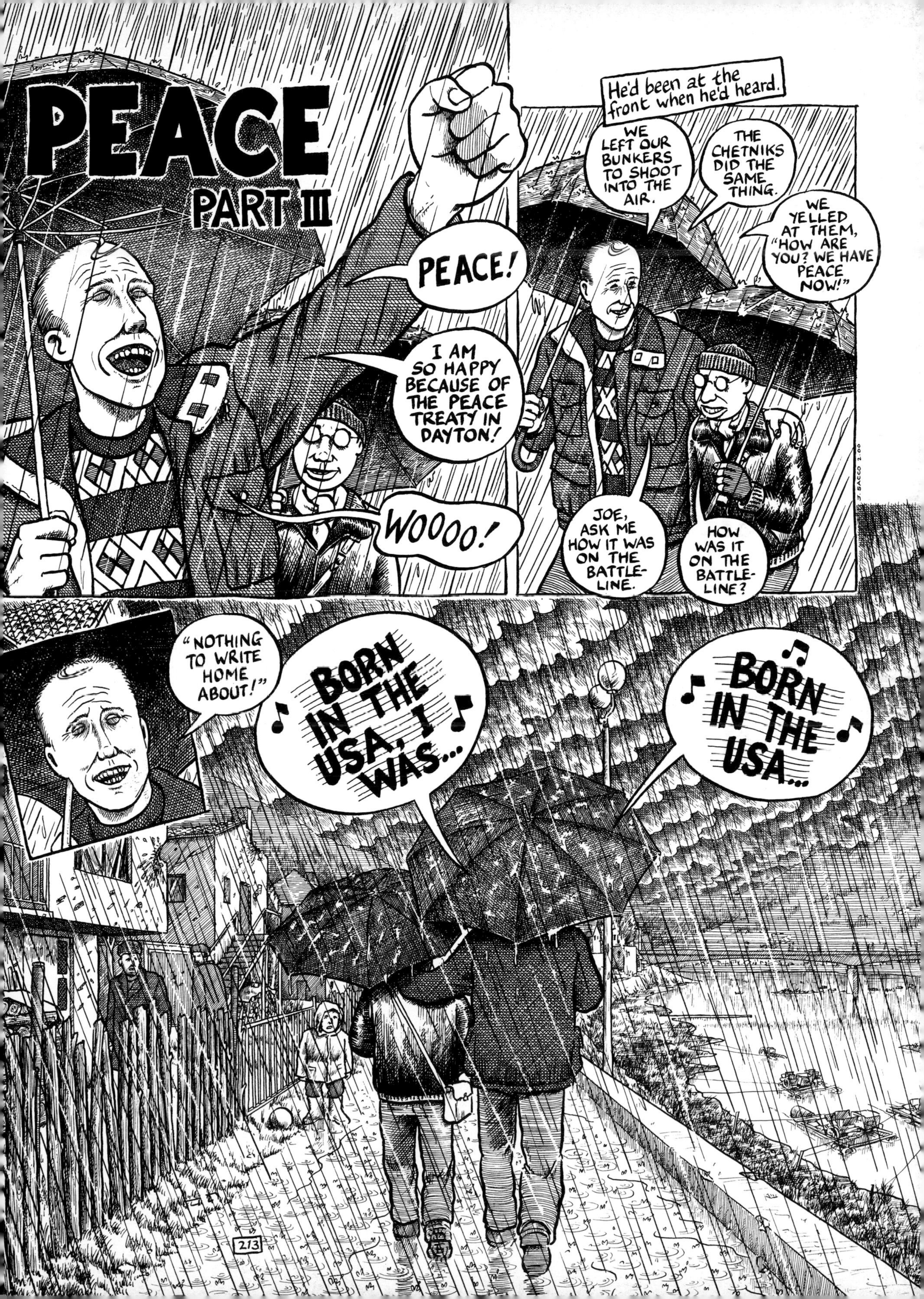
PEACE
PART III
PEACE!
I AM SO HAPPY BECAUSE OF THE PEACE TREATY IN DAYTON!
WOOOO!
He'd been at the front when he'd heard.
WE LEFT OUR BUNKERS TO SHOOT INTO THE AIR.
THE CHETNIKS DID THE SAME THING.
WE YELLED AT THEM, "HOW ARE YOU? WE HAVE PEACE NOW!"
JOE, ASK ME HOW IT WAS ON THE BATTLE-LINE.
HOW WAS IT ON THE BATTLE-LINE?
"NOTHING TO WRITE HOME ABOUT!"
BORN IN THE USA, I WAS...
BORN IN THE USA...
J. SACCO 2.00

Later, Riki and Edin discussed the peace...

REAL PEACE IS WHEN I CAN GO FROM HERE TO THERE...

WHEN WE HAVE WAGES.

WHEN I CAN DRIVE A CAR FROM HOME TO TOWN, WHEN I CAN GO TO A SHOP TO BUY WHAT I WANT, THAT'S REAL PEACE.

REAL PEACE WILL TAKE PLACE SHORTLY AFTER U.S. TROOPS COME THROUGHOUT BOSNIA.

SERB RADIO IS STILL TALKING ABOUT DIVIDING BOSNIA...

BUT WHEN THE MONEY STARTS COMING IN AND THERE'S A SINGLE CURRENCY, ECONOMICS WILL SOLVE THESE PROBLEMS.

But except for Riki and a few others, the mood of most people I knew, which had been growing progressively optimistic as the cease-fire held and regular convoys got through, suddenly darkened after Dayton.

I CAN'T BE HAPPY ABOUT IT.

MAYBE WE'VE LOST SOME EMOTION HERE.

THIS IS JUST A PAUSE IN THE WAR.

I'M WORRIED ABOUT RAISING CHILDREN HERE.

I'M AFRAID EVENTS MIGHT REPEAT THEMSELVES.

J.SACCO 2.00

Relief that the guns were finally silent was giving way to closer scrutiny of what the peace agreement did and didn't say.

THIS PEACE WAS IMPOSED BY OUTSIDE FORCES WITHOUT FULL REGARD TO JUSTICE AND THE WISHES OF THE PEOPLE WHO WERE VICTIMS.

MANY MUSLIMS LOST THEIR HOMES IN PLACES LIKE FOCA AND VISEGRAD.

WHAT ABOUT THEM?

Technically, Muslim refugees would be allowed to return to homes in territory still controlled by the Serbs...

but without any safety guarantees, everyone knew the idea of return was ludicrous.

214

MY HOME IS IN FOCA, AND THE ONLY WAY I'M GOING TO SEE IT IS IF WE WIN MILITARILY.

BUT I'VE HAD ENOUGH OF THE BALKANS.

I WANT TO GET OUT OF HERE.

For Muslims, the ugly truth of the Dayton agreement was that, though it provided for one Bosnia with a shared central government, it had divided Bosnia into two entities and accepted de facto the results of ethnic cleansing.

BOSNIA'S TWO ENTITIES FOLLOWING THE DAYTON ACCORDS

SERB-CONTROLLED TERRITORY

SARAJEVO

GORAZDE

MUSLIM-CROAT FEDERATION

And what did the peace hold for Gorazde?

Its industrial base had been completely destroyed...

So where would the jobs come from?

If people had a chance to leave, would they come back?

J. SACCO 2-00

In addition, the agreed-upon corridor to Sarajevo was only five miles across at its widest and had no road to Gorazde.

The construction of one was promised, but for the short term Gorazde was still dependent on the Blue Road running through Serb-controlled territory.

EVEN IF THERE'S NO WAR, GORAZDE IS STILL AN ENCLAVE.

215

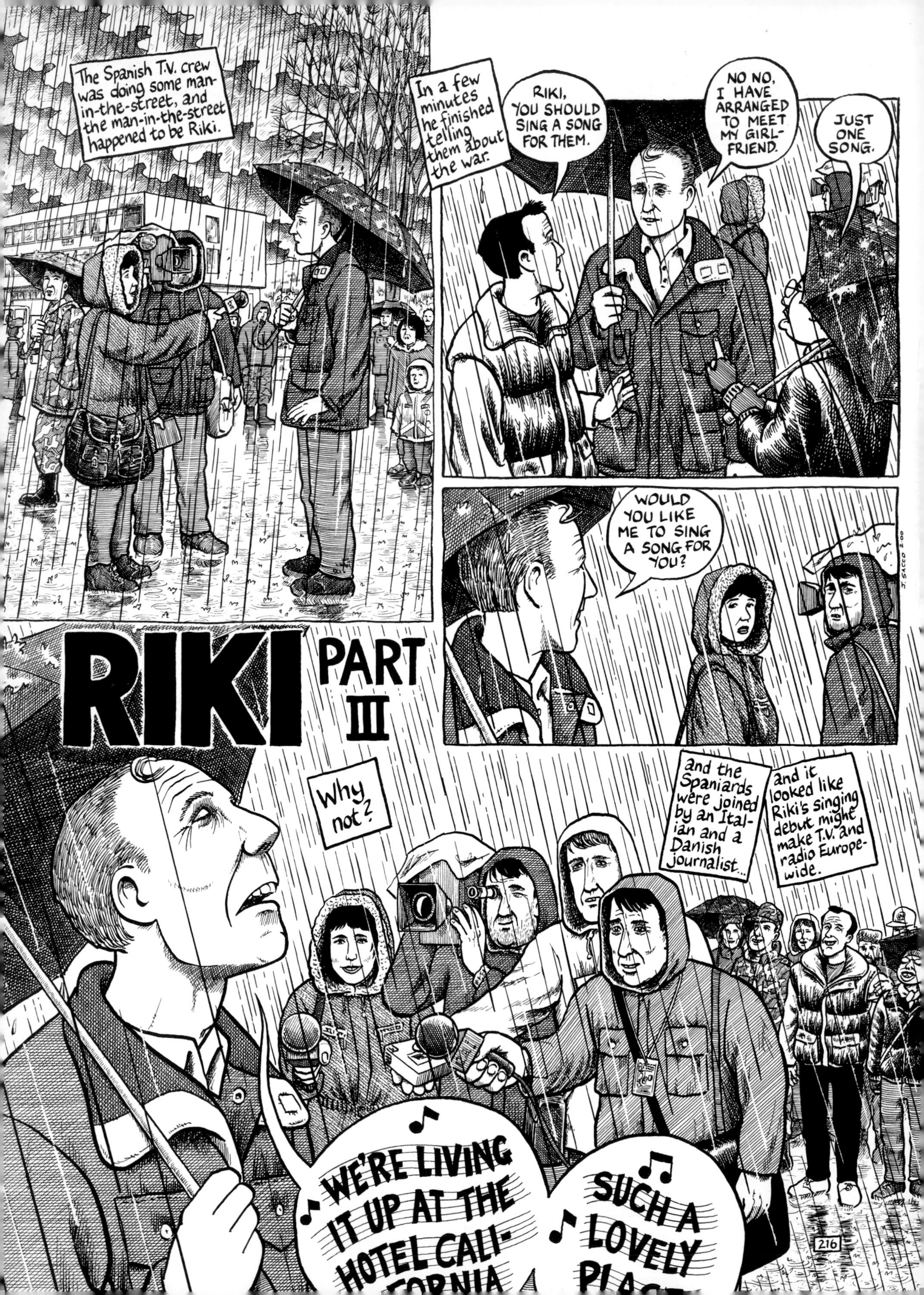
The Spanish T.V. crew was doing some man-in-the-street, and the man-in-the-street happened to be Riki.
In a few minutes he finished telling them about the war.
RIKI, YOU SHOULD SING A SONG FOR THEM.
NO NO, I HAVE ARRANGED TO MEET MY GIRL-FRIEND.
JUST ONE SONG.
WOULD YOU LIKE ME TO SING A SONG FOR YOU?
J. SACCO 2.00
RIKI PART III
Why not?
and the Spaniards were joined by an Italian and a Danish journalist...
and it looked like Riki's singing debut might make T.V. and radio Europe-wide.
WE'RE LIVING IT UP AT THE HOTEL CALI-FORNIA
SUCH A LOVELY PLACE

The journalists fell in love with Riki, they wanted him to take them around Gorazde.

I AM VERY SORRY, BUT I CANNOT HELP YOU NOW. I HAVE AN APPOINTMENT.

PERHAPS WE CAN MEET LATER.

BUT WE ARE LEAVING ON THE CONVOY IN THE AFTERNOON.

PLEASE HELP US.

WE WANT TO SEE SOME DAMAGED BUILDINGS.

LOOK!

THERE IS A HOLE IN THAT WALL!

THERE ARE DAMAGED BUILDINGS EVERYWHERE.

But Riki did go with them, acting as their translator, and when I met him the next morning, he told me they'd given him 100 dm.

100 dm!

He didn't want anything, he said, but they made him take it.

By the way, he said, this time he was paying for the coffee.

THE SPANISH JOURNALIST WAS VERY PRETTY. I KISSED HER TWO TIMES ON THE CHEEK.

I felt obliged to remind him about his new Bosnian girlfriend.

how did they meet?

I SAW HER WALKING ON THE BRIDGE.

I WENT UP TO HER AND MADE SMALL TALK.

I INVITED HER TO THE NEAREST COFFEE BAR TO TAKE A DRINK, LIKE BILL CLINTON IN SOME SMALL HOTEL.

I DROPPED MY TROUSERS AND PROPOSED THAT SHE PERFORM ORAL SEX.

J. SACCO 2-00

JUST JOKING!

Riki was in a good mood.

He was optimistic he would be demobilized...

that he would soon travel the Blue Road to Sarajevo to finish his studies.

He was sure that whatever international troops came to enforce the peace plan—

THEY WILL TAKE THEIR ORDERS FROM THE USA.

—and most of all that Bosnia would remain—

ONE COUNTRY, INDEPENDENT AND INDIVISIBLE.

WE HAVE SUFFERED IRRECOVERABLE LOSSES, BUT WE HAVE SUCCEEDED TO WIN THIS WAR.

Riki left for the front for a few days...

He got back as I was trying to arrange a lift on a convoy returning to Sarajevo.

I was tangled up in snafus, man.

While I'd been in Gorazde the NATO-led Implementation Force—IFOR—had taken over the U.N.'s military mission in Bosnia...

DID I SAY THAT RIGHT?

"IRRECOVERABLE"?

And unlike the U.N., IFOR wasn't letting journalists ride its vehicles.

J. SACCO 2-00

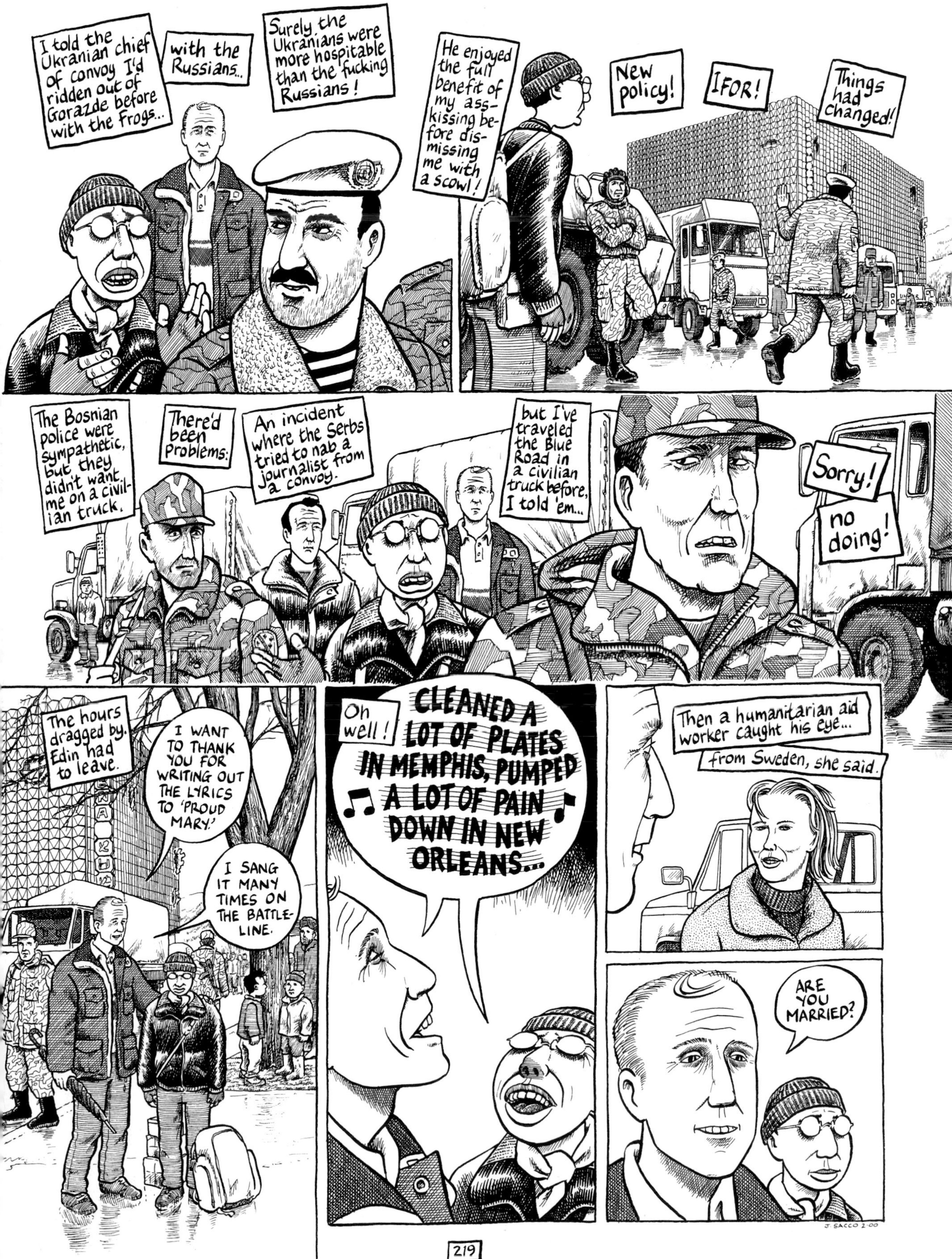
I told the Ukranian chief of convoy I'd ridden out of Gorazde before with the Frogs...
with the Russians...
Surely the Ukranians were more hospitable than the fucking Russians!
He enjoyed the full benefit of my ass-kissing before dismissing me with a scowl!
New policy!
IFOR!
Things had changed!
The Bosnian police were sympathetic, but they didn't want me on a civilian truck.
There'd been problems:
An incident where the Serbs tried to nab a journalist from a convoy.
but I've traveled the Blue Road in a civilian truck before, I told 'em...
Sorry!
no doing!
The hours dragged by. Edin had to leave.
I WANT TO THANK YOU FOR WRITING OUT THE LYRICS TO 'PROUD MARY.'
I SANG IT MANY TIMES ON THE BATTLE-LINE.
Oh well!
CLEANED A LOT OF PLATES IN MEMPHIS, PUMPED A LOT OF PAIN DOWN IN NEW ORLEANS...
Then a humanitarian aid worker caught his eye...
from Sweden, she said.
ARE YOU MARRIED?
J. SACCO 2·00

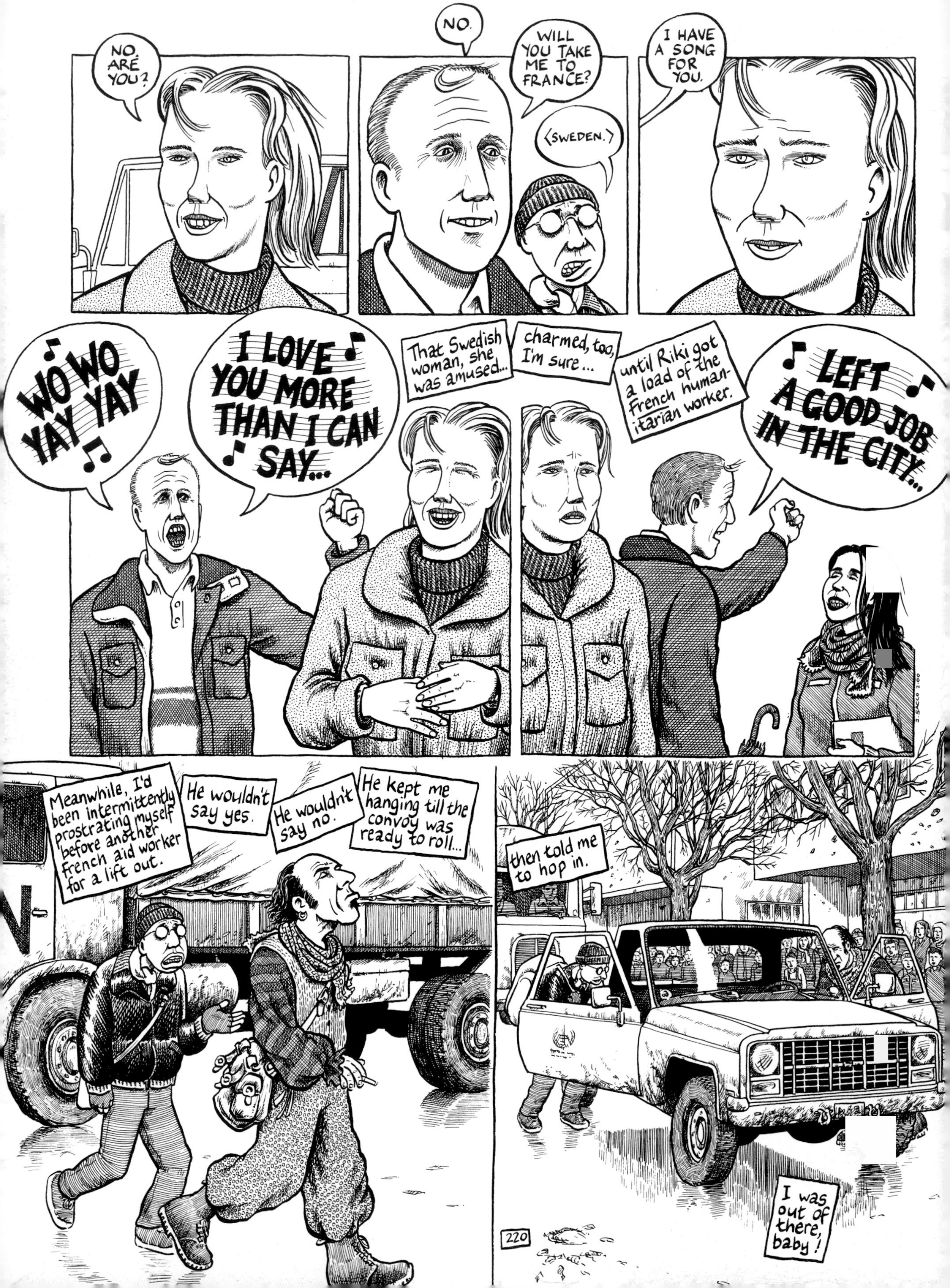
NO. ARE YOU?
NO.
WILL YOU TAKE ME TO FRANCE?
⟨SWEDEN.⟩
I HAVE A SONG FOR YOU.
WO WO YAY YAY
I LOVE YOU MORE THAN I CAN SAY...
That Swedish woman, she was amused...
charmed, too, I'm sure...
until Riki got a load of the French humanitarian worker.
LEFT A GOOD JOB IN THE CITY...
Meanwhile, I'd been intermittently prostrating myself before another French aid worker for a lift out.
He wouldn't say yes.
He wouldn't say no.
He kept me hanging till the convoy was ready to roll...
then told me to hop in.
I was out of there, baby!

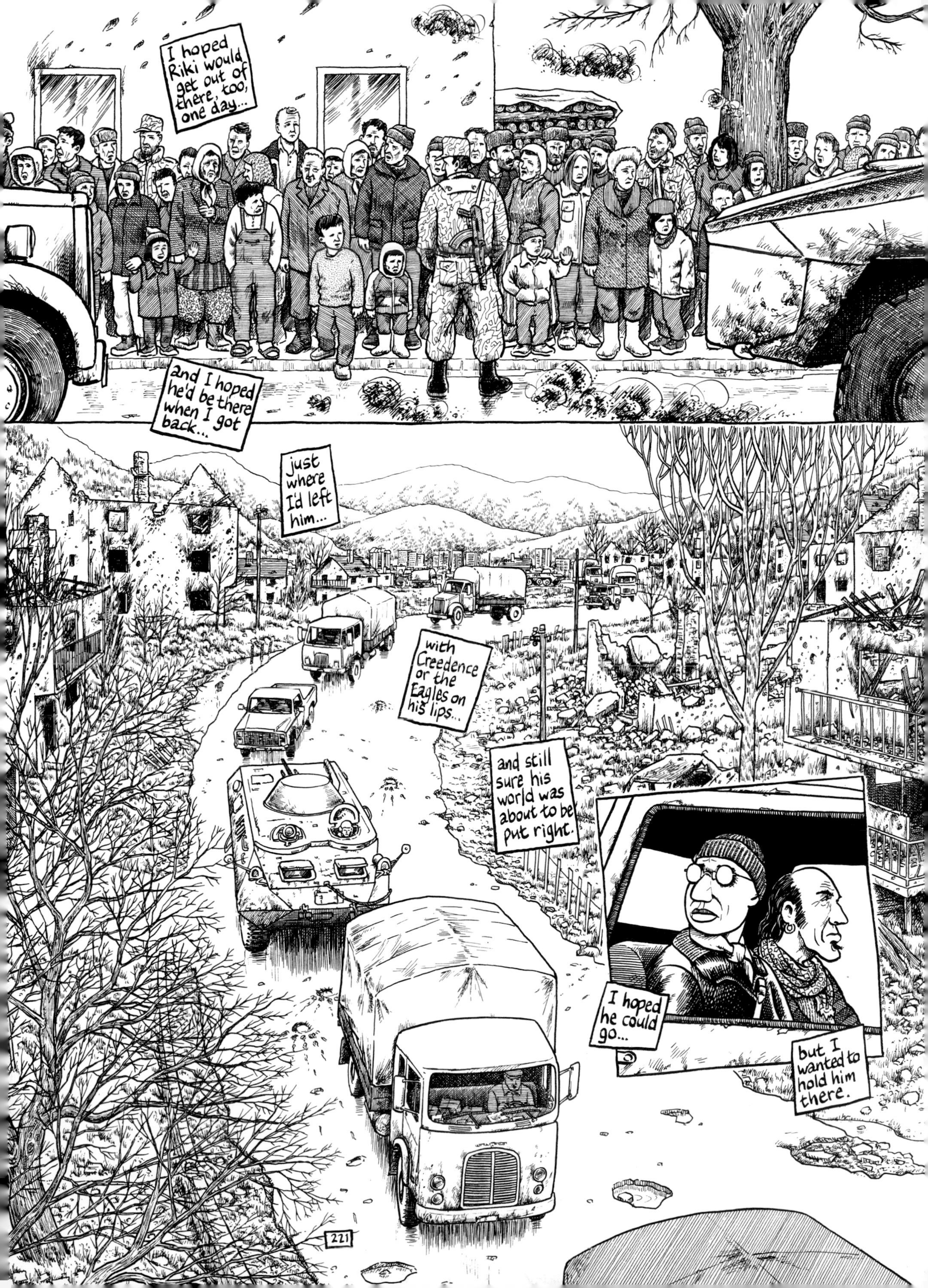
I hoped Riki would get out of there, too, one day...
and I hoped he'd be there when I got back...
just where I'd left him...
with Creedence or the Eagles on his lips...
and still sure his world was about to be put right.
I hoped he could go...
but I wanted to hold him there.

EPILOGUE PART II

Sarajevans talked wistfully about a time before the war when they couldn't walk down Marshal Tito Blvd. without running into everyone they knew.

But so many of their friends had fled Sarajevo, and so many were still leaving.

It was all new faces now, they'd tell me, refugees from Eastern Bosnia, bumpkins from cow towns, and most Sarajevans bristled at the sight of the strangers.

I hooked up with Edin in Sarajevo.

One day we walked down Marshal Tito Blvd. together. We couldn't go a few dozen steps without running into people from Gorazde — friends, students, and neighbors of Edin's who had just arrived.

Sarajevo was full of Gorazde.

J. SACCO 3-00

Lejla and Ema were beginning at the university.

Ema had found a job at a radio station.

They were both getting used to the traffic, to being in cars.

For them, even war-weary and shabby Sarajevo seemed a place full of life and possibility.

I GO INTO A STORE AND I WANT TO BUY EVERYTHING, EVEN THINGS I DON'T NEED.

I saw my friend Amra in Sarajevo on her first night out of Gorazde in years.

She was staying with a relative in Hrasno, a devastated neighborhood on Sarajevo's urban front line.

The electricity was off there when I went to fetch her, but not in other parts of Sarajevo.

ALL THE LIGHTS!

On the way downtown with a couple of my colleagues, we passed the Benetton, whose recent opening in Sarajevo had been much derided among foreign journalists as a crass publicity gimmick.

BUT I'M HAPPY THERE IS A BENETTON.

I WANT TO GO SHOPPING.

We took her to a real happening joint, Club Obala, and that's when she started to feel out of place.

EVERYONE LOOKS COOL.

ALL THE GIRLS LOOK 60'S.

THERE ARE NO GOOD-LOOKING GUYS.

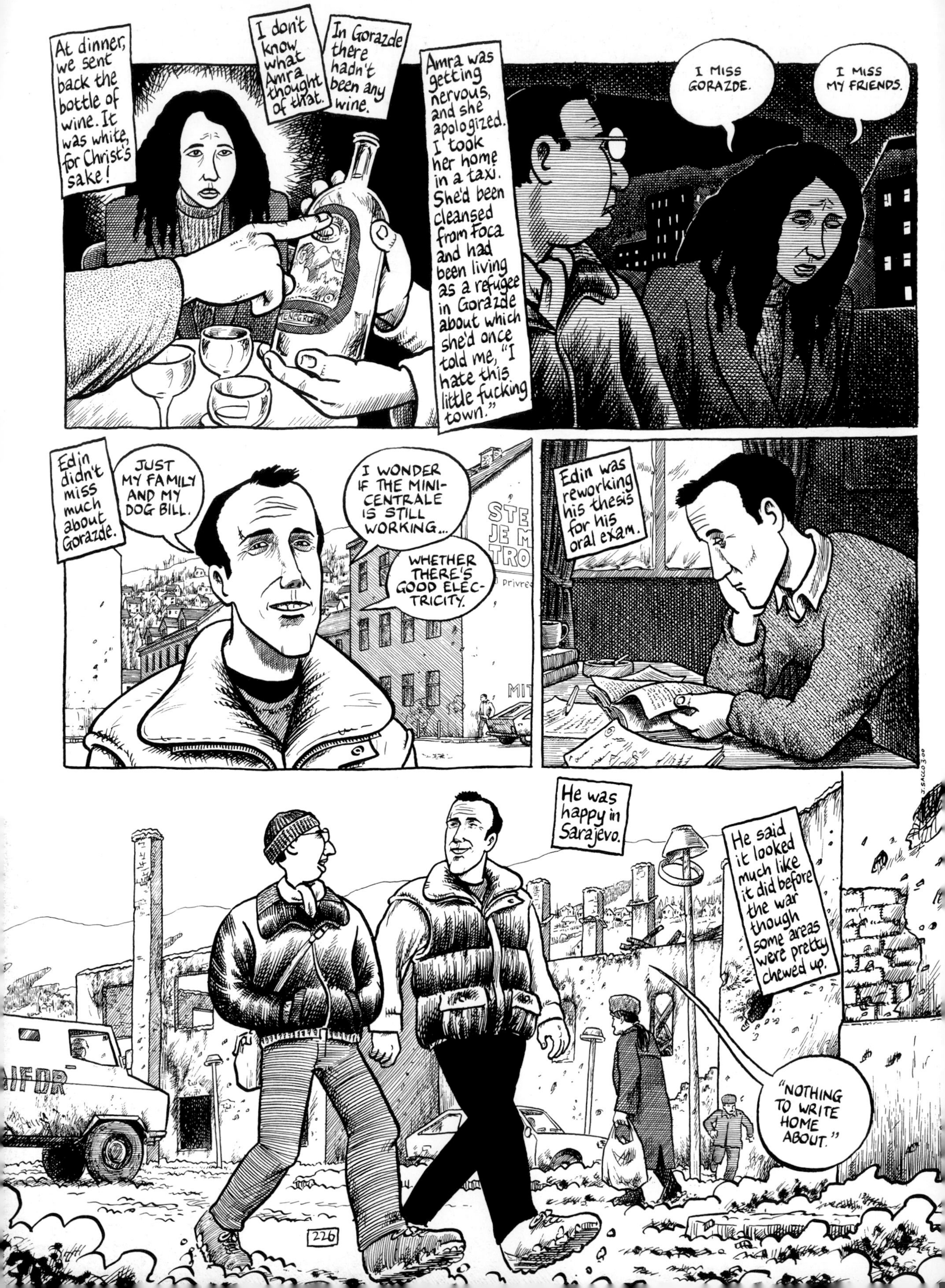

At dinner, we sent back the bottle of wine. It was white, for Christ's sake!
I don't know what Amra thought of that.
In Gorazde there hadn't been any wine.
Amra was getting nervous, and she apologized. I took her home in a taxi. She'd been cleansed from Foca and had been living as a refugee in Gorazde about which she'd once told me, "I hate this little fucking town."
I MISS GORAZDE.
I MISS MY FRIENDS.
Edin didn't miss much about Gorazde.
JUST MY FAMILY AND MY DOG BILL.
I WONDER IF THE MINI-CENTRALE IS STILL WORKING...
WHETHER THERE'S GOOD ELEC-TRICITY.
Edin was reworking his thesis for his oral exam.
He was happy in Sarajevo.
He said it looked much like it did before the war though some areas were pretty chewed up.
"NOTHING TO WRITE HOME ABOUT."
IFOR

Edin was staying with an uncle and aunt in a comfortable flat in the Skenderija neighborhood.

I DON'T WANT ANY NICE THINGS.

I DON'T WANT A NICE PLACE OR NICE FURNITURE.

IN THE END, PROBABLY IT WILL ALL BE DESTROYED.

If this war was over, and he wasn't sure it was, then there'd be another war within 50 years, he said.

Riki? He was elusive. I saw him only once in the next few weeks.

The university had changed the rules on him.

He'd thought he'd need a year to finish his studies, but he'd learned he needed more like two and a half.

He was searching hard for required texts and dealing with school bureaucracy.

He was very busy.

Edin was having more fun.

We hung out.

We had our laughs.

He told me about an invitation he'd just received from an old pal who'd settled in Germany to come and visit for awhile.

I encouraged that, I reminded Edin that he'd lived through the siege of Gorazde, I told him he ought to finish his thesis and then take a break.

No, he said, that was precisely what he didn't want to do.

He was in his late 20's and looking back on a hole in his life almost four years long.

This was no time for a break.

He wanted to get on with things.

227

BIBLIOGRAPHY

I never intended this book to be a comprehensive overview of the break-up of Yugoslavia and the war in Bosnia. However, I found it necessary to provide some context in order to tell the story of Gorazde. I leaned heavily on a number of books for background information.

Noel Malcolm's *Bosnia, A Short History* (New York University Press, 1994) is widely considered a masterpiece of scholarship, and rightly so. I had the pleasure to listen to Mr. Malcolm talk in Sarajevo in late 1995. Unfortunately, he was introduced for an hour by a professor, a parliament member, and a minister and only got 20 minutes to speak himself. He downplayed the role of the historian — his own role — saying that he'd heard a number of British politicians had read his book (Mr. Malcolm is himself British), but that Britain had changed its policy in Bosnia only after America had told it to do so. Anyway, I found Malcolm's section on World War II particularly helpful.

As far as World War II goes, I was also greatly helped by Matteo J. Milazzo's *The Chetnik Movement & The Yugoslav Resistance* (The Johns Hopkins University Press, 1975), which describes the different factions and changing allegiances in excruciating detail. I relied on the very readable *Tito And the Rise and Fall of Yugoslavia* (Carroll & Graf Publishers, Inc., 1994), by Richard West, for information about the Partisans and Tito's post-war Yugoslavia.

Mark Thompson's *A Paper House, The Ending of Yugoslavia* (Vintage, 1992) gave me a good overall feel for Yugoslavia and the thoughts of Yugoslavs at the time of the break-up.

As far as the politics of the disintegration of Yugoslavia, there is no better reference than *Yugoslavia, Death of a Nation* (TV Books, Inc., 1995 and 1996), by Allan Little and Laura Silber, which accompanied a television documentary. Little and Silber interviewed most all the major political players and their book is a triumph of reporting. It was on my desk at all times. I had the pleasure of meeting Ms. Silber in New York City, but she didn't come to a party I invited her to. Another excellent book on the break-up is Misha Glenny's *The Fall of Yugoslavia, The Third Balkan War* (Penguin Books, 1992 and 1993). Glenny has a real understanding of how the Balkans tick, though I read an essay or two by him during the war that pissed me off. I can't remember why.

I did need specific help in understanding the history of the arrangement between the U.N. and NATO in Bosnia and how that arrangement affected the safe areas. Chuck Sudetic's *Blood and Vengeance* (Norton, 1998) and David Rohde's *Endgame* (Farrar, Straus and Giroux, 1997) were more than a little helpful. Both these books, which I consider two of the best to come out of the war, tell the story of the fall of the Srebrenica safe area. Another useful book on Srebrenica is Jan Willem Honig and Norbert Both's *Srebrenica, Record of a War Crime* (Penguin Books, 1996).

For information on the end of the war and the backroom negotiations at the Dayton, Ohio, peace talks, I turned to Richard Holbrooke's *To End a War* (Random House, 1998). Holbrooke was a U.S. assistant secretary of state at the time of Dayton accords, which he helped design.

I am also indebted to the *New York Times* and the *Guardian* newspapers which provided me a day-by-day account of the war in Bosnia.

A NOTE ON THE POSSIBLE USE OF CHEMICAL WARFARE BY SERB UNITS AT SREBRENICA

I interviewed two men in Gorazde about their experiences breaking out of Srebrenica in July 1995. Both of them claimed the Serbs had used chemical warfare against the column of Muslim men trying to reach friendly territory. When I talked to these men in late 1995, I had heard no such accusations before. As a result, I was skeptical and didn't ask many follow-up questions. My mistake. Human Rights Watch has since collected many first-hand accounts in its Nov. 1998 report, *Chemical Warfare in Bosnia? The Strange Experiences of the Srebrenica Survivors*. Human Rights Watch concluded that the use of an incapacitating agent "cannot be ruled out" though "conclusive evidence remains elusive." I, for one, was convinced by the harrowing and detailed testimonials I read in the report. Those testimonials meshed with my own rather lazy interviews about the matter. As a result, I've chosen to present the accusations of the use of chemical weapons in the chapter that details the fall of Srebrenica.

SPECIAL THANK YOUS

My parents, Leonard and Carmen Sacco, and my sister, Maryanne, and her husband, Keith, encouraged me through the years I worked on this book.

Richard La Sasso, my friend since high school, spent many hours discussing Bosnia with me and always took an interest in the progress of my work. Beyond that, I relied on him often for grammatical and word usage questions.

Alena Nahabedian, Holly Cundiff, and Christi Guenther rescued me from personal despair though they probably didn't know it.

Almost everyone I met in Gorazde treated me with great respect and kindness. Edin and his family welcomed me into their home like a brother and a son. Till the last day I was writing this book, Edin continued answering my questions graciously. Believe me, I asked him a lot of questions. If it wasn't for him, this book would not exist. My deepest, deepest thanks go to him.

✤

ALSO BY JOE SACCO

More stories of the Bosnian War

Soba (1998) and "Christmas with Karadzic" (1997) contain further explorations
of the Bosnian War by Joe Sacco. The 41-page, magazine-format *Soba* focuses on
one of the fascinating people Sacco met in Sarajevo, while "Christmas with Karadzic"
(published in the anthology *Zero Zero* #15) shows Sacco's close encounter
with one of Bosnia's most prominent war criminals.

Tales from the rest of the world

Palestine (1992-1995), now complete in one volume with an introduction
by Edward W. Said, follows Sacco into the heart of the Middle Eastern conflict.
War Junkie (currently out of print) collects Sacco's earliest, shorter ventures
into comics reportage, including his sardonic take on the Gulf War,
"How I Loved the War"; "When Good Bombs Happen to Bad People"; plus
"In the Company of Long Hair" (tales of touring with a punk band).

Ordering information:
Soba: $4.95 postpaid
Zero Zero #15: $4.95 postpaid
Palestine: $26.95 postpaid
War Junkie: out of print

Available from FANTAGRAPHICS BOOKS, 7563 Lake City Way, Seattle, WA 98115;
or call 1-800-657-1100 to order by phone; or order from www.fantagraphics.com

Bookstores please contact W.W. Norton & Company, Inc. at 1-800-233-4830
for toll-free service in the continental U.S., or (212) 869-0856 outside the U.S.
In the United Kingdom, please contact Turnaround Distribution Services at 208-829-3009.